EVERYTHING

you ever wanted to know

ABOUT THE BIBLE

but didn't know who to ask

$+$

FLOYD HALE

Resource *Publications*

An imprint of *Wipf and Stock Publishers*

199 West 8th Avenue • Eugene OR 97401

EVERYTHING. . .
ABOUT THE BIBLE. . .

Resource Publications
An imprint of Wipf and Stock Publishers
199 West 8th Avenue, Suite 3
Eugene, Oregon 97401

Everything You Ever Wanted to Know About the Bible
But Didn't Know Who to Ask
By Hale, Floyd
Copyright©1999 by Hale, Floyd
ISBN: 1-49824-718-0
Publication date 4/20/2004

Other Books by this author:
Christian Superstitions (1990)
Saving Grace (1992)
The Gospel Truth (1992)

In Memory of
Jesus of Nazareth
Whose courageous witness to the rule of God
has changed the world

(By the editor when I left Benton, Illinois in 1981)

Odds and Ends *(Editorial)*

It is not often, so I am told, that the issue of a daily newspaper which contains its church listings and news of religious matters is the most eagerly awaited issue of the week by a good portion of its readers.

Yet as hard as it may be on the ego of the reporters and other columnists, that has been the case for The Benton Evening News. Each Saturday for some six years now many readers could hardly wait until the paper was printed, so anxious were they to read "what that preacher had to say this time."

The "preacher" is Floyd Hale, who writes the weekly "The Bible Says..." column for The Benton Evening News.

Though I don't like to jump the gun, tomorrow's column will be the final one for Reverend Hale. And the next day he will deliver his final sermon as the pastor of the First United Methodist Church in Benton.

The resignations were not entirely unexpected, though they came sooner than expected. After all, as as he said in a letter to members of the church, the departure of Methodist ministers is "as certain as death and arthritis."

I am not qualified to make any sort of comment on his service to the church. That is beyond my province. But I can say flatly that readers of his weekly column will feel something missing from the church page, unless I can come up with someone equally provocative. Especially missing those columns will be many readers who at first will say that they're glad they won't have to read any more of his at times unorthodox views. They always read them, however. Controversial? I suppose so, judging from the letters and comments which we have received since his very first article, No, 1, appeared. Tomorrow, No. 326 appears. It will be difficult to adjust to the knowledge that on the following Saturday some of the conversational staples of this area ("Did you ever?" "He does make you think, and don't he?") will be absent.

The Reverend Hale will be missed by readers. I rather think, however, that he will be missed most by the religious community, because he succeeded in achieving what may have been his principal goal: to make religion discussed and thought about, rather than just being accepted and forgotten.

Author's Preface

I believe these words of introduction will be a help to the reader of *EVERYTHING. . . ABOUT THE BIBLE. . .*

This volume is a compilation of some of the weekly articles which appeared in several different newspapers in Southern Illinois during a period of over thirty years. They are answers to questions sent in by the readers. When no questions came in, I'd ask my own--mostly the old standard "hard questions."

Putting these together in a book made me very aware that I had repeated myself a lot. There are two reasons for this. First, Some questions were from the same book in the Bible; thus some of the same background information was required each time. In writing a newspaper column you must be aware that the reader may not have read the previous ones.

Secondly, I notice that I repeated most on three themes which I feel have been neglected in understanding the Bible: 1) Jesus' gospel, 2) the Gospel of John, the book, and 3) the Apocalyptic literature. In book form this may become a bore, especially if you read right through. You might want to read these the way the original readers did. They had a week in between "pages" to think it over (or forget about it).

There is an index in the back of this volume which lists the questions by page numbers. You might want to pick and choose from this index according to your interest--especially if used as a group study.

My main purpose in writing "The Bible Says. . ." was not to teach the Bible. If I did that I'd be just one more preacher commentator blowing in the wind. I tried to convince people that a knowledge of Bible background is important to understanding the Book. This is a most neglected exercise. If people understood what the Bible is, they would not need anyone teach them what "the Bible says."

Most people, mainly believers, read the Bible through rose-colored glasses, or with blinders on. They either read it devotionally (mainly the Psalms) for their own spiritual (emotional) lift at the time, or they read those portions which support what they already believe. A small portion of the rest of the Bible they get from worship litany and sermons, or from books about the Bible.

Almost all the the books about the Bible sold in religious bookstores give it the traditional popular spin--because that's the only kind that sells. Those containing scholarly material are considered "confusing" and/or "controversial," don't sell, and are thus not carried.

You may find me often saying: "You have to know the *truth about the Bible* to learn the *Truth in the Bible*." (And that's the truth.) You don't read two pages into the Word until you find "knowledge" is a bad thing--the "knowledge of good and evil" of all things. I am not a scholar--nor the son of a scholar--but I apply the best of modern scholarship to this enterprise.

The newspaper editors received some pretty nasty letters about this column from time to time--some canceled publishing them because of it. I have included a fair sampling of these, not because I enjoy sharing them, but I think they help make my point. Some may enjoy these letters more than my answers. There were a few good letters (I didn't leave any of them out).

The pages of these "Letters" are scattered throughout and are all identified by abc's. I have left the names off so as to not embarrass anyone.

I was sometime asked why I had my picture in the column header; and I would say it was not my vanity, but for sticking pins in.

My share of the proceeds from the sale of this book will go to UMCOR (the United Methodist Committee On Overseas Relief).

The Bible Says...

By Floyd Hale

Question: Does the Bible say Jesus was ever in hell?

Answer: In the original Apostles' Creed it says (right after Jesus was "buried") "He descended into hell." This is based in part on Acts 2:27, I Peter 3:19 and 4:6.

Since the Christians came to believe only those who believed in Christ would be saved, this raised the question of what would happen to those who died B.C.--especially those who were victims of the Flood in Noah's day. The author of I Peter solved this by saying that Jesus--when he was "dead" those three days and nights--preached the gospel to all those in that "place where all the dead were being held captive."

That place was called "hades" by the Greeks, and meant only the "place of the dead," "grave," or sometimes "death" itself. Everybody who died went there--no punishment or rewards, just "sleep." The lake of fire "gehenna" (invented by the Apocalyptists for their enemies) and "hades" are both translated "hell" in the KJV. The RSV corrects this by bringing "hades" over into the English, and leaving "gehenna" translated "hell." So it was not the hot place where Jesus went.

All this stuff about Jesus suffering "in hell" for the punishment for our sins, is pure bull feathers.

The author of Acts contributed to this confusion by quoting Psalm 16:9-11 as foretelling that Jesus's body would not be left in the grave. In this Psalm "Sheol" (the place of the dead) is translated "hell" and "Holy One" is capitalized (in the KJV). The Psalmist is speaking of himself (as the RSV shows), not about Jesus. And what he is actually saying--and in a poetic way--the Lord will "sustain his life"--and show him the right "path."

In Acts 2:27 the RSV translates "hell," "hades," but does not correct the misinterpreted "prophecy"--that's not its job. It merely translates--as near as possible--what the original document says. We are supposed to know enough about our Bible to judge for ourselves in such matters.

I believe Jesus's death ended his preaching.

1

The Bible Says...

By Floyd Hale

Question: Is snake handling recommended in the Bible?

Answer: Mark 16:18 in the King James Version quotes Jesus as saying believers "shall take up serpents" in his name. "And," it goes on, "if they drink any deadly thing it shall not hurt them." You might note in the verse just before this, Jesus promised "these signs shall follow them that believe"-- including "tongues."

If you are not already aware of it, it is good to know Jesus said none of this. There is not only anything like this in the other Gospels, but this portion of Mark, from 16:8 on, was not in the original copy of this Gospel. These last twelve verses were added in the second century by some fanatical Christian sect. Phrases from the endings of Matthew and Luke (written later) were used in the composition of these added verses.

For a while it was believed the abrupt ending to this Gospel indicated that its original ending ("last page") had been lost, which caused other endings to be added, but now scholars see it as the author's design.

The Revised Standard Version (our present authorized version of the Scriptures) leaves this section (vv. 9-20) of Mark 16 out of the main text.

In the last century and a half many ancient manuscripts (copies) of the New Testament have been discovered which are older and better than those available at the time of the King James revision (1611), which show that Mark ended with 16:8. Although people are inclined to think of the RSV as a "new Bible," it really contains the oldest and most accurate text of the Scriptures.

There are other interesting instances where the RSV has "cleaned up" (I call it) the corrupt passages in the KJV. All this is important in determining exactly what "the Bible says."

Those who treasure the King James Version ought to know that their Bible has caused the death of about a hundred good people from snake bite in the last hundred years. You may say they should know better. But aren't believers supposed to do what "the Bible says"?

The Bible Says...

By Floyd Hale

Question: Why didn't the lions eat Daniel?

Answer: Anyone who has come up through "Bible School" would answer, "God sent an angel to shut the lion's mouths." And to this they might add, "That's what the Bible says."

As kids, like the Jewish children to whom this "story of Daniel in the lion's den" was first told, we were suppose to be good--and "obey God." Being faithful in religious practices does not pay off in divine protection. In fact Jesus suggested just the opposite--obedience to God's will would most likely result in hardship, suffering, even death.

Many a good boy and girl can testify that the "lions do bite" and "fire does burn." From counseling with college and university students who went through our Sunday Schools, I would conclude that the "Daniel in the lion's den" kind of theology has helped destroy more faith than it has strengthened. The subtle thing about this is it can happen unconsciously.

Instead of pushing dogmatically for people--especially children--to "believe the Bible from cover to cover," we should find out for ourselves what the Bible really is--and is all about.

Daniel is not just another "chapter in the Book;" it is an Apocalypse--and a Jewish one at that. It had its message for its day, during the Maccabean Revolt (171-164 B.C.).

To learn *when* Daniel was written, *to whom* it was addressed, and *in what literary form* it was composed, is to begin to understand how to treat the stories in it. But the average lay person has little or no access to this kind of information. Those who do are denied a voice in most congregations.

A misunderstanding of the the Son of Man figure in the book of Daniel by the first Christians also led to the corruption of some of the New Testament writings, leading to the false doctrine of the Return of Christ.

So, until we learn to use our Bibles intelligently we probably will go on blaming the "atheistic professors" in our colleges and universities and the "liberal preachers" in our pulpits for the breakdown in the faith of our young people.

3

The Bible Says...

By Floyd Hale

Question: Where did the Devil come from?

Answer: Coming home one night from a revival meeting service, in which the evangelist had said quite a bit about the Devil, one little boy said to his friend, "What do you think about that Devil person?" To which the second boy responded, "Oh, it's just like Santa Claus, it's your ol' man." The lad was more correct theologically than the Biblicists.

If Satan exists he would have to be of God's creating, or be coexistent with God. In many ancient cultures there was a god of evil. The "one God" faith of the Hebrews required that Yahweh handle both departments, good and evil, and most Old Testament writers found this a convenience. This has terribly distorted the good image of the Christian God.

According to Revelation 12 Satan got his start as a big red dragon in heaven, the angel who led a rebellion-- for which he was cast down to earth "to deceive the whole world." This shows that the Devil was a literary (expression) device for personalizing evil.

In New Testament times things were so bad that it "made sense" to conclude a Devil surely ruled the world. But Jesus would not buy this; he said "God is in charge"-- which was (is) his "gospel" (Mk. 1:14,15). But the Fundamentalists and Literalists will quote a lot of scriptures to prove Jesus believed there was a devil-- he even had a lengthy conversation with him in the wilderness (Mt. 4:1-11). Here's where one myth gets incorporated into another, and the biblical literature is further misunderstood. The story of Jesus' "temptation" at the beginning of his ministry is the Gospel writer's way of describing the basic challenge the Christ met in Jesus' life.

The evil imaginations of man need no help from a Devil. I think there's scripture to this effect (James 1:14).

The Devil is too important to traditional religion for him to be cast out of orthodoxy. But this also has its repercussions. If Christianity had not fostered the belief in a Devil (that he exists), there would have been no Satan worship going on in America. Think about this.

4

The Bible Says...

By Floyd Hale

Question: Did the sun really stand still?

Answer: It seems the Israelites (Joshua 10:13, RSV) needed this extra time in battle to finish "taking vengeance on their enemies." This brings to mind a couple exhortations from the New Testament: "Don't take vengeance" and "Love your enemies" (Rom. 12:19 and Mt. 5:44). This has nothing to do with the sun standing still, but if Christians did this, the world would stand still--at least long enough to take note of God at work.

For the sun to appear remaining fixed in one position, it would have to be the earth that stood still-- stopping its rotation. If this happened, can you imagine the super-hurricane effect this would have at the earth's surface? But it is easy for those who want to believe the sun actually stood still to go on and believe God could miraculously handle any other problems involved

When the author of the book of Joshua (writing about six centuries after the battle) was telling of the Israelites' victory over the Amorites, he said "it was sure a long day, but God was with them--overtime," and quoted from Jashar's poem about the occasion (written at least four centuries earlier). Knowing something about poetic expression and why some historians "rewrite history," you can begin to understand this passage-- and Old Testament history.

This solves the "sun standing still" problem, but what happened to the Jashar book of poetry? The author of II Samuel also quoted from it--at length (1:19-27, RSV). It, and several other ancient "books" (mentioned in this part of the Bible) used as sources by the "historians" as they wrote the six volume "Former Prophets" became "lost"--because they were no longer needed.

Later on this six volume "Former Prophets" (Joshua, Judges, I and II Samuel and I and II Kings) was used by the author of I and II Chronicles as his source for "rewriting" their History again. Since the "Former Prophets" was saved and-- along with I and II Chronicles canonized as Scripture, we have--right within our Bible--a way of seeing how "Bible History" was "improved on."

Check it out. It is most revealing.

The Bible Says...

By Floyd Hale

Question: Did God put the curse of slavery on the black race because Ham saw his father naked?

Answer: This false "Bible saying" (Genesis 9:25) was used by some Churches down south before the Civil War to justify the slavery of Negroes.

In the first place it was Noah, not God, who pronounced this curse. In the second place it was put on Ham's son Canaan, not Ham. And in the third place this whole story is a part of the mythical account of "History" from Abraham back to Adam (the first eleven chapters of Genesis).

In typical Jewish genealogical fashion the author of this part of Genesis constructed a "history of the origins of all the nations in the world" as the descendents of Noah. How convenient to name Canaan at the head of this list of the descendents of Ham, Noah's youngest son. This poem (vv. 25-27) was written to "justify retroactively" the abuse of the Canaanites by the Israelites who took over their land.

You will also notice among these "cursed nations" are Egypt (in which the Israelites were first captives), the Philistines (who battled Israel for the control of Canaan), Assyria (which took the ten northern tribes captive), the Jebusites (from which David took the city of Jerusalem), etc. And to take in the whole "tropical" (the meaning of the word "Ham") nations were included in this list as "Cush." Cush represented all of known Africa at the time (Egypt was then considered a part of the Asian Middle East). This is how the blacks got to be identified with Ham--pure myth.

Note also the warped view on sex revealed in this story. Something was ungodly about nakedness. And, instead of the "curse" being on Noah, the one naked--and drunk, it was on the innocent grandson whose father (Ham) had accidentally seen his father undressed.

What crimes have been committed in the name of the Bible? It is amazing that those who make the highest and most holy claims for The Good Book don't really know what it says.

6

LETTERS TO THE EDITOR

To the Editor:

Before you think this is just another crackpot, you need to know that I am the Pastor of a large respected Church (in this town), and I have several degrees that include a Masters in Biblical Communication.

I am writing to express my shock that *The Evening News* has a weekend column called "The Bible Says" that is written by a person that does not believe what the Bible says and probably does not know what the Bible says. Please let me illustrate from last week's column.

1. The writer begins his "response" to the question by saying "This (is a) false Bible saying" (Genesis 9:25).

2. He continues, "this whole story is a part of the mythical account of 'history' from Adam to Abraham (the first 11 chapters of Genesis)."

3. In the second to last paragraph he says the Bible has a "warped view on sex. Something was ungodly about nakedness."

4. Finally, in the last paragraph he says, "One who appreciates the Bible should be relieved to know that this 'curse' cannot be considered the 'word of God'."

The "Word of God" must be considered without error or it can not be considered the "Word of God." There are no myths in the scriptures. There are no warped views in the "Word of God." All parts of the Bible are inspired and without error or none of it is. The writer is nothing more that a pseudo-intellectual who believes he can discern what God has said without using the Bible and in fact contradicting the Bible. That in itself disqualifies him from writing about what "The Bible Says." I urge you to reconsider what your paper is printing from this so-called "expert."

A local Pastor

The Bible Says...

By Floyd Hale

Question: How did those sexy love Songs of Solomon get into the Bible?

Answer: Those eight secular love songs are in the Bible because the people treasured them as a part of their cultural heritage--the way most books in our Bible eventually became considered for Scripture. It was only late in Judaism that their sacred writings (with the exception of the Law) were all looked upon as "divinely inspired."

The Jewish poets seemed to brag of the sexual prowess of their ancient seers--Moses was credited with being yet able to cut the mustard at the age of a hundred and twenty (Deut. 34:7). Sampson was not condemned for his philandering. The great kings David and Solomon majored in this sport.

An organist once hesitated playing secular love songs for a church wedding, until I told her there were secular love songs in the Bible, the Song of Songs. Later I asked if she read them. She said yes--blushing. They get pretty erotic. In the fourth one the young man refers to his loved one's "rounded buttocks" being "like jewels" and her "breasts" being like "young twin deer." In the last Song the female lover boasts that her breasts were "like towers," complaining (or bragging) that her younger sister was flatchested.

These "Songs" were not written by Solomon, but his name got attached to them for two probable reasons. They reflect his romantic spirit, and, to justify their being included in the "Writings" (the third, and third rate section of the Jewish Scriptures).

In some of the Bibles of the last century there were headings put to these Songs which explained them as symbolizing Christ's love for his Church. "The Church and Christ Congratulate One Another," "The Church's Fight and Victory in Temptation," "Christ Sets Forth the Graces of the Church," etc. For obvious reasons, of late these captions were left off-- though worse explanations of scripture have been made by those who believe everything in the Bible is the "Word of God."

It is thought that these were popular wedding songs and thus treasured.

7

The Bible Says...

By Floyd Hale

Question: Is the story of the Great Flood in the Bible true?

Answer: Most communities in ancient times lived in such isolation that an unusually large flood anywhere would go down in their tribal lore as "covering the whole world," and archeology shows there were some large ones in most parts of the world. Do you realize how much water it would take to cover all the mountain peaks on earth fifteen cubits? And where did it all that water go when it "subsided"? But questions like this don't apply when you are dealing with myth.

Literary research in early Bible times traces this story back through the Canaanite legends to Babylonian origin. The Hebrew author of Genesis 6-8 edited this tale to his own purpose--to declare God's judgment on the wicked. To most of the Old Testament writers natural catastrophes were inflicted by a wrathful God. They are yet called the "acts of God."

Think of the task Noah had getting two of every species--elephants, tigers, snakes, skunks, bees and ants--into his boat. If this story were true there certainly was a time the lion laid down with the lamb. Which raises the question, what did the carnivorous animals have for food while aboard?

When this flood story was injected into the Abraham back to Adam "history" (the first 11 chapters of Genesis), it left a telltale mistake. Shem was born 100 years before the flood. In 11:10 it says Arpachshad was born to Shem when he was 100 years old-- "two years after the flood."

We might (in our more pessimistic moments) conclude that man has been a sorry lot, but to say God repented that he created him makes a wimp out of God. Destroying the millions of animals just to get at man? In the story of Jonah God gave as mercy on the animals in Nineveth the reason for not destroying that "wicked city."

Why should children in Sunday School still be told this "Bible Story" as true? Think what that does to their image of God. There can be a lot of difference between the kind of character attributed to God in a "Bible story" (for effect's sake) and the true character of God.

8

The Bible Says...

By Floyd Hale

Question: Was it one blind man or two Jesus healed as he was leaving Jericho?

Answer: Mark (10:46) says it was *one* blind man; Matthew (20:29) says, it was *two*. Luke (18:35) agrees with Mark about there being only one man, but says it happened as Jesus was entering, not leaving that town. The difference in these reports was not just "each Evangelist telling it as he saw it." Combining all three certainly does not give us a "full account." God surely did not inspire one to plainly contradict the other.

One must remember both Matthew and Luke used Mark as their primary source. It is rather easy to see why Matthew reported two blind men, for he had a habit of embellishing Mark's record--if one was good two was better. (Some of the Old Testament writers were really good at this.) The one man possessed of demons in Gerasaenes (Mk. 5:2) becomes two in Matthew (8:28). Matthew goes so far as to have Jesus riding two donkey's into Jerusalem instead of one. Numbers in biblical literature serve more the purpose of emphasis than accuracy. When Luke said 3,000 joined the church on the first day it opened for business, and 2,000 more came in a few days later, he was saying more about the growing strength of the church than reporting the number of converts.

It is unimportant that we know whether it was exactly one or two blind men? Or this took place entering or leaving Jericho? Or that it really happened at all? Not really. But we do need to understand that such stories were the writers' way of "bragging on Jesus"--and he deserved every bit of it!

When the fundamentalist literalists explain that such discrepancies (and there are many in the Gospels) result from different writers reporting events or words of Jesus differently, "as news reporters do the same event," they need to know they are actually violating their view of the "plenary inspiration" of the Scriptures. If one writer saw two men and the other saw one-- and they are excused for that for being "human"--you might justifiably question their "human" accuracy in reporting the rest of their Gospel stories.

9

LETTERS TO THE EDITOR

To the Editor:

This is to let you know how pleased I am that you are again running Floyd Hale's columns. Eighteen years ago his articles led me back into church and a new relationship with God. This was after 10 years of wanting nothing to do with organized religion.

Floyd's articles showed me there was a church (unnamed) that would allow one to use his or her brain in building faith.

After a class on Revelation with Rev. Hale, I understood that this book was written for the people under persecution some 1,900 years ago. The "way out" symbols had definite meaning to the people of that day. They referred to the oppressors of Christians at that time, in a secret symbolic language those oppressors did not understand.

That book encouraged those early Christians to persevere under horrible conditions. When it came time for the early church to put the New Testament together (i.e. canonize certain of its writings), Revelation, after much debate, made it into the Bible.

I know you will catch a lot of flak from Christians whose faith is so narrow that they can't allow themselves to even read something that may challenge the way they have believed things to be for so many years. On the other hand, there are probably many people out there such as I once was, who will benefit from the research of the scholars of the Bible.

Open minded study still continues at the (unnamed) Church where I attend the Eternal Learners Class,

If any of the readers are fed up with force-fed religion, I would encourage them to come study with us, and then make up there own minds how things really were back when the writers of the Bible were living and trying to keep faith in God strong among people who were just as human as we are today.

A Reader

b

The Bible Says...

By Floyd Hale

Question: What was bad about eating the fruit from the tree of the knowledge of good and evil in the Garden of Eden?

Answer: The bad part (according to the story) was that Adam and Eve disobeyed God by eating of it. The question arises, if they did this before they "knew right from wrong," how could they be morally responsible for doing it? But myths do not have to make sense. Yet it is not hard to see the primitive reasoning back of this myth. That is, all the bad things in the world began when man learned the difference between good and evil.

You can sense the logic that "there was a time, way back when," before people had a conscience, life was free and easy, no burden of guilt. Here's the envy of living morally (immorally) like cats and dogs. (I think the proper word is "amorally.") Someone has said if this was a "fall," it was a fall forward; for morality (however that may be knocked) makes meaning and purpose serve life--civilization.

Since there is a tendency in the scriptures to put down "man's knowledge"--if he hadn't got so smart we'd still be living in the "garden." (Actually we would have remained in the jungle--eating each other.)

The mythical thinking of the author of this story is that the prime evil involves sex. As long as Adam and Eve didn't "know" they were naked they were OK. But the minute they "saw skin" they covered their private parts with a few fig leaves and hid from their Creator. Islam yet applies this to their women's dress--just the eyes showing. (The eyes of men is the problem, but Islam is a man's religion.)

Death (in this myth) came because of "Adam's sin." Evidently the fruit from the "tree of life" in that garden would have kept them alive forever. Their being chased (and a guard put at the gate) was to keep them from eating that fruit and living forever in a sinful condition. But it is folly to try to make sense out of a myth--although some try to do it.

Forget the myth but remember its Truth: If God were obeyed--his will done--this world would not be in the mess it is in.

10

The Bible Says...

By Floyd Hale

Question: Is there fiction in the Bible?

Answer: As sure as I answer "Yes" someone will say I said "The Bible is fiction"--but I'll say it anyway: Yes, there's fiction in the Bible.

Fiction is a very legitimate literary form for getting an author's view across. Fiction at its best is very realistic, which makes parables a most effective teaching tool. This gets the "truth" in the little book of Jonah (which is fiction in parabolic form) mistaken by those who take it literally.

The little book of Ruth is fiction, but since it is about some ancient historical characters, it is more properly called a historical novel. Daniel and Revelation are Apocalypses--a most unique form of fiction. The "biblical" blunder of taking these literally spawned the "Christian" false beliefs about the end-of-the-world and Jesus' second coming.

Esther is the best example of pure fiction (I should say "impure") in the Bible. The story is set in Captivity (during the Persian period), but none of it is factual. A Jewish girl--even if she took a foreign name and beat out all the foreign girls in the beauty contest for the crown--was never the queen of a foreign empire. A Jew never became the prime minister of a foreign government and had the former prime minister hanged on the gallows he built on which to hang him. The Jews never slaughtered thousands of foreigners--by permission of their king.

I could go on, but any reader of the book of Esther could right away recognize it as fiction if it were not in the Bible. The Fundamentalists have beat it into our heads that everything in the Bible is literally true--or its false. Odd that something most unbelievable in the Bible is defended as true "because that's the way God works."

The book of Esther was written to fan the flames of "foreigner-hating." It is most interesting that Ruth was written (also in fiction) to put those very same fires out. Recognizing fiction in the Bible is a great (necessary) help to those looking for Truth in the Scriptures.

This last statement is not fiction made by a Liberal to help "destroy God's Word." It just has to be said, and that's why I say it.

11

The Bible Says...

By Floyd Hale

Question: How did the Davidian Cult in Waco, Texas use their Bible? (Date 5-5-93)

Answer: They accepted without question the biblical view of their charismatic leader. He used the Bible to gain his own "irreligious" ends. In going too far he dared not stop.

A "cult" easily gets paranoid in its defensiveness. This "persecution complex" automatically suggests the book of Revelation as its spiritual guide. Revelation was written at the beginning of the Roman Persecution (ca. A.D. 100) to encourage the Christians to *remain faithful unto death.* Revelation's symbolic and violent apocalyptic language can easily be misinterpreted to apply to just about any "desperate" (real or imagined) cultic situation. The government made the Waco situation desperate.

The Seven Seals (Rev.16) had to do with the supposed wrath of God which was to be released on those who recognized the Roman Emperor as "Lord." The Christians refused to do that and Rome turned on tnem.

The Waco group saw themselves as being "persecuted by the government." After the ATF's aborted attack, Koresh concentrated with the group on (his revised version of) the "Seven Seals," wherein you have the "last showdown battle"--Armageddon. The initial assault by the ATF and continued harassment only strengthened the cult's "faithfulness (to Karesh) unto death," and the the final attack by the FBI simply brought on the "apocalyptic fulfillment." David Koresh was truly in charge. The winners in that game lost it.

The largest factor leading to the tragic end of this episode was the complete absence of any *religious* or *political* pressure on the "law" to accomplish its purpose some other way. Koresh could easily have been arrested on one of his weekly trips into town before this stand off started. The clan would have caved in without him.

I hope our government learned its lesson at Waco. But I am afraid it didn't. The Law has the "law" on its side. It is no accident that the Oklahoima City bombing happened on the anniversary of the Waco debacle.

The Bible Says...

By Floyd Hale

Question: Is "speaking in tongues" in the Bible?

Answer: "Tongues" was the uttering of an unintelligible gibberish which the "spiritual clique" in the Church at Corinth claimed as a "gift of the Spirit." This caused a serious problem in the fellowship, which brought a letter from the founder of that congregation, in which a lengthy lecture (I Cor. 12, 13, and 14) tried to get them to stifle it. In Paul's tolerance of the immaturity of these good people he made several statements which have been later lifted out of context and used as "Scripture" supporting this aberration.

If the modern Bible reader knew all the background of Paul's exhortation in 12:1 and 2, he would see that "speaking in tongues" and the ecstatic experience accompanying it came from the "revivalistic" practices prevalent in the pagan Mystery Cults of that day; not from the teachings of Jesus--nor the Scriptures.

The person who believes (even subconsciously) in "tongues" and believes religious experience is consummated with an ●emotional high, is a good candidate for this "gift." The primary problem in this is not so much the "tongues," as it is the misunderstanding of what is spiritual. When people who expect feelings of elation and euphoria from religion, it tends to sanctify their emotional insecurity. They are then tempted to form the habit of spiritual masturbation--repeat "religious experience" for the bang they get out of it-- rather than get on with the the creative doing of God's will in life (as discipleship demands).

Although some may not believe it, my sympathy is with these very well-meaning Christians. If I have been plain-spoken in my comments, it is because I have tried to tell it like it is-- not only to be of help to those who may "speak in tongues," but to any who may be tempted in that direction.

The grace of God is a forgiving and comforting medicine to the guilt-ridden and depressed--and should be taken in large doses, but to use the scripture to repeat an ancient practice which this "scripture" actually discouraged is to misuse the Bible.

The Bible Says...

By Floyd Hale

Question: Has God ever spoken to you? If he has, how did it happen and what did he say? From a reader.

Answer: Yes, He has, and this is how it happened.

Back when I was in seminary my Bible professor got me very confused about the Scriptures. One day I got so mad I picked up my Bible and ran out of the building.

Fleeing very swiftly in my befuddled state of mind, I stumbled and fell into the goldfish pond there on the campus. Before I could get up and get out of the water a little goldfish swallowed me. While in the belly of that fish, God spoke to me. I knew it was God, for He used perfect King James English.

He said, "Floyd, I perceive thou art troubled about your Bible teacher suggesting there some parts of the Bible which is not literally true. Thou doest well to be troubled, for I will tell thee why I put it there.

"My people, you know, are critically inclined, and will pick up very quickly on things like that. There are several errors, contradictions, and inaccuracies sprinkled throughout my Book (my writers were human you know) to catch their attention and get them investigating. That way they will discover that I used many different literary forms in composing the various documents--poetry, fiction, epistle, sermon, and even apocalyptic. Once they discover this and start interpreting each writing in keeping with its particular literary form, they will come closer to getting my Word."

After three days and nights in the belly of that little goldfish I heard a big rumble and was tossed to and fro mightily. The fish had belched. I think I made it sick at its stomach, for the next thing I knew I was regurgitated up on the campus lawn--right in front of several other theology students.

I quickly picked up my Bible and ran straight--and I do mean straight--back into that seminary class and learned all I could about the Scriptures.

(That part about a reader. sending this question in is not true. I made that part up.)

The Bible Says...

By Floyd Hale

Question: Why in your column last week did you doubt the truth of Jonah and the whale by your irreverent parody of the scripture?

Answer: I don't doubt the truth of the story of Jonah one bit; I believe it. That's why I want people to understand it. That small pamphlet was written to counter the prejudice and hatred demonstrated against "foreigners" at that time. It is as modern as medicine--and as much needed.

Is was not until after the fish ordeal that God told Jonah he was going to destroy Nineveth. This gave Jonah a motive for "crying out against that wicked bunch." In this very pregnant little *parable* God "changes his mind" (repents), but Jonah doesn't--he still wants to see the Ninevites burn--even after they were all converted (down to the last cat and dog in town). Here's where the original readers of this "story" were very subtly challenged to change their minds about foreigners--as God did--or, like Jonah, rather die. What a punch line!

In my seminary days I struggled with a real prejudice against my professors who were teaching me the truth about the Bible. My fundamentalist view of scripture was being threatened, and "changing my mind" about that was not easy. I thought I was putting myself down (in my article) by being so small a little goldfish could swallow me, but my Mark Twain humor was probably a bit brash--sorry 'bout that.

My article was an "irreverent parody of the scripture" only for those who refuse to change their mind about Jonah being a parable. I am sure Jonah was originally considered irreverent by those who didn't like God's changing his mind about foreigners. Its becoming Scripture shows that enough people liked it to treasure and save it.

If the author of the Jonah story had signed his name to it, his publisher would not have received "letters to the editor"--he'd have been taken out and stoned. I'd kinda like to think "The Bible Says" is a modern day Jonah. The stones are much softer now than they were back then.

15

The Bible Says...

By Floyd Hale

Question: Is there humor in the Bible?

Answer: Some have tried to find humor in a few of Jesus' sayings. E.g. "How can you see to get a speck of sawdust out of your brother's eye, while you have a saw log in your own eye?" Speaking of eyes, "It is easier to drive a camel through the eye of a needle, than it is for a rich man to enter the kingdom." Or, on the subject of camels, "Hypocrite, you will often gag at a gnat in your drink, but at other times gulp down a camel in it." This type of saying is called "hyperbole"-- exaggeration to make a point unmistakably clear. By these Jesus was not trying to get a laugh.

A few of the Proverbs border on humor. 25:24 says "It is better to live up on the edge of the roof alone, than down in the house with a contentious woman." I doubt if women will find any humor in this--especially contentious ones. 1:26 suggests that God Himself occasionally has a laugh--at your calamity. I am afraid the author of this barb was attributing too much human nature to the Deity.

I woldn't recommend the Bible as a fun book. It's dead serious. Because it takes every aspect of life seriously, it deserves to be taken seriously. This does not mean that one should shift his/her mind into neutral in reading it. It requires all the intelligence one can apply to it.

There just might be some subtle humor in Exodus 33:23, where Moses is wanting to see God. God had spoken to Moses a lot but never "showing His face." Moses finally asks God to put in his appearance, but God says that's a "No no." Then, because Moses has found favor in His sight, God condescends to give him just a little peek. The author of this story says God has Moses stand in the crevice of a rock, and holding His hand over Moses' eyes, removes it as he streaks by. Moses gets just a glimpse--of God's "behind." The King James translates this "back parts," and the Revised Standard Version cleans this up still further, just "back."

If this is not humor, it might at least have a moral in it: Be careful about wanting to see God; you might succeed, but you'd come away with the wrong image of Him. I Know some who did.

16

The Bible Says...

By Floyd Hale

Question: Should children be taught the Bible stories?

Answer: No part of the Bible was written for children. The "stories" in the Bible are a mixed bunch of heavy theological works most adults don't even understand--mainly because they learned them as a child.

There are parables (e.g. Jonah and the Whale); myths (e.g. Adam and Eve), propaganda (e.g. Esther); fiction (e.g. Young David Kills a Giant--With a Slingshot); apocalypse (e.g. Daniel In the Lions' Den), to name just a few. Taken literally these corrupt even an adult's concept of God.

It hurts me to see a Pediatrician's office full of "Bible Stories for Children" books. I took a large one off the bookshelf in one of the big chain discount stores the other day, and it had 242 "Stories" from the Bible listed in its table of contents. Can you imagine what all these were?

If. . . if a child be told a Bible story, its unique literary form should be explained. Knowing the purpose the author had for writing it centuries ago is also important. Often the "moral" of a Bible story is not "in the story" if taken literally. And the "moral" of a story in the Old Testament doesn't usually come up to Christian standard.

Very damaging to the child's image of Jesus--and to his/her future faith--is for her/him to take the "Birth Stories" (at the beginning of Matthew and Luke) as literally true. When little children are used Christmas after Christmas to "act out" these stories, how are they going to ever get Jesus straight in their minds when they grow up (if they stay in the Church which did that to 'em)? Visions, dreams, a traveling star, angels, a virgin, etc. have no place in a child's tender faith. A child can not be expected to understand the deep meaning in these two very different myths--simply because they were not written for children.

If you have a question about a particular "Bible Story," send it in. I'll answer it as fully as space allows-- and honestly. (You don't have to put your name to it if you choose not.)

17

The Bible Says...

By Floyd Hale

Question: What do the "Four Horsemen of the Apocalypse" represent in the book of Revelation?

Answer: The *first* of the seven major visions in Revelation begins with these four horsemen riding out. In the very first scene the rider on a *white* horse rides out--conquering and to conquer. In the second the rider on the red horse rides out to remove peace from the world--war. In the third a rider on a black horse makes food scarce (famine). And in the fourth scene a rider on a pale horse inflicts death (6:1-8). All four relate to what was going on at the time John was writing.

But there is a "fifth" horse which rides out in the first scene of the *last* (7th) major vision in this Apocalypse. It is a *white* horse also, and the mission of its rider is made very clear. He is to *"conquer"*-- the nations with a *"sword"* which issues from his mouth. The riders on the "two white horses" form a parenthesis around this whole body of visions, suggestion they are one and the same, "the beginning and the end," who has been riding throughout this whole drama--*conquering with his two-edged sword.*

Don't let this apocalyptic militant language throw you off. The "sword" is the "word of God." From the Gospels it is clear that Jesus' "word" was his gospel--the Kingdom (Rule) of God. When "declared," it comes out in the present tense, "God IS in charge." This was John's basic message to the Christians at the beginning of the Roman Persecution, when evil (Satan) sat squarely on the throne of the "whole world."

John ends each of the first six "letters" to the persecuted Churches in Asia Minor with the same exhortation,*"Conquer!"* He ends the seventh "letter" by explaining *how to conquer--* the same way Jesus did, by preaching and practicing the gospel, "God is in charge," and paying for it with their lives if that need be

They "followed Jesus (o n *white* horses) whithersoever he went" (14:4b, 19:14). The message to those endangered Christians was very clear--"Mount your horses!"

The Bible Says...

By Floyd Hale

Question: What is the mark of the beast, "666"?

Answer: Boy, has this been played with too much down through the ages.

Like most symbols in Revelation it is explained therein (13:3, 16-18 and 19:9-11), but, as John warns, getting it straight requires a few extra smarts.

The Emperor Domitian (81-96) was to the Christians at the end of the first century what Nero had been to the brethren a generation earlier. He was "Hitler come back alive" (as President Bush called Sadam Hussein). Nero had blamed the Christians for setting the city of Rome afire, so he burned a few hundred of them and had their leader, Paul, beheaded.

Domitian pushed his divine title as "Lord" too much to suit the Christians and they refused to participate in his Roma cult, which meant the loss of a lot of privileges and some economic hardships--plus being suspect of sedition.

John right off got an Apocalypse (Revelation) dispatched to "the churches" as a strong exhortation to not participate in any of the "Beast worship"--even if they kill you. Victory was promised to the faithful. Martyrdom was a quick ticket to heaven (so the symbology went).

Domitian is identified as "Nero come back to life." (There was rumor that Nero had faked his enforced suicide and was yet alive.) They might not have heard too much of Domitian yet, but they sure remembered ol' Nero.

In an explanation hard to follow, John reviews the seven Caesars, with this "eighth" one, identified by adding up the numerical value of the letters of his "name." Neron Caesar came out exactly "six hundred sixth-six," the "mark of the beast." Some think if John had named Domitian outright that might have made this document obviously subversive, hindering its getting spread around.

To say this is the number of some future antichrist is to really not take this sacred book at its word. It sure would have meant nothing to those endangered Christians (to whom this was first addressed) to tell them their tormentor was coming on the scene about nineteen centuries later.

The Bible Says...

By Floyd Hale

Question: Why are two different resurrections mentioned in the book of Revelation?

Answer: The "first resurrection" is for the martyrs who "come back to rule the nations with Christ" (20:4-6), and the second one (20:11-13) is for everyone else on "Judgment Day." But what does this mean?

Revelation is an Apocalypse; therefore *not to be taken literally.* It would take far more space than available here for me to explain the apocalyptic form of expression, but it must be learned by Bible believers-- if they are going to understand their Bible.

John is writing to the Churches in Asia Minor which are just entering (ca A.D. 90) that horrible period known in history as the Roman Persecution, when Christians were on trial for "subversion" (refusing to pledge allegiance to the state). John encourages them to keep the faith--even though executed for it. He says if they are beheaded that will only "guarantee the victory" over the "Beast." The number 144,000 dramatically warned them *this may take a lot of dying."*

These martyrs were promised a "first" (special) resurrection (anybody could get in on the "second" one). *This symbolized the effect their martyrdom would have on the world---*"as if" they actually came back to life and helped Jesus rule the nations ("with a rod of iron" no less). Their Crosses did prove effective. The number of Christians mushroomed, and in 323 the "Beast" (Constantine, the emperor at the time) received Christian baptism (for his own political purposes) and officially lifted the persecution. His son, Constantius, went one better (actually worse), outlawing all other religions, setting into motion the "Holy Roman Empire." John's promised "end" had come.

Notice, those whose names are found in the "book of life" at the "second resurrection"*don't go up to heaven.* Their God *comes down to earth* and leads them in the ongoing mission of "healing the nations" (22:1-5).

The "end" in revelation is just the beginning, as John saw it.

The Bible Says...

By Floyd Hale

Question: Enjoy your column . . . Each week it is thought provoking. Are their any other books or writings you could recommend to help a lay person better understand what there is to be learned from the Bible?

Answer: Most of the books on the Bible available are sold in religious bookstores. Even the best ones promote the author's interpretation of the Bible--or some book in it. A person should learn enough about the background of the Bible--or some particular book in it-- to "interpret" it for him or herself. But that requires the approach of a student--but why not?

To begin with you might borrow volume I of *The Interpreter's Bible* commentary (the older set) from almost any minister. (Some public libraries carry these.) The first 171 introductory pages are 11 articles "about" the Bible. The first one is "Its Significance and Authority." There's a good start. The fourth one, "*The Canon of the New Testament,*" could come next. It is by Edgar J Goodspeed, one of the best of the older Bible scholars (he even has a very good and popular translation).

There is no more interesting exercise than studying Bible background-- when, why, to whom, and in what literary form the various books in the Bible were written. Then the very interesting subject of when, why, and how the four groups of books became "Scripture." First the "Law," ca. 400 B.C. Then the addition of the "Prophets" ca. 200 B.C. (making the "Bible" of Jesus' day, "The Law and The Prophets"). The "Writings" were canonized in A.D. 90, finalizing the Jewish Scriptures (our Protestant Old Testament).

Then the amazing story of how Paul's Letters, the Gospels, the other Epistles, and Revelation made their way into Scripture as a "New Testament."

To learn the *Truth in* the Bible you have to know the *truth about* the Bible.

The Bible Says...

By Floyd Hale

Question: Where is Hell?

Answer: I ought to know, I've been there.

The first time Dorothy and I toured Israel, our hotel was a little to the south of Jerusalem. As our bus entered the city the first day through a small valley, the guide said, "You are now going through Hell." After studying the expressions on our faces, he added, "This is the Valley of Ge-Hinnon, which gave its name to the apocalyptic hell in the New Testament."

There are three different words translated "hell" in the King James Bible, and it is worth knowing the meaning of each. In the Old Testament the Hebrew word is "sheol," and means simply "the place of the dead"-- sometimes just "the grave"-- without any reference to punishment or reward. The Revised Standard Version leaves this "sheol" in the English.

In the KJV New Testament there are two Greek words, "gehenna" and "hades," both translated "hell." "Gehenna" (the Greek pronunciation of the Hebrew "Ge-Hinnon") comes from the name of the valley I mentioned above. At one time the Assyrians forced the Israelites to offer human sacrifice in that place. Being "unclean" it became the city dump, which burned continually (as all old city dumps used to). The carcasses of lepers (and other "sinners") were sometimes incinerated there. The hardhearted apocalypticists just before the time of Christ gave the name of this place to the "lake of fire" where they promised their enemies "everlasting" punishment.

The other word in the Greek New Testament, "hades," similar to the Hebrew "sheol," simply meant "the place of the dead," with no suggestion of anything taking place there. The RSV does us the favor of bringing this word "hades" over into the English, while leaving "hell" where the word "gehenna" was in the Greek text--and there it is a figure of speech..

It was an injustice to the O.T. for the KJV translaters to translate the Hebrew word "sheol" "hell." However cruel the God of the O.T. was at times, at least He never promised to roast anybody-- forever.

LETTERS TO THE EDITOR

To the Editor:

I would like to share a different answer to the question, "Where is Hell?" on your 25 editorial page.

The word "hell" in the New Testament is the Greek word "geheena." It is a region. The character of this region is the eternal fire where the fire is not quenched and the worm does not die.

In Luke 12:5 Jesus is speaking to the religious elite who appear righteous outwardly but are "rotten" inwardly. (See verse on of this same chapter.) Jesus says not to fear the hypocritical Pharisees, for they can only kill the body.

Then in verse 5 Jesus says, "But I will warn you whom to fear: fear the One who after he has killed has authority to cast into hell: yes, I tell you, fear Him!"

Those guilty of hypocrisy will suffer in torment, where the "worms and fire" in their eternal souls in the region of hell.

The region of hell is experienced after death and is not a reference to any earthly location.

In the Old Testament the actual reference to hell itself is not used. Instead the word "sheol" (Hades is the corresponding word in the New Testament) is used. It is the region of the departed spirits of lost souls. It represents the place the lost will be after physical death and before sentenced to hell and its terrors. The only exception to this is those who trusted in the Messiah in the Old Testament times.

When Jesus, the long awaited Messiah, came He was crucified, buried, and arose from the dead. He overcame the power of sheol, hell in hades!

After his bodily ascension back to heaven as the resurrected Christ, all those in sheol who trusted in Him as the messiah were released to be with Him in heaven-- also a definite place.

Jesus as the Messiah, the Christ, made this possible for all who trust in him. Jesus without sin, died, was buried and went to hell in our place. When He arose from death, it was for us!

This is the good news. When those who trust in Jesus as the Son of God die, Jesus will be there to receive them and take them to the glory of heaven, not to sentence them to hades or the torment of hell.

A local pastor

c

The Bible Says...

By Floyd Hale

Question: Do you have to know the truth about the Bible to learn the Truth in the Bible?

Answer: If one does not know *about* the book of Jonah being a parable, and when and why it was written, the Truth in it is missed--and God is credited with planning to do something "evil" to the Ninevites (and then "repenting" of it).

If one does not know *about* the book of Job being a poetic drama and why it was composed, its Truth is missed--and God is credited with letting the Devil do anything he wishes to a certain man--except take his life (and his wife--who became a part of his misery).

If one does not know *about* the book of Daniel being an Apocalypse (a very far out expression form), one would believe God saved the young man Daniel from the lions den and his three friends from the fiery furnace because they trusted in Him, thus getting another false image of God.

If a person does not know *about* the unique literary form of the book of Revelation, he/she will believe it foretells the future, when "prophecy" in that book actually means a "message" to the Christians who were beginning to be persecuted by the Roman government at that time.

If a person does not know *about* how the Gospels were written, the true image of Jesus is missed, because the Gospels are not biographies of Jesus--especially the Fourth Gospel. All the lectures ascribed to Jesus explaining himself in John's Gospel are of John's own composition.

This suggests just a small bit of what must be learned *about* the Bible if it is to be used as a proper guide for faith.

Some have insisted I should teach in this column strictly what "the Bible says." But I would not be fair to the Bible nor honest with you if I did this; for sometimes there is a lot of difference between what the Bible says and the Truth in the Bible.

Divine Truth is beyond the printed page anyway. The Scriptures, when properly understood, only point to it. From there on it is a leap of faith.

The Bible Says...

By Floyd Hale

Question: Did Jesus really walk on water?

Answer: From what I have learned about him I would say, "He could!"--figuratively speaking; but I do not believe he actually did. It was a common practice for those of that day (especially in Jewish "Bible" tradition) to "glorify" their heroes with "wonder stories." The narratives were in very realistic prose. To support my bias in this matter I would point out another "wonder story" which got edited into this one--which illustrates my point.

In the oldest version of this "story" (Mark 6:45-51) Jesus walks on the sea, out to where his disciples are, and "he" alone gets into the boat with them. In another version of this same story, reported years later by Matthew (14:22-32), using Mark's gospel as his source, Peter sees Jesus coming and asks if he may join him. Jesus says, "Come on," and Peter steps out on the waves--doing pretty good for a while, but then starts to sink. Jesus grabs him by the hand, and "they" both get into the boat with the others. Mark didn't just "forget" about Peter.

If the "story" about Peter walking on the water originated between A.D. 70 (when Mark wrote) and 85 (when Matthew wrote), why could not the story about Jesus walking on the water have originated between A.D. 30 and 70? This is not just a baseless guess. The gospel authors had a "doctrinal reason" for almost every detail of their writing; not just to record a biography of Jesus. Here's where a critical study of the Gospels is a big help. This would also give us a more accurate picture of who Jesus was and what he really said and did.

By the end of the first century Peter was being acclaimed as Christ's Vicar (successor) on earth. The inclusion of Peter's feat into this story by Matthew was to "glorify" him. His failure to stay afloat (keeping him from being rated "up there" with Jesus) does not overshadow his partial success.

The story of Jesus walking on water is one more way Mark had of "glorifying" Jesus. I like it.

The Bible Says...

By Floyd Hale

Question: Dear Mr. Hale, does Floyd Hale believe that Jesus was actually born of a virgin, that he actually died on the cross, that he actually rose from death to life on the third day, and that he actually ascended back to God in heaven some forty days later?

Answer: In your lengthy letter you suggest that I give a simple yes or no answer to your questions. (This is like asking me if I have quit beating my wife.)

Since your question is in four parts, I will have to answer each separately. My one-word answers are: to the first part, "No;" to the second, "Yes"; to each of the last two, "No." You also suggested the other 299 words of my column be given to "what the Bible says."

I do not--as you do--go by what the Bible literally "says." I have to interpret it in each part in light of what is known about it. To give as much space as possible to my answer, I will, in the three following weeks, explain each of the above "No's." I think I can explain the "Yes" one in just a few lines below.

The New Testament is full of *theological* and *doctrinal* explanations of the death of Jesus--for the purpose of establishing the fundamental "beliefs" of the new religious sect which was immediately established in his name.

Jesus died because of the way he lived. He openly ridiculed the traditional religion of his day. For this the self-appointed defenders of the faith charged him with blasphemy--which was punishable by death according to their Law (the Scriptures)--yet a part of the Christian Bible.

(The day is not over when those who challenge traditional religion are supposed to be silenced.) The secular ruler, Pilate, was glad to honor their wish and have Jesus executed, for "messiahs" were considered political threats--the temple today, tomorrow the palace.

Yes, I have no trouble at all believeng Jesus died on a cross.

How such a thing could happen got his followers into picking out some "Scriptures" (which did not apply) to explain it; and this started the Church off on a false doctrine of salvation.

25

The Bible Says...

By Floyd Hale

Question: (Mr. Hale) do you believe Jesus was actually born of a virgin?

Answer: I do not believe Jesus left out of his teachings anything important to Christian living, and he never mentioned his birth. The first Gospel written, Mark, saw no reason to even mention the birth of Jesus. Paul--on whose doctrines the Church was actually established--knew nothing of a virgin birth. If he had he would have surely loved it. Paul had completed his writings and was martyred before Matthew and Luke were written, in which the Virgin Birth Stories appear-- and they are just that, "Stories."

Instead of concentrating on the mission Jesus began, the early Church leaders in their lack of "orthodox" traditions argued among themselves about *what Christians had to believe.* As a solution they generally agreed on "The Apostles' Creed," basing it (they thought) on the "teachings of the Apostles." But there is no mention of the virgin birth in any of the writings of the Apostles. Matthew was not an apostle, and his account of the virgin birth (misinterpreting Is. 7:14) made it "Scripture."

Matthew and Luke used the idea of a "virgin birth" as *figurative* of the Spirit of God in Jesus. Jesus' followers "saw" the Spirit in Jesus-- because of the way he lived and died as a man. This is the way Christians are to "see God" (actually, "see God's will") in Jesus. This brings them to a *faith commitment,* of discipleship (or it is not real faith).

To *believe* the Spirit was in Jesus because God impregnated Mary is to put one's faith in a myth, instead of looking for what it was in Jesus that caused them to describe his birth in this fashion.

To show you how mythical these stories are, Matthew says Mary not only conceived without Joseph's help, she didn't even "sleep with him" until after Jesus was born (1:25). Otherwise it would not have been a "virgin birth." If Protetstants can believe this, they should not criticize Catholics for believing Mary never did "sleep with Joseph" after Jesus was born.

See what happens when a myth is taken for true?

26

The Bible Says...

By Floyd Hale

Question: (Mr. Hale) Do you believe Jesus actually rose from death to life on the third day?

Answer: This is the explanation of the second "No" answer I promised you two weeks ago.

The apocalyptic "end-of-the-world-ism" dominated the "kingdom" thinking at the time Jesus lived. It held that a "Son of man" would come from heaven ("on the clouds"), bring Judgment, and establish the rule (kingdom) of God. Jesus' disciples (or their disciples) believed he would fulfill that "Messianic" hope.

In the literal apocalyptic drama, the *martyr* in God's cause would be *resurrected* and help establish the *kingdom* in the "end-time." Because of the unique role Jesus had played in the "kingdom" business, his death was thus proclaimed as his *victory*. God had *elevated* him ("raised him up") to the place of *Power*--at the same time he would "remain with his disciples" until the the end (Mt. 28:20). (Jesus' physical remains--dead or alive--would actually have nothing to do with this.) Thus it was that Jesus' *death* saved his *life*--and mission. Revelation (an Apocalypse) explains how all this works in detail.

Very soon the popular resurrection view of "life after death"--so desired by religious people--gave to this story a *literalness,* and the Apostle Paul made this the foundation of his gospel--"because Jesus came back to life, the believer in Christ would also." This Gnostic *hope* replaced the true hope Jesus inspired--*in the rule (kingdom) of God* coming on earth (expressed symbolically in apocalyptic).

By the time the Gospels were composed (out in the Gentile world), some of the oral traditions about Jesus on which their writers relied were edited to reflect Paul's interpretation of Jesus. This established a "scriptural" tradition which almost completely hid the meaning of the original apocalyptic affirmation *about the influence the crucified Jesus would have on history (through his disciples).*

The Bible Says...

By Floyd Hale

Question: (Mr. Hale) Do you believe he (Jesus) actually ascended back to God in heaven some forty days later?

Answer: What I say here follows--and supplements--my last week's article on the "resurrection" of Jesus originating as the apocalyptic explanation of his death--as *insuring his victory (actually the victory of his cause).*

You will recognize this as the fourth (and last) part of that lengthy question a few weeks ago in "The Bible Says." I flatly answered it "No" then, promising an explanation later.

It was hoped somehow by Jesus' followers (or their followers) that he would fulfill the "Son of Man" mission of bringing in the kingdom (midrashed from Daniel). This being apocalyptic, the death of his physical body did not end this hope; his *martyrdom* only confirmed it. This meant that "any day soon" (in these "last days") he would yet complete that work. Obviously he did not, and by the time the Gospels were written the "delay" alone began to make out of this a "second" coming.

Since the apocalyptic placed the Messianic *martyr* in the seat of Power--*"at the right hand of God."* The "ascension" story merely gets Jesus "up there" in that position (elevated, "raised"). To illustrate that this is a "faith story, not the reporting of historical "facts," Luke has Jesus ascending on the afternoon of his "resurrection" at the close of his Gospel, while in Acts he says it is forty days later.

Real Bible Truth is never going to be learned until people understand the *story form* in which so much of the scriptures were written--especially the apocalyptic. A Bible "story" and the truth it teaches can be two entirely different things. You might ask, "Well, how do I know the Bible is not just one big 'made-up' story?" To this I would answer, "Learn all *about* your Bible and you can answer that question to your own satisfaction."

Those who are afraid of "myth" in the Bible ought to wake up to the fact that they have swallowed--without gagging--a much bigger myth about the Bible, laid on them by the Literalists--"God wrote it."

28

The Bible Says...

By Floyd Hale

Question: Where in the Bible does it say an ass spoke? What did it say?

Answer: The account of an ass talking to its master is found in the book of Numbers, Chapter 22.

To me it is just as amazing that its rider talked back to it. The story goes that the king of Moab was afraid of the Israelites who were passing through on their way from Egypt. Balaam--a master at putting curses on those he (and God) didn't like--was called by the king of Moab to come put the whammy on the Israelites. God told Balaam not to go, and then He changed his mind and told him to go. Then He got mad at him for going, and sent a sword swinging angel to stop him. The ass Balaam was riding saw the angel in the road and balked, upon which Balaam set to beating his faithful beast. After the third flogging God "opens the ass' mouth" and it pleads its case with its owner (22:28). Then the Lord "opens Balaam's eyes" and he sees the angel also.

The author of this story was doing a very common thing in his day, speaking to the "present" situation by giving a "romantic history" of the past. After the Babylonians had left Judah a weakened state the Moabites were raiding the land at will. The writer was telling the Moabites they were "fooling with God's chosen," whom He had protected from them at their first meeting centuries earlier. This story became a part of the Hebrew traditions and was later included in the Pentateuch--"The Story of the People of the Law"-- when it was composed about 500 B.C.

That this story is not true is a problem only for those who hold a narrow view of the authority of the Scriptures. Those who have pushed "God's Word" all the way to include every word in the Bible have done the Bible, God and the rest of us a great disservice. It takes a lot of researching the background of the Scriptures to know what they were all about when they were written. The lack of this leaves the uninformed not knowing their relevance (if any) to today.

The real problem is not so much that an ass spoke in the Bible, but that far too many asses have been speaking on behalf of the Bible ever since.

29

The Bible Says...

By Floyd Hale

Question: Did God send two bears to mangle forty-two little boys for calling one of His prophets 'Ol' Baldy'?

Answer: "The Bible says" in II Kings 2:24 this happened as a result of Elisha's putting a divine whammy on these children. Because they had shouted at him--twice, "Get out of here ol' baldy," two she-bears tore up forty-two of 'em--in the name of the Lord. You'd think that a "man of God" would have ignored this jeer, but men of God (in the Bible) are not to be fooled with.

What if a minister on Sunday morning in worship, for his children's sermon, read this story ("from the Word of God") and then said: "So you kids had better be careful not to make fun of your preacher?"

You say that's Old Testament stuff. But what if that minister (because the offerings had been falling off) read from the New Testament the story of Ananias and Sapphira's getting laid out cold--and I do mean cold--for withholding part of their pledge to the church (Acts 5:1-11), and then he went on to preach a "stewardship sermon" to the adults?

You notice the author of Acts ends his story by saying, "Great fear came upon the whole church, and all who heard about this." Here I think is the key as to why such "stories" are in the Bible--to promote the "fear of God" (not the love of God).

I am glad to come to the defense of the good character of God by saying flatly, none of this happened--at least with God's help or blessing. Somehow God just can't be trusted to motivate people by His love, to get his work done. I guess an "example" has to be made out of someone once in a while. I have no problem believing men wrote the Bible, for they couldn't keep from injecting a bit of their own human nature into the God who inspired them.

I am dead serious when I say we need to clean up the Bible. It is too great a Book, in which we have the story of the greatest man who ever lived, to let it be dragged through the mud of Literalism.

30

The Bible Says...

By Floyd Hale

Question: I would like it explained to me where in the Bible (it says) that the Sabbath is the 8th or 1st day of the week? The fourth commandment says it is the 7th day.

Answer: To be strictly biblical, it says nowhere that the Sabbath is the 8th day or the 1st day of the week. That explains that.

When this Sabbath law was first established by the Israelites, how did they know that their 7th day was actually the 7th day of the week? They went by the traditional calender of the time, and that calendar was man made. The calendar has been completely changed since then (I forget the circumstances of why and when), so how do you know what day of the week is really when? Does it make any difference?

The Jews (and some Christian Biblicists) keep the 7th day as the Sabbath. Christianity in general keeps the 1st day. In each it is the "religious tradition" which determines this.

In any discussion like this "legalism" sticks its ugly head up and takes over. The spirit of the law of the Sabbath is "a day of rest." It was what was good for "life" when the Deuteronomist and the author of Proverbs wrote. Now people have more rest than work time. Furthermore our keeping the Sabbath is not to make God smile nor gain His stamp of "righteous" on our souls. Mowing the lawn and washing the car could be good "rest" for the person whose job all week is not physical work. To really keep that fourth commandment one would have to "labor" all those first six days of the week (which makes me want to change the subject).

If you think I am getting a bit frivolous, I admit it. Legalism in religion leads to this. Without it the Scribes and Rabbis would have had little to do--all week long.

I could go into detail on what Jesus and Paul said about the Sabbath, and its honoring Jesus "Resurrection," but I think God is far more concerned about what you do all during the week, than what you don't do on Sunday.

31

The Bible Says...

By Floyd Hale

Question: Do you really believe an angel troubled the waters of Bethesda, giving them healing powers (John 5:2-9)?

Answer: Modern discovery of many manuscripts of the New Testament not available to the King James revisors reveals that the last part of verse 3 and all of verse 4 of the 5th chapter of John was not in the original document. When this interpolation is removed (as the RSV has done) you see that the only mention of troubled waters is made by the cripple Jesus spoke to there. You will notice that he said he "had no one to put him in; when the waters were troubled another stepped in ahead of him."

If you did not have the explanation in verses 3b and 4 (KJV) you would wonder what he was talking about. Jesus certainly didn't stop to discuss this superstition with him, for if he had I think he would have had some unkind things to say about a god who did his good deeds in this manner. Can you imagine the scramble of a hundred or two paralytics, cripples, and litter carriers piling up near the water (or in it), all coming in second to a sprinter who got his acne cured?

This does not mean that there were no cures at Bethesda--there are many such "healing spas" around the world today, and healings take place at all of them. It's the perfect set up for certain illnesses--and people with a certain kind of faith. But I'm glad neither Jesus nor John gave any credence to the work of this water rippling angel. There's too many stories like this in the Bible already.

When it was noticed that the copies of John originating in North Africa were in the only ones carrying this interpolation, it was easy to guess that some church scribe in that area had gone to Jerusalem to make a copy of this Gospel for his home congregation. Knowing folks back there would know nothing of the Bethesda Tradition he added this "explanatory note" in the margin of his copy. As other neighboring churches made copies from his they added the "marginal" into the main text. Old manuscripts reveal this to have been a common practice before they became Scripture.

The Bible Says...

By Floyd Hale

Question: Is Jesus coming back someday?

Answer: Matthew 28:29 says he never went away: "Lo, I am with you *always,* to the close of the age." But some would see in this (by quoting other scriptures) his returning at the "close of the age."

The confusion comes from "the end of the age (world)" sayings in the Gospels and the "prophecy" in Revelation. Apocalyptic (a most unique expression form) was the popular religious language of the first Jewish Christians. It expressed the *power* of Jesus' continuing ministry in and through his followers. The first three Gospels combined all of the *coming-crucifixion-resurrection-ascension* into an apocalyptic "Son of Man" cycle. This figure (mentioned in Daniel 7:13) would "come on the clouds" (from heaven), be martyred, and *raised by God to His right hand of Power.* " The Gentile Church (not understanding Jewish apocalyptic) took this literally, repeating the first phrase of that cycle as yet in the future. It must be said, the "second coming" is actually a false Christian teaching.

Jesus--through his witnesses' preaching his gospel--was to *continue* "ruling" (and "judging") as Son of Man. Revelation perfectly explains this "cycle" in detail. In Revelation Jesus is continually "coming." This is why that cycle stopped at the right hand of God--the place of Authority and Power. Acts explains that "power" as the spirit of Jesus (the Holy Spirit) working *in the disciples.*

Before the Church could de-literalize its apocalyptic, it found itself out in the Gentile world, growing rapidly. It's first "creed" took shape from Paul's apocalyptic language adapted to Greek Gnosticism. The apocalyptic resurrection of the human body (considered inherently evil by the Gnostics) was replaced with the redeemed human "spirit" (the real person) returning to the Spirit World "above"--its original home. The task of the Son of Man was no longer to establish his kingdom on earth, but to "rapture" his saints at a future "return."

If this is confusing it is because we have not kept up on our Bible.

33

The Bible Says...

By Floyd Hale

Question: In regard to Mr. Hale's column on the Bible, who does he think he is, picking the Bible apart as he does? It's a wonder God doesn't strike him down. He's nothing but an advocate of the devil.

Answer: I know my style of writing is threatening to some, but I seem to be getting several readers' attention. If I simply quoted some scripture and preached a little sermonette, I'd be just one more "Bible preacher" espousing one more view of "thou shalt and shalt not" There's enough of that going on--and in the pulpits every Sunday. I believe there is a shortage of preachers who will tell the truth about the Bible. So, I volunteer to fill that niche.

I am convinced that learning the truth about the Bible is necessary to understanding the Truth in the Bible. When I point out an error or contradiction in the Bible, that indisputable fact has to be dealt with as "the truth." It may cause a person to doubt his/her faith in the Bible, but a doubt can be the first positive step in learning the truth, if it is treated as such. If one opens up to learning more about the Bible it may change his/her view of the authority of the Scriptures--

I think it should. At least seventy-five percent or more of the traditional view of the Bible conforms to fundamentalistic literalism, which makes "every word" in the Book the "Words of God." This does great damage to the image and will of God in the mind of the average person--religious or no.

We have ignored too long what the scholars in this field have to say about the Bible. Their method of research can be followed by anyone with an open mind and a good set of commentaries (I'd recommend *The Interpreter's Bible*.) This requires that, *first*, before concluding about the meaning of a given passage the background of the book in which it is found be studied--when, why, to whom, and especially in what literary form it was written .

One of the sad things about not understanding one's Bible it can cause a person to make such awful accusations as this.

The Bible Says...

By Floyd Hale

Question: In your writing you show a preference for the Revised Standard Version of the Bible over the King James. Why?

Answer: These two Bibles reflect two different ages, cultures, and even ways of doctrinal thinking. The KJV was the "Scripture" of the Church during the development of our nation-- the 16th through the 19th centuries. When it was first published (1611) very little real research had been done in the different ancient manuscripts of the scriptures. In fact most of the oldest and best of these sources had not been discovered yet.

The traditional beliefs at the time had a great influence on the translators of the KJV--it was the product of the Church. A good example of this is Daniel 9:25,26. The title "Messiah" appears in both verses. The Hebrew word literally means "an anointed one," and is translated as such in the RSV in this place--and properly so.

Then (1611) these two verses were thought to "foretell" the coming of Christ and his crucifixion. Since Jesus had been proclaimed "THE Anointed One," and the Hebrew word was pronounced "mashiah,"

the KJV brought it over into English in this place as "Messiah" (with a capital M). Yet they translated it "anointed one" in all the other places where it appeared in the rest of the Old Testament.

Anyone holding a sacred office--prophet, priest, king, etc--in Israel was considered "an anointed one" ("one of God's anointed"). When Daniel was written this was especially the popular title for a priest; just as "reverend" is today for a minister. The KJV translators were not aware that these two "anointed ones" in Daniel were two priests--one (Joshua ben Jozadok) who came back with the first Returnees in 540 B.C. and the other (Onias III) assassinated 369 years later (about "62 hebdomads"--weeks of years).

I could give many other examples where the RSV is an improvement over the KJV. In the RSV you actually have the "oldest" Scriptures.

The Bible Says...

By Floyd Hale

Question: Does the Bible account of Creation conflict with evolution?

Question: Far too much has been made of the "conflict" between the Genesis account of Creation and the theory of evolution--by both sides. First, it should be pointed out that there is no such thing as one consistent theory of evolution. The scientists in this field differ widely in some of their theories. But the Creationists should not take quick joy in this, for the Scriptures disagree on how God did it.

There are two Creation Stories in Genesis, 1:1-2:4a and 2:4b-4:25. The first story is a beautiful affirmation of the sacredness of life--"it's all good." The second seeks in true mythological form to explain what's wrong with life--"it's all bad." The men who put the Pentateuch together probably chose them both in order that "both sides of the story" are told.

These two Creation Stories literally contradict each other in a number of places. Notice in the first one the animals are created *before* man and woman (1:25,26), while in the second they come *after* Adam (2:18-22)-- with Eve coming in third.

Those who say the second story just fills in the details left out of the first one, without attention to order, just haven't read these stories--with their eyes open. The first story has an error in it, there are three "days and nights" before God creates the sun and moon. But myths do not have to walk on all fours.

These Creation Stories deserve serious study and appreciation in keeping with the unique form and purpose of each, but they were not written to reveal scientific data, to tell *how* God did it. Yet I find a marked similarity between the pattern of progression outlined in the first story and that suggested by evolution. Why should one rule out the other? God didn't leave His fingerprints on everything--and He's not finished yet.

I like to think evolution is the smart but free method God used in developing good physical bodies into which He could finally put His children.

Life is a miracle--that's Creation. Evolution is just the way God did it.-- and keeps doing it.

36

The Bible Says...

Question: Should "Creation Science" be taught in public schools?

Answer: Those who are pressing state school boards to include the Bible account of creation in the children's science books along with (even in the place of) the theory of evolution don't realize this would defeat their purpose.

In the first place there are two Creation Stories in Genesis (1:1-2:4a, and 2:4b-3:24). If both were included the children would easily see they do not agree on the way God did it. In the second account the man was created, then the animals, and then the woman (from the man's rib bone). In the first the man and woman both came after the animals. In a science class these accounts would undergo this kind of scrutiny.

If the first story--the Seven Days one--were chosen alone, it would be obvious to a child that "day and night" could not have operated for three days and nights before God put the sun in the sky--"to separate the day from the night."

If only the second story--the Adam and Eve one--were selected, you would have the fruit of a certain tree, when eaten, giving people the knowledge of good and evil. Magic just could not pass for science in a public classroom. Also some smart aleck eighth grader might ask how a snake could talk to a woman--and the woman talk back to it. And how would the teacher explain that first snake's smooth talking is what caused all snakes thereafter not to have legs--and eat dust?

Neither could a school teacher mix these two separate accounts together as Fundamentalists do, for that would really confuse things.

The Creationists should be glad these Bible Stories are not taught in the public schools. They would soon learn--from their children--that these accounts could not be true.

Let these Stories be taught in the church school, where the teacher can point out what the authors of these myths were teaching about life, and not *how* God went about creating the world and all that's in it.

It is also worth pointing out that these Stories, composed in heavy theological jargon, were not written for children

The Bible Says...

By Floyd Hale

Question: Did God have Jesus killed?

Answer: The followers of Jesus had a tough time explaining the death of their Master. If he was God's man, why was he charged and executed as a criminal? If he was the Messiah (as they were claiming) why did the Jews not only reject him but push blasphemy charges against him? Having been tried in a Roman court, what was subversive about his ministry?

Since his life was lived sacrificially, it was easy for his followers to say his death was sacrificial. They "proved from the Scriptures" it was the fulfillment of the Levitical system of animal sacrifices--"for sin." Paul worked this into the Christology of the early Church. Taking this "doctrine" literally makes God guilty of the murder of Jesus. This is very blunt, but when said this way it obviously makes God having the best man who ever lived killed--because He had to? Jesus was considered the "perfect, spotless" sacrifice--meeting the Levitical standard. But this can be countered by saying this makes human sacrifice "better than" animal sacrifice.

I purposefully make this confusing--which it really is, to show you how "doctrines" get out of control when they get believed literally--which is the traditional way the Scriptures are taken. In reading these Scriptures in worship or preaching on them, what minister ever explains the way this mess developed from the death of Jesus of Nazareth? If this were explained it would ruin the sermon--and the minister who did the explaining would also be "ruined." But it would reveal the truth about what happened to Jesus.

The truth about Jesus, being killed for proclaiming the prophetic gospel "God is in charge" (the kingdom of God), and more especially for living that way, is what ought to be central in the Christian Faith--that's what started it all.

It would be OK to say Jesus had "the sins of the world laid on him," if the "sins" in all those involved with him and his death were pointed out. But "doctrine" is fascinated with the magic of it all--at the expense of God's true character.

38

The Bible Says...

By Floyd Hale

Question: Where was the "place" Jesus said he was going to prepare?

Answer: At the end of the first century the Gnostic Christians held that heaven, and not this world, was their "home." One purpose of this Fourth Gospel was to counter the Gnostic heresy. In John "everlasting life" is "now."

To ease "heaven" out of the picture as the goal of faith, John opens his 14th chapter by saying "Where God is their is much space." (He wants to show that God can be anywhere--not just "up there.") Then Jesus says he is going to prepare a place, and he will return and receive his followers to where he is. (This purposefully sounds like heaven, but don't stop here. John is setting up his readers for some other "place")

"We don't know where you are going, nor the 'way' to get there," a "dumb question" put on a disciple's lips by John to bring Jesus' answer, "I am 'the way.' You get to the Father only through me." The goal now becomes God (who can be everywhere, as pointed out in verse 2) and not just heaven. "You know the Father for you have seen Him (in me)," John has Jesus saying. "The Holy Spirit is going to come and remain with you forever." Jesus says he will not leave his followers "orphaned"--he will "come to them."

"In that day (when he comes), Jesus says, "you will know I am in my Father, and you in me, and I in you" (John's theology). Instead of taking them to heaven, he comes back from heaven to get inside them--that's the "place" he has been preparing. To make this clear John says--for Jesus, "We--my Father and I--will come and make our home with you" (the believer). John's word for "home" (or "abode," KJV) in this 23rd verse is the same Greek word for "house" in the 2nd verse (where God dwells).

In what may be a confusing manner John is trying subtly to change the minds of a lot of his readers about three things: 1) Heaven, 2) the Second Coming, and 3) the Coming of the Holy Spirit.

John 14 should be understood for what it says, and not changed to agree with other "Biblical" views on heaven.

39

The Bible Says...

By Floyd Hale

Question: What does the Bible say about itself?

Answer: The Bible could not refer directly to itself, for the simple fact the book in which the Bible ("Scripture") might be mentioned was not in the Bible yet. (A writing was not looked upon as "Scripture" until centuries after it was written.) The "all scripture" mentioned in II Timothy refers to what we now call the Old Testament--that was the "Bible" of the early Church.

The comment, "all scripture is inspired by God (II Tim. 3:16)," was written at a time when the Church (which had become mainly Gentile) wanted to do away with its "Jewish Bible" (their only "Scripture" at the time) and form one of their own--a "New" Bible. This reference (in II Timothy, written at that time) shows that the author was opposed to this move. Neither did this author have in mind that his--and the other books later included in the Bible (as the N.T.)--were "scripture"--or ever would be.

The "authority of scripture" has been far over stressed. I haven't heard any of my fundamentalist brethren complaining about Martin Luther taking fourteen books out of the Christian Bible in the 16th century--after them having been in there from the beginning. The Hebrews got along until 400 B.C. without "Scripture." The Church was organized and well on its way before it had a New Testament--which it produced, and later canonized. It is not a matter of whether the Bible is of God, but whether the Church is (which canonized the Bible). This should leave one free to research the Scriptures with an open mind--and do it in Church.

In the New Testament the phrase, "word of God," does not refer directly to the "Bible"--the two terms are not synonymous (as popularly believed). "Word" means "(divine) Truth." Jesus was also called the "Word," and he certainly was not the personification of the Bible of his day. Jesus told his disciples to "preach his gospel," not the Bible.

Too high a claim for something sacred can be just as damaging to faith as too low a claim.

40

The Bible Says...

By Floyd Hale

Question: Did Isaiah write all the book which bears his name?

Answer: No. An "unknown prophet" wrote chapters 40-55. Bible scholars refer to these great "servant poems" as "Deutero-Isaiah."

He might not have left his name, but he was one of the greatest inspirations in all the Old Testament, writing in Babylon during the late hard years of the Exile. He cried out for the restoration of his nation. It was so real to him he sang of it as though it were already accomplished. A highway in the desert (between Babylon and Palestine) is being prepared over which the Lord will lead his people homeward (40:3-5), leveling the mountains and filling the valleys, making the path smooth underfoot for the weak and weary pilgrims. His imagination raced on ahead of the caravan and announced to the city of Jerusalem their coming (40:9-11).

How did his document become a part of the book of Isaiah? About a century and a half earlier a "school of the prophets" was formed by Isaiah's disciples. Some of this school wrote "in his name" (and properly so) for years to come. If their works were treasured they were added into the portfolio called "Isaiah." The last 11 chapters are called "Third Isaiah" by some scholars, and were written even later. The first 39 chapters contain Isaiah's words.

Finally twenty-one of the "prophetic (important) writings" were collected into one group and called "The Prophets." Some of these had no authors' names attached to them, such as Judges, I and II Kings. In order to have exactly "twelve" of the smaller ("minor") books, a little unnamed document was included and later called "Malachi" ("my messenger," from the opening line). By 200 B.C., without official canonization, these had come to be treated as "Holy Writ"-- but less sacred than the Law, till then their only "Scripture."

It needs to be remembered that the tradition of a "book" in this group was called a "Prophet," without any reference to its title or author--or even whether it was written by a prophet or not.

LETTERS TO THE EDITOR

To the Editor:

I can't understand why you're putting that "Hale" person in the paper under the "Bible Says." I can't believe our Southern Illinois local newspaper is allowing a person to come into homes trying to destroy the "Holy Word."

No wonder crime is taking over, young people can't read what Hale says and take God's word seriously and they have no fear of consequences.

Also don't you have a anything better to put in the paper? It has gone down hill for the last months, since you started with "Hale" and quit the Friday evening paper.

A Reader

To the Editor:

When Rev. Hale's column resumed, I was pleased. I had missed his scholarly, sometimes humorous explanations as to what is myth, history or parable in the Bible, though I enjoy it more when it is spontaneous.

A Reader

To the Editor:

I am writing in regard to Floyd Hale's column (notice that I left off his title of "Reverend." "Reverend" means worthy of reverence which, in my opinion, Floyd Hale has not).

I have yet to read this column when he didn't suggest that something should be omitted or disregarded completely. He makes it sound like the Bible is full of fairy tales.

A preacher or teacher who gives God's TRUE message will never contradict or explain away anything in God's word. If Mr. Hale will turn to Revelation 22:19, it plainly states that if any man takes away from the words of the Bible, God shall take away his part out of the book of life and out of the holy city and from the things which are written in this book. This warning is given to those who might purposefully distort the message in the Bible that warn about changing the word.

How could any human being, with limited wisdom and knowledge, edit God's perfect word? There is a certain Mrs. O'Hare who is an atheist and who publishes an atheist newspaper. It is my opinion that Floyd Hale's columns would fit in quite well in her paper.

A reader

d

The Bible Says...

By Floyd Hale

Question: When and where is the Battle of Armageddon to be fought?

Answer: It has been popularly thought of as the "last battle on earth"--at the end of time. It gets its name from "Meggido" (I've stood on the mound). That place--because of its strategic position at a pass in the Carmel Mountains--was where the decisive battle was usually fought for the control of Palestine. This made it a very fitting *apocalyptic symbol* of the "decisive" battle between good and evil (God and Satan). It comes from the Apocalypse (the book of Revelation) which was written to the Christians at the beginning of the Roman Persecution.

To treat it as a battle to be fought in the future between armies is to misunderstand its message to those refusing loyalty to the Roman Emperor ("worship of the Beast") in favor of loyalty to their faith ("Jesus is Lord")--which usually meant death. Armageddon is mentioned near the end of the Fifth Vision (16:16). The "kings of the whole world gather there for battle." Then the Sixth Vision celebrates the judgment and destruction of the "Harlot Babylon" (Rome).

Then the Seventh Vision opens with the "Faithful One" riding out of heaven on a white horse to "make war." With a "sword issuing from his mouth," he slays all the gathered kings and their armies--who do not get to do any real fighting. This heavenly "victor" then rules the nations for a thousand years--*with the help of all the resurrected martyrs*.

Satan is then let loose to go out and gather "the whole world" together, to make war on the saints one more (last?) time. Before they can attack the "the *beloved city*" (20:9), they are all incinerated with fire from heaven. "Judgment" takes place, and the *Holy City* is freed to continue its mission--"the healing of the nations"--world without end (22:1-5)!

The fearful Christians, huddled together in secret, who first heard this prophetic message read (1:3b) knew for sure when and where Armageddon was *being fought--right then, right there!*,

42

The Bible Says...

By Floyd Hale

Question: In your article last week you said the book of Daniel was an "Apocalypse." What is an Apocalypse?

Answer: As a literary form the apocalyptic originated in Persia several centuries B.C. It fantasized that the gods would get so fed up with the injustice people were suffering that they (the gods) would call history to a halt, bring judgment, and punish. the oppressors most severely.

Israel was spared this "bitter hope" because of its "covenant with the JUST god Yahweh." The Israelite kings failed to govern by that covenant, and, according to some of the prophets, this is why Babylon took over (598 B.C.). Persia soon relieved the Babylonians of world custody and allowed the Jews (short for "JU-deans") to return to their homeland-- but without kings. Under the two centuries of Persian domination (539-330 B.C.) the apocalyptic became familiar to them.

When Alexander the Great took the world away from the Persians, the Jews began to feel that the apocalyptic applied to them; for the Greeks not only introduced the Western ("satanic") culture, they forced it down the throats of the Semitic "barbarians." The Jews strongly resisted, and the Syrian governor of the area, Antiochus IV, took a small army to Jerusalem and tried to literally wipe out the Jewish religion. Holy terror ensued.

At the peak of this persecution (165 B.C.) an unnamed Jewish Hasidim penned an Apocalypse and "sent it into battle against the Syrians." He wrote as though he were one of the legendary heroes of their Faith, one Daniel, encouraging faithfulness and "foretelling the END" of their tribulation in just three and a half more years, with God setting up his "everlasting kingdom"--the Jews dominating the whole world. That book got credit for inspiring the success of the Maccabean Revolt (162 B.C.). That Apocalypse (Daniel) was immediately looked upon as an "inspired" book and set off the plague of "end-of-the-world-ism" which dominated the man-in-the-street religious language at the time of Christ.

43

The Bible Says...

By Floyd Hale

Question: Where did Cain get his wife, since there were no other living women except his mother at the time?

Answer; This is an age-old question, and considered to be a stumper. The answer in this Bible story--and it is a story--is that he "knew her in the land of Nod," just next door to Eden (Gen. 4:16,17). Another stumper in this story is, why did he build a city when there were no people to inhabit it? (He could at least have started with just a village.)

In Babylonian Captivity (beginning in 587 B.C.) the priesthood put together a "Story of the People of the Law," to inform the "Exiles" as to who they were, so they would keep from losing their sacred identity "in a foreign land" (not intermarry with Gentiles). This lengthy "Story" (Genesis-Exodus-Leviticus-Numbers) attached onto Deuteronomy was made up of ancient Hebrew customs and traditions, with a lot of "editing" done to them. The first eleven chapters of Genesis was the most highly edited part, a mythical account of "history" from Abraham back to Adam.

This was not just senseless fiction. One of its purposes was to answer certain troubling questions: How did the human race begin? Where did evil come from? Why is it snakes look evil and have no legs? Why do men have to labor? Why do women have labor pains? Why was there a big flood at one time? Why are there so many different languages? I do not say these are correct answers.

You will notice that this prehistorical "history" followed a Jewish fundamental genealogical scheme. Abraham was the nineteenth direct descendent of Adam. To make this appear realistic, not only the names but the ages and dates of birth are given for each patriarch. When these numbers are added up they date Adam's creation at 4004 B.C.

All this may seem as though I am rambling to evade answering the question about Cain's wife. But I think all this helps those who appreciate the Bible understand the fact that the answer is irrelevant. A basic literary rule is, a myth does not have to walk on all fours.

44

LETTERS TO THE EDITOR

Dear D. (Editor):

Now your invitation to explain where Cain got his wife, which has puzzled some people who have read the English Bible down through the years and probably so because of the overly modest translation of the passage of Scripture in Genesis where Cain's wife is mentioned. Just after the record of Cain's murder of his brother Abel and his being driven out from the homeland, the record says in those older translations of the Hebrew into English, "And Cain went out from the presence of the Lord and dwelt in the land of Nod, on the east of Eden. And Cain knew his wife and she conceived and bare Enoch..." (Genesis 4:16-17). Translated this way, some read it as ACQUAINTED with women living in the land of Nod.

The word "knew" here means "sexual intercourse with."

This meaning of "know" is generally not understood by modern readers of the Bible.

The record says, "Now Adam KNEW his wife and she conceived and bore Cain *Genesis 4:1). Adam and eve were the parents of the whole human race. Genesis 3:20. Of Adam's children only Cain, Abel and Seth are mentioned by name, yet the record says of Adam in Genesis 5:4, "and he had other sons and daughters."

Since it is declared then that all people are descended from Adam and Eve and that they had other sons and daughters, Cain had to marry one of his sisters. God had told Adam and Eve, "Be fruitful and multiply and fill the earth" (Genesis 1:28).

Adam and Eve were the parents of all people. We are not told the name of any of Adam's daughters nor Cain's wife nor of their daughters, but we are told that all are the family of Adam and Eve.

A Minister from Cincinnati

Editor's note: As you notice in the account, it was not until after Cain had left home it is mentioned that Adam "knew" Eve and she conceived and had other children.

The Stokes trial jury is still out, although the teacher was convicted. "Instant creation" is in conflict with genealogy traced in the Bible would make the earth only 6,000 years old, and carbon traces place the age of the earth in the millions.

D.B.

e

The Bible Says...

By Floyd Hale

Question: Are there mistakes and errors in the Bible?

Answers: Yes, many. Proverbs 26:4 directly contradicts the next verse, 5. The author of II Kings 26:8 and the author of Chronicles 36:9 (both writing the history of Israel at different times) disagree on two or three points related to King Jeroiachin, and in many other places.

Such does not destroy the authority of the Bible; it only destroys some people's Bibliolatry. Damage is done the Bible in making too high a claim for it, as much as making too low a claim for it. Biblical truth is not always synonymous with a Bible quote. God's truth is in the Bible but it is discovered only when a most critical examination is made of its literature. Errors in the Bible actually become helps to understanding the Bible if they are properly researched.

The student of the Bible who looks into the Proverbs "problem" will, if he or she goes to scholarly sources, find that Proverbs was not in the first Hebrew Bible (called the "Law")--nor in the second one (when the "Prophets" were added about two hundred years later).

Proverbs was in the third (and considered third rate) portion (called "The Writings"), added to the Hebrew "Bible" much later.

When the mistakes made by the Chronicler are cataloged, certain of his motives for "rewriting" Israelite History become obvious. This leads the Bible student on into interesting insights into the mistaken beliefs and hopes of the religious leaders just prior to the coming of Christ. Some of these beliefs were carried over into Christianity and yet haunt us today.

These are not full explanations, for those can come only when open and proper study is made of the development of the Biblical literature, making full use of modern scholarship on this vital subject.

In the weekly "question and answer" articles in this newspaper we will be taking an honest look at this whole issue of Bible Authority. I hope it will be your questions which will guide us. Please send in any questions you may have on the Bible or religion in general.

45

LETTERS TO THE EDITOR

To the Editor:

A few weeks ago in answers to questions of the Bible, was one, is there mistakes and errors in the Bible? The answer was yes.

Let me say there are no mistakes or errors in the Bible, of course I am talking about the King James Version of 1611, not the versions out in the last few years.

The Bible is God's word and God makes no mistakes, you can stake your life on that. Man is the mistake.

But God can take the mistake and make it right, as the potter did the broken vessel

What is it that is missing from our Churches today To use an Old Testament term, it is the burden of the Lord. The tragedy of it all is that the voice of the prophets is no longer heard in the pulpit.

Where is the lamenting for the lost? Jeremiah was so concerned for the lost in his day that he wept day and night over them.

Let us face the facts, who weeps anymore? The Bible says in Joel 2:17, Let the Priests, the Minister of the Lord, Weep between the Porch and the Altar.

Do you ever see the minister of today weep for the lost? Most of them never speak of sin or wrongdoing today. The word repent is never spoken from the pulpit, except by a very few.

All that is needed today is just decision. No wonder the Bible is declaimed by some to have mistakes and errors. They say anything goes today, but God says in his word, Sin is in the world and must be repented of.

So you do not believe the Bible is true, the complete word of God without mistakes and errors, there is no hope for you, for God says in Heb. 11:6, He that cometh to God must believe that He is and is a rewarder of them that diligently seek him.

A reader

f

The Bible Says...

By Floyd Hale

Question: Is Jesus going to come back soon?

Answer: "The Bible says" he is, and evangelists major on this, but the Bible said this nineteen centuries ago. How soon is "soon" in the Bible?

The promise of Jesus' soon return is made by Jesus himself(?) in his "closing remarks" in Revelation (22:12 and 20). The author of Revelation also said, in his opening lines (1:1) what was being "revealed" in this book would "soon take place"--and it did. So, Jesus was mistaken or there is some other meaning to the word "soon" in Revelation.

To correct this "mistranslation" the literalists have given "soon" the meaning of "quickly" (and it has been translated such in some of the unauthorized Bibles). Thus what was "foretold" in Revelation might come much later, but when it came it would happen "quickly." Jesus' coming--regardless of when--would then be a "quick" operation. This midrashes what John was saying instead of looking for what he meant by "soon."

The "tribulation" John was "foretelling" (in lengthy visions full of violent language) had already set in. It was the Roman Persecution--which lasted two more centuries (until 323). In John's apocalyptic form of expression Jesus' coming "soon" was saying "he is here now"--*live this way!*

Apocalyptic preaching was to secure radical faithfulness at a time when that might mean death; the survival of the Faith depended on it. In the Gospels we have Jesus requiring this of his disciples. In very militant (apocalyptic) terms John was preaching Jesus' gospel, "God is in charge!" Believing this they could "hope" for victory--and bet their lives on it.

If I read Jesus right, he "comes" every time God's will is done--justice is served for the oppressed. And in a more apocalyptic way he also "comes" every time the needs of others (both personal and social) are ignored by those who think they are righteous. Followers of Jesus--and that's what Christians suppose themselves to be--stand in a very unique place in all this.

46

The Bible Says...

By Floyd Hale

Question: How did the Bible begin?

Answer: The "Story of the Bible" begins in exactly 621 B.C. with the official adoption of a "legal code" in Jerusalem as "God's law for the nation." There were many earlier writings considered somewhat sacred, but none had yet been looked upon as "Scripture." (II Kings 22-24 sketches this historic event.)

In 700 B.C. a young king by the name of Manasseh came to the throne of Judah--the only remains of the Israelite Kingdom. Judah was spared destruction by the cruel Assyrians, because this king did their bidding--paid extravagant tribute ("protection fees"), shut down the temple ceremonies, enforced the worship of the Assyrian gods, and outlawed prophecy--the traditional "protesting" exercised by prophets. There is a tradition that he had Isaiah put to death.

The "Prophetic Party," the product of the great 8th century (B.C.) prophets (mainly Isaiah) then went underground to work for much needed national reform. They had more than enough time, for Mannaseh ruled 54 long years. They drew up a lengthy document of "laws" in the name of Moses, hoping the next king would adopt them as "God's law." That "manifesto" makes up most of our present book of Deuteronomy. That title literally means "back to the law (of Moses) a second time."

In 621 (B.C.), after the "good king" Josiah had ruled for some time, this "book of law" was conveniently found in the temple. On the advice of the prophetess Huldah, the king decreed that document to be "God's law of the land." That resulted in this first Jewish document to be recognized as "Scripture." It didn't become a "Bible," but in Captivity, *only one generation later,* it did inspire the creation of the first Jewish Bible.

Ths story of why and how this happened is a most interesting story.

I hate to say "to be continued," but next week I will try, in far too short fashion, to chart the evolution of this "little book of law" (Deuteronomy) into the "big book of Law" (Torah), in, of all places, Babylonian Captivity).

47

The Bible Says...

By Floyd Hale

Question: What was the first Bible?

Answer: Last week I told how the book of Deuteronomy became decreed as "God's law of the land"--just one generation before Babylonian Captivity. As true of human nature, it was in Captivity that the first real interest was shown in the "law of God." This interest was not dulled any by being told they were there because they had "broken that law."

Being set free by the Persians (539 B.C.), some of the Jews returned to their home, but not allowed self-rule. Several, being no longer "captives," just "exiles," remained in "Babylon" because it was economically inviting.

So as to not lose their *identity* there, the priests put together a "survival kit" for them--*The Story of the People of the Law"* (Genesis-Exodus-Leviticus-Numbers) and attached it onto Deuteronomy. They were promised if they kept these "traditions of their ancestors," God would return the land of their ancestors to them. Since the Deuteronomic Law was nationalistic and temple-centered, it could not be practiced in a foreign land, but *"The Story"* could be-- and was, meticulously.

"Sabbath" (previously being only the "Day of rest") became the weekly Day of worship--in Babylon. Synagogues for the first time sprang up in exile as "Churches." All this gave birth to "Judaism" as a formal religion, and was "imported" back into Jerusalem by Ezra's getting this "Story" (Torah) adopted there as the "Law," in ca. 400 B.C (Nehemiah 7-9). The *prophetic* law of Moses, majoring on JUSTICE, was thus subtly replaced with a *priestly* religion of RIGHTEOUSNESS--in the name of Moses.

"Ezra's Reform" was an ethnic cleansing of the Jerusalem community from all "foreign elements." This "separateness" ("holiness"), practiced in Exile as a "necessity(?)," thus became "God's law" for the Jews in Jerusalem--and everywhere. This hardened Torah into "Scripture."

Understanding how this "first Bible" evolved should help modern believers better understand how to use--and not use--their Bible to practice their "identity" as God's people today.

The Bible Says...

By Floyd Hale

Question: Why was Peter not so good at walking on water?

Answer: It might not have been because of his "little faith" (Mt. 14:22,23). If you look at Mark's older account of this (which Matthew used as his source) you see that Peter most likely didn't try this stunt (Mk. 6:45-52). Then why is this in Matthew?

As the Christian movement became an "institution," tradition required that it, to be valid, have proper succession in leadership. Matthew, written long after Peter's death, was here (as in 16:17-19) "grooming" him for the office of "Vicar of Christ"-- Jesus' successor as head of the Church. As foolish as you may think this sounds, Matthew's having him "walk on water" was a way of supporting this tradition. Protocol would call for Peter's failing to do it as good as his master.

Compare these two accounts closely--Mark's (the older one) with Matthew's (the later version)--and you'll see this explanation makes sense. You will notice in the original story, Jesus calms the disciples' fears and "he" gets into the boat with them.

In its revision, after Jesus saves Peter from going under "they" (Jesus and Peter) get into the boat.

This can lead to another insight the student of the Gospels may get from this. If Peter is reported as walking on water to give him "special status," could it not be that Jesus was originally reported as walking on water to credit him with "special status"? This was a common way of praising great men (posthumously) in the Mediterranean culture of the first century.

When such miracle stories about Jesus are interpreted as "proof" of his deity, the real Jesus becomes a victim of a creedal faith based on magic. The believer then misses seeking the answer to the important question: "What was there about Jesus which caused his followers to so eulogize him this way?" Answers to this lead one to the place of decision, to--or not to--be one of his followers. This decision can be evaded by simply believing a bunch of stuff about Jesus--and "be saved" (play it safe).

49

The Bible Says...

By Floyd Hale

Question: Were Adam and Eve the first two people on earth?

Answer: According to the Old Testament chronology they began the human race in the year 4,004 B.C. This (second) Creation Story (Gen. 2:4b-3:24) was not written to explain when--nor how--homo sapiens first appeared on this planet; it very vividly declares that the awful predicament we have gotten ourselves into is due to *not doing the will of our Maker.*

Why are we in the mess we are in was not the only question answered in this myth. Why do women have labor pains? Why do men have to go through the pain of labor? Why do snakes have no legs? Why do people have to wear garments? Why do people die? Where did sticker weeds come from--we don't plant them? (And to think some people want their children to study this in their science book in the public school.)

No amount of quoting other references in the Bible to Adam (and/or Eve) helps answer this question. It only illustrates further how we need a whole new understanding of our Bible.

True to life, those involved in the spoiling of paradise, rather than confess responsibility, blamed someone else. The man blamed the woman; she blamed a talking snake. In a modern Adam and Eve myth I suppose the monkey would be charged with the "fall"--it disobeyed god by walking upright.

What can be done about the mess the author of this story is telling us we are in? I think this prophet was also taking a sly shot at those who think the solution is to "become like God." This could be the snake's most subtle temptation--be "religious" as a counterfeit for "obeying God."

When Jesus walked out into this mess (and it was much worse then than now) he began with his whole heart mind and strength to do something about it--by radically *"doing God's will."* And that's what he asked his followers to do--not believe a bunch of stuff about him.

This is the real challenge the Bible lays on us. One way of not seeing this is to make the whole Bible a true story and get lost in all its religiosity.

50

The Bible Says...

By Floyd Hale

Question: Where does the term "Pearly Gates" come from?

Answer: In Revelation the twelve gates to the Holy City are mentioned as not only made of pearl, but each is made from a single pearl. Can you imagine the size of the oysters which birthed those precious stones? Before you accuse me of making fun of the Scriptures, let me point out more of this kind of what I call "outlandish" language in Revelation.

The mountains and islands will all disappear. The stars in the sky will fall to earth. (Do you know how big and hot just one star, a sun, is?) Blood will flow out from a certain city about four feet deep for two hundred miles . (Do you have any idea how much blood this will be?) 200,000,000 cavalrymen come out of the Euphrates Valley and kill a third of the earth's population--just by the fire and smoke from the mouths of their steeds. Jesus will someday ride out of heaven on a white horse and slay all the nations with a sword sticking out of his mouth, with all the vultures of the air gathering to feast on the carcasses of these armies-- this is called "The Great Supper of God."

A second time all the people on earth gather to make war, and are incinerated with fire which falls from heaven. A city 1,500 miles square will come down to earth out of heaven. (Can you imagine a city which is not only about equal in size to all the territory of the United States east of the Mississippi, but is also 1,500 high--a perfect cube?) To understand what this book is all about, one must first understand what all this is actually "saying."

Otherwisie good people become sucked in by people like Hal Lindsay who tell them all this will actually happen in the future. But this book of "Scripture" must--and can--be understood. Not only for its own sake, but for understanding how this kind of Apocalyptic "end-of-the-world-ism" influenced the Gospel writers strongly.

One good reason for underanding Revelation is because it inspired Christians to die as martyrs in saving the early Church from extinction during the Roman Persecution.

51

The Bible Says...

By Floyd Hale

Question: Was it James and John or their mother who asked Jesus to appoint them to the number one and two positions in his kingdom?

Answer: It depends on whether you read Matthew or Mark. Mark (10:38) says they did, but Matthew (20:20,21) says it was their mother.

No one's salvation depends on knowing the answer to this question, but those wondering about how contradictions like this could be in the Bible just might like a straight answer. I'd say it was the brothers, not the mother.

I have mentioned before (a number of times) that Matthew later did a lot of "improving" on Mark's version--which was his primary source in composing his Gospel. Evidently Mark was a bit too forthright for him. How could a disciple of Jesus be so self-seeking? Since it fit right into a typical mother's concern for her boys, Matthew gave her credit for the asking.

In one place Mark (6:52) says the disciples' "hearts were hardened." Matthew (14:33) replaces this with "they worshipped him (Jesus), saying, 'Truly you are the Son of God'." Matthew (13:16) has Jesus pronouncing a blessing on the disciples for "seeing and hearing," replacing Mark's statement about Jesus' scolding them for "not understanding" (4:13).

When Matthew edits Mark's script he occasionally leaves a telltale blunder. In this place where the request is made by the mother, he gets back to Mark's version (10:38) of Jesus response without changing the "Are *you* able to drink the cup that I drink" to "Are *they*..," to make it grammatically correct.

Some may say this is foolish tampering with the Scriptures, but this is the best way I know how to impress interested people with what the Bible really is. It is not "God's Word." When approached intelligently it points toward God's Word. The quest from there on in is all personal.

Do you think Matthew knew his and Mark's Gospels would be included in the Bible--and them both be taken later as literally true?

The Bible Says...

By Floyd Hale

Question: Is it true in Genesis 11 that God confused the human language because the tower of Babel was built?

Answer: No, but let me explain how that story got into the Bible (Gen. 11:1-9). The authors of the first Jewish Bible (the Law) felt they needed to write a "history" covering prehistorical time--from Abraham on back to "the beginning." So we have the first eleven chapters of Genesis.

Many legends and myths--answering the major puzzling questions about life at the time--served as sources for this literary project. By this time (ca. 500 B.C.) God was the prime mover in Hebrew writings, so it was natural that He be the guiding figure in these stories.

One of the obvious questions to be answered was, "If there was one language after the Flood, why are there so many now?" Well, it was like this: To remain together and show off their superior intelligence, they built themselves a city. God seemed to be against cities (and you can understand why). In that city they built an Empire State Building--"that reached to the heavens." And God said "That's enough of this humanistic genius;" so he "mixed up" their language--no one could understand anyone else. (It must have been like a hill of disoriented ants.) This is the way people got scattered out over the earth (where they were supposed to have gone to begin with). And this, my child, is why there are so many different languages.

They named their city Babel (Hebrew for Babylon), from which our word "babble" comes--unintelligible gibberish. At the time of the writing of this story there were the remains of a huge ziggurat (tower structure) in the Babylonian city of Etemenanki. At its top was a temple to the pagan god Marduk, making it a good symbol for "confusion."

Wouldn't it be wonderful if our children in Sunday School had their Bible Stories explained to them this way. Then they would not have a "confused" image of the God Jesus called his "Abba" (Dear Father).

The Bible Says...

By Floyd Hale

Question: Was the wine Jesus made from water at Cana the real stuff?

Answer: The people at that wedding thought it was not only the real stuff but better than the usual (John 2:1-11).

Those who say the word for "wine" in this place means "unfermented fruit of the vine" don't know their Greek language--nor their wine. But to argue this point is to fall into the old trap of taking the Bible for what "it says"--literally--and going on from there.

As with any book in the Bible, the literary form of the Gospel in which this story appears must be first understood. John's Gospel is a "historical novel" written in Gospel form. This gave the author a free and unique way of explaining the relevance of the Spirit of Christ to the "faith" of the Greek (non-Jewish) Christians--in their own "spiritual" idiom.

To develop his theme, "Life with a Capital L," John chose five of the miracle stories from the earlier Gospels, added two of his own composition (this and the last one), used these as "The Signs of Life," and scripted an "I Am" lecture for Jesus on most of them. This means that Jesus did not actually perform this water-into-wine piece of magic. I don't say this to eliminate the alcohol issue, nor to deny Jesus the ability of working miracles. You just don't take a myth as fact--or you miss its point.

Anyone with any perception of the Cana situation would see that more than 150 gallons of "spirits" made by Jesus (for a small village crowd which had already been drinking), was pure extravagance--*but this is the very point John is making.* This "first" miracle story perfectly introduces Jesus as "more than the water of life"--he is the "Wine of life"--*in abundance.*

If the reader would examine the Gospel of John carefully--as one would any other important document--he/she would see many more "signs" that this is not just "another Gospel"--a fourth "Life of Jesus." In fact it should not be treated as a Gospel at all. It is the most misunderstood book in the Bible, because in it John explains Jesus by having him "explain himself."

54

The Bible Says...

By Floyd Hale

Question: Did Jesus actually raise Lazarus from the dead?

Answer: This "miracle" (KJV, called a "sign" in the RSV) is recorded in the Fourth Gospel only. Do you think a deed of such magnitude would have escaped the attention of the other three Gospel writers? If this were the only thing unique about the Gospel of John it might be insignificant, but this is just one of its many characteristics which separates it from the other three.

Looking closely at this Gospel we find this story replaces the cleansing of the temple at the end of Jesus' ministry in the other Gospels. John moves the cleansing back to the beginning of Christ's mission (to show Jesus' authority right at the start), and uses this story at the close of Jesus ministry to climax his theme, "Life"--in Christ. In the former Gospels it is the temple cleansing which causes the Jerusalem authorities to decide to "destroy" Jesus (Mk. 11:18); in John it is the raising of Lazarus (11:47-53).

That John fabricated this story about Lazarus (as he did the "water to wine" sign at the first) may surprise (even shock) some readers, but this is because we have thought this was just "another Gospel." To know *what* John is saying we must know *how* he said it--and *why*.

This "story" provided a "live illustration" for Jesus' last "I Am" lecture. John has Martha setting this up by saying she knows her brother will "rise in the last day." Then Jesus says, "*I am* the *resurrection* and the *life* " (now). John transforms Jesus into the "Life-bringer"--and has him killed for this. What a dramatic play on words!

This does not deny what Jesus--or God--could or could not do. Neither does this make a liar or deceiver out of John. When you understand his literary freedom to choose this unique expression form, and study the theme of "Life" in this Gospel, you can appreciate it. But to identify John's Jesus with the real one is to make a serious mistake--changing the image of Jesus entirely. *This is what the Church did to Jesus,* and John gave them the "Scripture" for it.

The Bible Says...

By Floyd Hale

Question: Who are the '144,000' in the book of Revelation?

Answer: This is the *symbolic* number of those who refuse to "worship the beast" (wear his "mark"); they remain "faithful to Jesus"--unto death.

John saw the Roman Persecution (then beginning) becoming very severe, increasing to "apocalyptic" proportions.

In the First Vision the "souls under the altar in heaven cry out for vengeance," and are told to "wait until the *number*. . . is complete" of those "who will be martyred even as they were" (6:9-11). The author then injects an Interlude Vision (7:1-12) at this point to explain very clearly that there will be "144,000 sealed in faithfulness" from all across the Church (the true Israel)--wear the "mark of God" (7:3,4). This Interlude Vision is followed by another one (7:13-8:5) explaining that "these are they who will come out of great tribulation; having washed their robes in the blood of the Lamb"-- *dying as Jesus did* (7:14). In the Fourth Vision the 144,000 are again mentioned as "the redeemed from the earth . . , bearing the mark of God" (14:1-4).

In Rev.19:7,8 these martyrs are the "bride of the Lamb," who finally come back with Jesus "riding on white horses" (19:14), making up the "first resurrection" (20:4-6), "reigning over the nations with Christ 1,000 years" (20:4-6)--and eventually "forever and ever" (22:5).

It is not hard to see, in this *apocalyptic symbology*, John is saying "faithfulness unto death" (the way of the Cross) will conquer injustice. The "end" (of the Beast) that John "envisioned" finally came in A.D. 323, when the Persecution was officially lifted by the emperor Constantine (who for political reasons received Christian baptism).

My interpretation of this--or anyone else's--should not be accepted blindly. Revelation can--and should be--understood by anyone who will learn *when, why,* and *in what literary form* it was written.

The apocalyptic 144,000 told the faithful "there's going to be a lot of dying going on."

56

The Bible Says...

By Floyd Hale

Question: Is it true that God created the world in six days?

Answer: That's what it says in the first chapter of Genesis--and it was twenty-four hour days. "A day is as a thousand years" doesn't apply here, for a thousand years' period doesn't have "an evening and a morning." The author meant the first six days of one week--but this is a "story." A story which gets Scripture off to a very positive start.

Bible scholars identify this First Creation Story (1:1-2:4a) with the "P" (Priestly) traditions scattered throughout the "Five Books" of the Law. The Sabbath Law ("going to Church on Sunday") was of prime interest to the priests, and by this law the whole of life was prescribed and judged ("Sabbath" means "holy"). This could well have been the "call to worship" in the temple, for it recognized all of life as sacred--something people miss who do not worship the Creator.

This also meant life was "good." Life as a whole is good. When God made man He recognized both sexes, "male and female created he them," and he said they were "very" good. "In his own image" declared their moral nature.

Putting all the rest of creation in man's custody may not have been so good, for exploiting and ravishing it may just be man's worst immorality (the "rape of the planet" someone has called it)--time will tell.

This being myth does not rob it of its Truth--it really adds to its beauty. The priestly poet of these lines never let there being no sun until the fourth day interfere with his "evening and morning" staccato from the first day.

It's hard to think of God getting tired, but if He did all that work in six days he deserved to rest. If God needed a "day of rest," surely man does too--which was the author's inference. This makes me want to invite you to go to Church next Sunday. Tell the preacher I sent you.

(Don't write me; I know I should have said "Synagogue on Saturday" instead of "Church on Sunday" in the second paragraph above. I just wanted the emphasis related to our situation.)

The Bible Says...

By Floyd Hale

Question: My question to you is, where have you gotten all your information that makes you dispute what is written in the bible? I am not a bible scholar but I can read, and it plainly states that "if a man shall take away from or add to the words of the book of this prophecy, God shall take away his part out of the book of life and out of the holy city.

Answer: "This book" refers to the book of Revelation, and not to the whole Bible--it wasn't in the Bible yet. It was written in a highly symbolic language (apocalyptic)--*not to be taken literally.*

Apocalyptic writings flourished at the time, and each apocalypticist edited and borrowed at will from the apocalyptic writings of others. That was legitimate. John himself used several apocalyptic sources in putting together this very misunderstood masterpiece. Because of this, the serious warning you half-quoted is "apocalyptic," highly bombastic, for John did not want any of his words deleted or others added to as copies were made from church to church. That might change or confuse his very important "message" (prophecy), which was "hidden" in all those symbolic terms. The lives of those to whom John was writing depended on their getting his message straight, for he was asking them to give their lives--literally--during the beginning of the Roman Persecution (ca. 90).

Most of the "information" I share in these articles comes mainly from treating the Bible realistically--and from knowing a little about when, to whom, why, and *in what literary form* each book in the Bible was composed. Anyone who wants to could learn this.

I don't mean to be personal, but one of the things about understanding passages like this is it saves a sincere person like you from making very severe and false charges (in your lengthy letter) against a brother.

The Bible Says...

By Floyd Hale

Question: Do you believe the book we call the Bible to be the inspired word of God?

Answer: I believe it is obvious that God was the inspiration leading most of the authors of the scriptures to write the books in our Bible. If the words are His, dictated, the authors would not have to be inspired.

Did God "inspire" Mark to say Jesus, after his baptism, "went immediately into the wilderness, staying forty days and nights"? Did God also "inspire" John to say Jesus left the Jordan and attended a wedding up in Cana "three days later"? The Doctrine of the Inspiration of the Scriptures has to take this--and many other similar passages in the Bible--into consideration.

The "inspiration" of the Scriptures can not mean that the Bible is "infallible and inerrant." Inspiration has more to do with the effect the Bible writings have on the reader, and that's where God's action (the Holy Spirit) comes in. This makes it most important that those writings be treated very realistically. This requires learning when, to whom, why, and in what literary form they were originally written. Most of the books now in the Bible are there because they individually "inspired" their first readers, being treasured and handed down by a religious movement, and thus finally being officially canonized by the leaders of that religion.

To prove that "all scripture is inspired by God" II Tim. 3:16 is often quoted, and applied to our whole Bible. II Timothy was written during the second century (not by Paul) when there was a movement on in the Church to do away with the Jewish Old Testament (the only official Christian Scriptures at the time) and replace it with a "New Bible" made up of the Christian writings--which were becoming more used and popular than their "Bible." The "Old Bible" was not rejected, but this led finally to the addition of a "New Testament"--which the conservative author of II Timothy had opposed--and his writing was included in it. Now tell me how "Inspiration" figures in that?

59

The Bible Says...

By Floyd Hale

Question: Have any books ever been removed from the Bible?

Answer: Yes. In the sixteenth century Martin Luther removed twelve books and parts of a few others from the Scriptures which the Christians had been using as a part of their Bible for fifteen centuries. This literature remains in the Catholic Bible, but not in the Protestant version.

These books eliminate what has been called the "Intertestamental Period," since they were written just before and after the time of Christ. Some of this material supported the priestly hierarchy in Jerusalem, and Luther was contesting the authority of a similar ecclesiastical system in Rome. A few of these books seemed to support other goings on in the Church to which he was also objecting.

Luther found that these books were not in the oldest (Hebrew) version of the O.T., giving him the "grounds" for removing them. But to be consistent he had to remove all fourteen, and not just the few which were offensive.

But the Christians never used the older Hebrew version of the Old Testament. From the beginning they used the Septuagint (Greek) version (which the Jews used outside of Palestine), which contained these extra books. Luther moved these books to the appendix of his German Bible and called them the "Apocrypha" (meaning "of questionable authority") This set the Bible tradition for Protestantism. The second edition of the KJV (1629) dropped the Apocrypha altogether from its appendx.

It would be good if all of us had these books as a part of our Scripture heritage, for it would greatly help us understand how the Old Testament evolved, illustrating how additions were made to older books (such as Esther and Jeremiah). I Maccabees is a historical report of the Maccabean Revolt described by Daniel in that crazy apocalyptic expression form--which we have mistaken for prophecy.

It is also one of these books (II Maccabees) which contains the passage used by the Roman Church to support its doctrine of Purgatory burning out dead people's sins.

The Bible Says...

By Floyd Hale

Question: What is the gospel?

Jesus never preached "about" the kingdom; he preached "it." He *declared it--to be--right then.* This was the fundamental affirmation of ancient Israel--"The Lord God Jehovah reigns!" This was the message of the great Old Testament prophets. But the popular priestly cult substituted for this a "formal religion"--with all kinds ordinances and ceremonies.

Anyone who proclaimed "the rule of God" ("God is in charge") to make it ring true, would also have to "live that way." This Jesus did--with his whole mind, soul, and strength--all the time. This is what was unique about him.

At first his "good news" drew great crowds, for the common people were not in charge--of anything--even their own lives. The poor--and that was the vast majority--were convinced the rich were in charge; but Jesus declared, "God is in charge!" The sick and afflicted believed the demons were in charge; Jesus told them "God is in charge"--and it worked wonders. The sinners believed the priests were in charge; Jesus said "God is!" The women were convinced the men were in charge; Jesus said "God is in charge!" Everybody knew the king was in charge, but Jesus declared, "God is in charge!" Talk about good news! But to those who were in charge--of wealth, politics, and especially religion--this was threatening, "bad news." And Jesus would not shut up and go away.

Answer: It depends on whose gospel you are referring to. The Apostle Paul's gospel was, "Jesus Christ died for our sins (so we could go to heaven)." Jesus' gospel--and the gospel he sent his disciples out to preach--was "the kingdom (rule) of God" (that there might be heaven on earth).

When it followed that "believing in" Jesus' gospel included "doing God's will"--his way--the crowds fell off. It is not hard to understand why Paul's gospel won out over Jesus.' Neither is it hard to understand why those in charge had Jesus put away.

Jesus' gospel--what he actually "preached" ("proclaimed, declared, announced")--has been confused with his "teachings."

The Bible Says...

By Floyd Hale

Question: Do the good people go to heaven after the Judgment?

Answer: "Judgment Day" is found only in Revelation. According to the author of that book the souls of the people who are killed for their "faithfulness to Jesus" go directly to heaven, where they "rest" until "enough" of them get there. Then there is a "first resurrection" in which these martyrs come back and help Jesus "rule the nations."

After the "thousand years reign" the devil leads another attack on the "saints" and fire falls from heaven and consumes them. Then comes a "second resurrection" in which all the rest of the dead are brought back to life and go through the Judgment (but not the living). The bad ones are cast into the "lake of fire," but the good ones don't go anywhere They stay right here and God "comes down to earth" to dwell with them. The medicinal leaves from the tree of life in the Holy City are used for the "healing the nations." The peoples of the world (nations) will bring their "treasures" into that Holy City. And life will go on--"for ever and ever." There is no "end" of the world or time in Revelation (22:5).

The above is a brief summary of the last three and a half chapters of Revelation. It is written in the apocalyptic literary form John chose for getting his message out to his fellow Christians in Asia Minor, who were just entering the Roman persecution. ("apocalypse" is the way the word "Revelation" was spelled and pronounced in John's language, Greek.)

If the apocalyptic form of expression is not understood, John's message is then taken literally as foretelling the future, and missed, and this great book of Scripture lies hidden to the Church. This also allows the prophecy hounds and cultic nuts to use it to prey on the minds and faith of good but uninformed believers.

If Revelation were understood, it would be easy to go on to properly interpret the "Son of man" (apocalyptic Messiah) sayings in the Gospels. This would help eliminate the "Second Coming" and better clarify the Christian task for the right now.

The Bible Says...

By Floyd Hale

Question: Is it true that a Jewish girl in the Bible became the queen of the Persian Empire?

Answer: It makes for a good story--and that's just what is.

I doubt if even those who are most familiar with the book of Esther are aware of the not-so-happy ending to this happy story.

By decree of the Persian king (shrewdly secured by Esther) the exiled Jews were given the right "to destroy, to slay, and to annihilate"-- even "the women and children" of all those who sought their hurt. So, in retaliation they killed thousands of their enemies across the empire (according to this "story").

Esther is not only fiction (thank goodness), but a unique kind of fiction, jingoistic fantasy. To the Jews of the 2nd century B.C., who had been backhanded by every swing taken in the Middle East for centuries, this book gave a euphoric feeling that there had been "a time when we got our licks in--but good!" This could not help but inspire them to "do it again."

Some of the Jews had brought back from the Persian Exile a pagan holiday, a fun festival which centered in a game of "dice" ("pur"). Esther was written to give that celebration "Jewishness." This was the origin of the Feast of Purim. This book gained such popularity that it was canonized into Scripture (against the better judgment of the Rabbinical Council passing on it in 90 A.D.). This Story is yet read in its entirety annually in most Synagogues on this Feast Day.

The main objection--then and now--to this book's being in the Bible is, it is in no way religious. It contains no mention of God, prayer, faith, righteousness, or the like.

Although the Bible student is not to take Esther as the Word of God, it helps one understand the sad plight of the Jews. Being the very last book of the Old Testament to be written, it also offers insight into the spiritual bankruptcy of Judaism just prior to the time of Jesus.

This is certainly not a "Bible Story for children."

LETTERS TO THE EDITOR

Dear D. (Editor):

Having read the barrage of negative letters to the editor about Rev. Hale's column, I just wanted you to know that he has at least one big fan out there among your subscribers.

I wasn't always such; in fact, the original title of his column caused me-- thinking it another religious column of stale piety--to read right past it. But thanks to his critics, I discovered his column last year and now look forward to it each week.

Rev. Hale's column is a real gem of religious brevity and sanity, which is far more interesting than columns that appear in our local newspapers.

Contrary to the impression the critics would like to give, his views are not radical, rather seems well within the mainstream of modern biblical scholarship.

I would also like to applaud your courage as an editor of a small town newspaper to stand for pluralism on your religious page. Your readers include moderate and liberal Christians as well as outspoken fundamentalist "true-believers."

Yet, after all is said, our behavior toward our fellow men and women are a hell of a lot more important than beliefs about the virgin birth, bodily resurrection and so forth.

To paraphrase one religious sage, religion is not really about words, names and doctrines, it is about spiritual realization. And there are many paths to the mountain top.

An (out of town)
Reader

Editor's note: I needed that. D.B.

To the Editor:

The congregation of the (unnamed small rural) Church would like to commend the Management and the Staff of the (unnamed) newspaper on the removal of the 'Floyd Hale column' in your weekly paper. We fail to see how anything positive can be accomplished by what we consider derogatory remarks about the Bible.

(The above letter came in just after one paper stopped carrying "The Bible Says." Signed by 34 members of a small rural Church, but not by the pastor.)

The Bible Says...

By Floyd Hale

Unusual Bibles.

The Bible which sold a few years ago for $2,000,000 certainly was an unusual Bible. It was the first book to be printed on the newly invented printing press. Movable type made work much easier for printers, but for some it made headaches. Their mistakes have ended up in producing some unusual Bibles.

There was the printer in the 17th century who--having his own profession on his mind no doubt--changed Psalms 119:161 to read: "printers persecute me without a cause." Then there was the printer who created a very unusual Bible and paid a 300 pound fine for his blunder. He left the "not" out of the seventh commandment. (Look that one up.)

A proof-reader had a question about a comma in an 1805 edition of the Bible. His editor scribbled "to remain" in the margin of the rough draft. The printer moved the marginal note into the main text, and Galatians 4:29 came out like this: "But as then he that was born after the flesh persecuted him that was born after the spirit *to remain,* even so it is now."

This is the way many "marginal explanatory notes" got into the scriptures--back before they were looked upon as "Scripture."

In a 1717 Bible Jesus told a "Parable of the Vinegar," Luke 20:9. Do you know what the correct title is? In an 1806 Bible the printer had "fishes standing" by leaving the "r" out of "fishers" in Ezekiel 47:10. "Murmurs" was misprinted "murders" in Jude 16 in an 1801 edition of the Word.

I like the Geneva version which said Adam and Eve "made themselves breeches"; but my favorite "unusual Bible" of all time is the 1810 Bible which came to be called the "Wife-Hater Bible." In it a (Freudian?) slip caused the printer to make one of Jesus' conditions for discipleship in Luke 14:26 that of "hating his own wife."

I don't know if unusual is the word for it, but the Bible is the book most stolen from public libraries.

64

The Bible Says...

By Floyd Hale

Question: Does the Bible say there were giants on earth at one time?

Answer: Yes, in Genesis 6:1-4. A part of the "wickedness" for which God flooded the world was the marriage of the "daughters of men to the sons of God"-- giving birth to giants, called Nephilim. Some of their descendents are mentioned as inhabiting Canaan at the time of the Israelite invasion, so the flood evidently didn't drown all of them. (It would be too frivolous of me to suggest maybe they could hold their heads above water?)

The construction of this text is very awkward, showing it has been redacted (edited by the authors who put the Pentateuch--"Five Books"--together creating the first Jewish Bible, the Law). One can only wonder what was omitted and/or added. Especially since hanky-panky is suggested by the deities' "eyeballing these fair human damsels." .

Most ancient literatures contained references to giants. It was probably a mythological way of accounting for exceptionally tall people. There might have been tribes known for their height. It was also common mythology at the time that gods came down and mated with earth females--accounting for legendary heroes, kings, etc.

The Bible student is not to credit the first eleven chapters of Genesis as history. Something compelled a Hebrew scribe to fill in the gap from Abraham back to Adam. It all reads as real, but there are enough "stories" in the rest of the Bible which need proper attention--forget these.

One should be very careful of the theological lessons glibly espoused from Genesis 1-11. Never should these stories--Adam and Eve, Cain and Abel, Enoch's Ascension, Noah Building the Ark, The Flood, The Tower of Babel, and this one about Giants--be taken literally. And above all, these "Bible Stories" should never be taught to children as true. Growing up believing the Bible is all literally true makes it very hard for one to later adjust to the adult method of looking for the Word of God in it.

The Bible Says...

By Floyd Hale

Question: Did Jesus really use a whip to drive the money-changers out of the temple?

Answer: I do not believe he did.

Mark reports that Jesus "drove out those who bought and sold and overturned the tables of the money-changers." The only Gospel which speaks of a "whip" is John. And since John is not a factual report of events, we may conclude that the whip thing was added for emphasis sake--"against Jews." (John didn't like Jews.)

Jesus cleansed the temple by the authority of his own personality. Boldness and firmness in a right cause do not require physical force. Furthermore, according to Jesus the use of violence defeats its own cause. Parents who make a habit of whipping their children--or swatting them across the face in emotional rage--are actually teaching them (among other things) violence is the primary solution to problems.

Jesus was performing a prophetic service. He was doing something more than correcting an ecclesiastical procedure in the temple; he was striking a heavy blow at the whole sacrificial system. More than one of the older prophets had found it repugnant. It was actually superstitious. The Israelites originally borrowed it from their pagan neighbors. For Christians to theologize that the blood of animals was a "type" of the sacrifice Jesus would make, is to both misunderstand scripture and the blood of Jesus.

In cleansing the temple Jesus was not proclaiming he was the Messiah. His daily preaching in the "cleansed" temple was the final "opportunity" Israel was getting to accept his gospel, "God is in charge" (Lu. 20:1). The challenge courageously created by Jesus forced the issue and demanded action. To stay "in charge themselves" the authorities had to get rid of Jesus. This gave his death its significance.

It is also interesting to learn why John left the cleansing of the temple in his Gospel but moved it back to the beginning of Jesus' ministry.

The Bible Says...

By Floyd Hale

Question: Does the Bible say a fish actually swallowed a man, Jonah?

Answer: This raises the basic question of the method of interpretation of the Scriptures. Those who strongly defend the "inspiration of the Scriptures" say that every statement in the Bible is to be taken literally--true, "God said it." But those who are informed in Bible background realize that this is not only erroneous but damaging to biblical Truth in many instances.

The interpretation--meaning--of a statement from the Bible is determined first of all by the literary form of the particular writing from which it is taken. There are many and varied literary forms in the Bible--poetry, law, fiction, parable, proverb, sermon, epistle, even apocalypse. When these are mixed up together, either by reading the books of the Bible as though they are merely chapters in one long story, or picking "texts" from different places in the Bible to construct some theme, this violates the rule of propriety, and it usually ends in misinterpreting biblical Truth.

Jonah is such a piece of biblical literature. It was written in parabolic form (and for a very important reason). This can not be a bad form of expression for our Lord used it almost exclusively in teaching. The truth of a parable is not identical with any or all its parts--such as: Jonah was in the belly of the fish three days and three nights, God repented, or Jonah wanting to die (because he had been the world's most successful evangelist-missionary?). The "truth" of a parable is the insight its writer wishes his reader to get in a delayed action sort of way. In the story of Jonah it is couched in the last (and punch) line of this little pamphlet (4:10-11). The person who reads this story as history must stop here and deal with the conclusion this surprise ending has suddenly thrust into his/her mind.

If the author had begun his book by saying he wanted to set his readers straight about God accepting foreigners, he would have lost them right off. His parable was a much more effective way of convincing them.

LETTERS TO THE EDITOR

Dear Sir (Editor):

I have had the dubious privilege of reading 24 on the columns written by Floyd Hale, "The Bible says."

Readers without formal theological training will have no way of knowing that Mr. Hale is presented anything but "what the Bible says." What he does present, disguised as (to use his language) "critical (honest) analysis of the text and its background," is a particular approach to the Bible called Higher Criticism.

Only against this background can one understand Hale's reduction of Jonah to parable (many scholars have pointed out that the Book of Jonah reads just like any other Old Testament prophetic book and sets forth the actual ministry of a prophet as historical as Isaiah or Jeremiah). It's the miracle of being swallowed by the beast and surviving that sticks, not in the whale's throat, but in Hales; and his denial of Jesus' virgin birth, physical resurrection, and actual ascension to heaven (the New Testament accounts clearly present every one of this events as factual, and they are included as such in all three Ecumenical Creeds of the church, defining Christian faith for Eastern Orthodox, Roman Catholic, and Protestant Christians).

Mr. Hale's approach thus only represents heresy and disqualifies him from legitimate Christian ministry; it is also a travesty of scholarship. Higher Criticism has been jettisoned in other disciplines because of its subjectivity and unreliability: only liberal theologians of a previous generation are still (religiously) committed to it.

It is too bad Hale seems incapable of giving the Bible even that much benefit of doubt. It is even worse that your paper continues a column by a non-expert who foils his unbelief on unsuspecting readers disguised as "scholarship" which it certainly is not).

A College Professor
London, England

Editor's note: Professor, your term "unsuspecting readers," is degrading--they have the ability to make up their own minds. Your belief that Jonah survived three days without oxygen and giving it the same rating as Isaiah or Jeremiah would have about the same believability to many as your opinion of Hale's views.
D.B

The Bible Says...

By Floyd Hale

Question: Some time ago you had an article about the book of Jonah being a parable and not a true story. Did Jesus know this when he referred to Jonah as being "three days and three nights inside the whale" (Mt. 12:40)?

Answer: Research in the development of the Gospel traditions concludes that this saying about Jesus' being in the earth three days and three nights was a product of the early Church (after his death) to support their claim of his "resurrection." If Jesus had said this he would have been incorrect, according to the resurrection stories, for it was one day, two nights, and parts of two other days. If you think this is being too picky, you have to be if you want to know what Jesus really said.

Even if Jesus had mentioned the fictional Jonah in a teaching, it would have been proper, the way outstanding literary characters are referred to as "real"; but there is hard evidence in the Gospels that Jesus never mentioned Jonah at all. In Matthew and Luke you have Jesus referring to Jonah--in various ways. These were written years after Mark's Gospel (which both of them used as their primary source). But in Mark--the oldest Gospel--Jesus not only doesn't mention the "sign of Jonah," he says very sternly to those "seeking a sign," "No sign shall be given" (8:12), and went on to condemn "sign-seekers." Isn't it rather odd then that Matthew retains (from Mark) this condemnation, while having Jesus go ahead and say there would be a sign--"Jonah"?

Quoting a Bible text while ignoring one that may contradict it, and lining up verses from different books in the Bible literally, can lead to serious doctrinal error. When the Bible is properly understood it does become a trustworthy commentary on itself. This takes a knowledge of Bible background lay people are not exposed to. That's regrettable. "The Bible Says" is trying to do something about that.

LETTERS TO THE EDITOR

To the Editor:

I've enjoyed the running controversy being carried on in your letters column over "The Bible Says. . ." feature I hope they continue (both the column and the letters).

I think the letters illustrate a curious double standard on the part of those who take such offense at the efforts of Mr. Hale. I say this because on the same page as that column there is another, authored by the Reverend Robert J. Hastings. The Reverend Hastings is a highly respected spokesman for the Southern Baptists. And I should think that that denomination should be fundamentalist enough for even the most rock hard upholder of the faith.

Yet, I have not seen any letters commenting on points raised by Mr. Hastings by the fundamentalists, nor have I seen any letters from the more liberal followers of Jesus Christ, or even from non-believers, upbraiding the newspaper for daring to run his columns.

Could it be that people just see what they want to see? And what they don't see, doesn't bother them

A pleased Bystander

To the Editor:

I read your paper every day and find it interesting. With the exception of the little column of "The Bible Says..." My Bible happens to be filled with "truths," not "myths or misunderstandings" as quoted by this educated preacher.

The last letter has gotten under my skin and I would like to express my opinion.

The book of John in my Bible has quotations that "Jesus says." When I read these I know that they are what Jesus said. Mr. Hale has a way of confusing the word of God--that I will agree. If being educated gives a person his outlook on the Bible, all I can say is "Praise the Lord for uneducated people."

Thank you for letting me get it off my chest.

A Reader

The Bible Says...

By Floyd Hale

Question: I hear the expression, "Bible Prophecy." Exactly what is that?

Answer: The pure meaning of "prophecy" in the Bible is "God's truth proclaimed"--relevant to the present situation (at the time it was "preached"). A corrupt meaning of the term is "the future foretold." This latter one is very fascinating, thus more popular. It has dominated the interpretation of the Bible, to the detriment of much truth in the Bible.

One good help in understanding "Bible Prophecy" is to see how some of the New Testament writers quoted from the Old Testament (their Bible at the time). Matthew said Jesus' birth and return out of Egypt as a child "took place to fulfill what the Lord had spoken by the prophet. . ." That's very strong language, but the "prophecies" quoted (Isaiah 7:14 and Hosea 11:1) have nothing to do with Jesus--as they plainly show in their context. Matthew does this in other places also where the "prophecies" do not apply (e.g. 2:17, 3:3, 27:9).

This is not "Floyd Hale's view"--nor the view of "new theology" (whatever that is); it is an obvious fact. Matthew did what was commonly practiced then, called "midrash." It found a scripture which could be treated as though it had a second (hidden) meaning, making it apply to ("foretell") a current event or teaching. This is yet done to-day by quoting a whole bunch of Bible verses, each out of its context, to prove some preconceived or denominational doctrine. Those who do this could justify their twisting the scriptures around by saying it is "Biblical"--Matthew did it.

Doesn't it strike you as odd, that the Bible is so well known by most and loved by many, yet so little is known "about" it? What's odder to me is so few are interested in learning this important information.

My prayer is that those who love the Bible will learn all about it, that they may discern the Truth in it, and share that Truth with the world which so desperately needs it. Christians fussing with each other about what "the Bible says" is certainly not the way this is done.

The Bible Says...

By Floyd Hale

Question: Are there love stories in the Bible?

Answer: The little book of Ruth is sometimes called a love story. As a young widow Ruth was very devoted to her widowed mother-in-law, and she carried on a quite a romance with Boaz to get him to marry her. But all this "story" was to get the readers "liking" this "foreign" grandmother of King David. This novel was penned about six centuries after Ruth and Boaz lived, and was designed to try to get the Jews to quit treating the "foreign" wives in their midst unjustly as a result of Ezra's Reform.

The book of Esther is sometimes called a love story. The relationship of the Persian Emperor Ahasuerus and the beautiful Jewish maiden Esther was somewhat romantic, but the last three chapters of that "story" are full of jingoistic hatred released in fantasized slaughter of the enemy. One thing is for sure, there is no love of enemy in this little book.

King David is quoted as saying his love for his close friend Jonathan was most wonderful--"surpassing the love of women." Some have thought there might be a unique love story in that, but who knows? Who cares?

Love stories--even in the Bible--tend to follow the habits of romance-- infatuation, sex, bonding in relationship, etc. Not that these are bad, but there is a "more perfect way"--love which is demonstrated strictly for the benefit of those loved. The unique New Testament word for this was "agape," and was expressed (perfectly, I believe) in Jesus. He looked upon the poor, sick and oppressed with *compassion*. Without the "I love you and God loves you" and that sort of gush, Jesus tried with all his heart and strength to do something to alleviate the misery of people.

Because of the sociopolitical situation at the time there was very little he could do, but his teachings and bold living has inspired much change for the better down through history--more than he could have imagined. Because of him millions--literally millions-- are far better off. To me his story is the greatest--if not the only--true love story in the Bible.

The Bible Says...

By Floyd Hale

Question: Did King Saul commit suicide or was he slain?

Answer: This may seem unimportant, but seeking the answer to this could lead a person to a better understanding of the Bible as a whole.

In I Samuel 31:4 the Bible says Saul, severely wounded in battle, asked his armor-bearer to "thrust him through," so the Philistines (who had just won the battle) would not capture him. The armor-bearer would not, so Saul "fell on his own sword." One chapter later, in II Samuel 1:10, the Bible says an Amalekite (who "just happened to be in the area") slew Saul, and reported this to David, taking him the crown from off Saul's head.

An easy answer to this contradiction could be, Saul's armor-bearer was an Amalekite. But in the first account Saul's armor-bearer, following his lord's example, also fell on his sword, could not have taken word to David. Another easy answer is that it could be considered "suicide" in both accounts, since Saul also asked the Amalekite (he said) to "slay him." But suicide or murder is not the issue here; it is what the Bible actually says in both places, and why the conflicting stories.

When the background of Samuel-Kings is researched as to when and why these accounts were written, it is discovered that these traditions got "amended" a number of times to improve on David's character (when Saul was actually the far greater man). II Samuel 1:10 and 4:10 are just small examples of the way this was done during the passing centuries.

During that time I and II Chronicles were penned completely reediting Samuel-Kings, in which David is painted not only as the George Washington of Israel, but as the patron saint of Judaism. To help understand how all this could be, one should know Samuel-Kings was not considered "Scripture" yet when the Chronicler edited it. And the Chronicler had not the slightest idea that his version of "history" would centuries later appear side by side with the older version (Samuel-Kings) in a "Bible"--and then be looked upon as the "inspired Word of God," literally.

The Bible Says...

By Floyd Hale

Question: I have seen a bumper sticker which read, "In case of the Rapture this vehicle will be driverless." Where in the Bible is the Rapture mentioned?

Answer: This exact word is not in the Scriptures. It comes from Paul's statement in I Thes. 4:17 about the Christians' being "caught up" to meet Jesus in the air at his return. In that passage Paul used the apocalyptic language profusely, without its apocalyptic meaning. The apocalyptic had a proper interpretation, and its wording was not to be taken literally.

In Revelation--the one formal Christian Apocalypse in the New Testament--the souls of the martyrs are *taken up to heaven,* to return with Jesus and help him rule the nations. After 1,000 years Satan is released and makes one last futile effort to take over. Then comes the "second" resurrection and Judgment Day. But those who "pass" don't go *up to heaven.* John adds a postscript vision. God "comes down to earth" to dwell with them--*for ever,* and they continue their mission of "healing the nations."

When Revelation was written it had a here and now relevance. The message was for those just entering the Roman Persecution (ca. 90); and they understood it clearly. The "martyrs ruling the nations" symbolized their faithfulness--especially in dying--helping change "the kingdoms of this world into the kingdom of God and His Christ."

The Apostle Paul used this popular apocalyptic language, but wed it to the Gnostic philosophy of his audience, making it come out: When Jesus returns he will take his saints *up to heaven (rapture)* where they will remain with him *for ever.* Instead of God's kingdom coming on earth, the future becomes centered in the "next world."

This can be a very confusing subject. As a result of our not keeping up on our understanding of the apocalyptic in our Bible. Jesus's gospel has actually been replaced by the gospel of the Apostle Paul.

The Bible Says...

By Floyd Hale

Question: Do you believe "Literally" in the 9 gifts of the Spirit and in the manifestation of the Gifts of the Holy Spirit in believers in Church according to the Instructions for use in I Corinthians Ch. 14?

Answer: Out of your lengthy letter I can deal here only with the first question--which may make the answers to the others unnecessary.

Paul wrote I Corinthians to a *specific* group about *particular* problems in their fellowship *at that time and place*. What he said to them is to be understood in light of this. The nature of the paganism in their cultural background (especially one certain Mystery Cult) contributed to the "spiritual" immaturity being demonstrated by them.

The "workings (gifts) of the Holy Spirit" in I Corinthians are Paul's own concepts and evaluations, and he had founded that church. The Christian Faith was just then taking shape in the world. Why was Paul discouraging the practice of a "gift" causing trouble which he also recognized as "of the holy Spirit"? Etc.

Years after Paul wrote his personal advise and instructions to that group, this, and all his other "personal" letters, were being used to guide "all the Churches" in the forming of the doctrines of the whole Church. Their continued use put them on the level of "Scripture," which finally resulted in their being officially added to their Bible (which up until then was the Old Testament). The Established Church then took over and treated Paul's words as the Word of God--for all time to come.

The Church today may learn much from I Corinthians, but Paul's detailed instructions to the Churches he served should not necessarily be a "literal"--and Divine--guide for the Church now.

There are many reasons for this, but space doesn't allow me to comment on all of these here.

73

The Bible Says...

By Floyd Hale

Question: Why did Jesus put a curse on a fig tree for not having figs on it, when it was not the season for fruit?

Answer: A close examination of these three gospel accounts, Mt. 21:18-19, Mk. 11:12-14, and Lu. 13:6-9, shows rather clearly what happened. Luke is the only gospel which reports the parable about a barren fig tree, but no cursing thereof. Mark and Matthew are the only gospels reporting the cursing of a fig tree, but no parable.

A Bible student familiar with how the gospels were written can readily see that Mark worked the parable used by Luke into an "action parable," and placed it near the cleansing of the temple, where he thought it better made its point. Matthew adds to Mark's account Jesus' telling his Disciples they will do miracles like this if they have faith and never doubt.

Mark was a bit clumsy in his reshaping the material in the parable. To give Jesus a motive for looking for figs on the tree he has him "hungry." To explain why the tree was "barren," he says "it was not the season for figs." But leaves indicated it was the season for figs. (Some scholars believe this "for it was not the season for fruit" was injected into Mark's text later. It's not being in Matthew gives weight to this.) It being in season (with leaves) but bearing no fruit better illustrates Luke's parable about Israel's barrenness. This is just one example of how we need a better understanding of how the Gospel traditions evolved.

The point of both of these passages was the claim that the Church was the new trustee of the Kingdom, replacing Israel. During the 40 years before the first gospel was compiled the Church developed a lot of "oral traditions" about why things had gone as they had--and would go in the future--and worked these "explanations" into some of Jesus' sayings and doings which went into the Gospels.

Bible scholars are good at determining more nearly what the authentic sayings and doings of Jesus were. This is the only academic field in which its scholars are ignored if not rejected altogether.

The Bible Says...

By Floyd Hale

Question: Did Jesus actually say the world would come to an end in his generation?

Answer: If you believe what the King James "Bible says" is true, you'd have to admit Jesus said this--and was also mistaken.

The 24th chapter of Matthew in the KJV is a kind of "countdown to the end," in answer to the Disciples' question, "Tell us, when will these things be? And what will be the sign of your coming, and of the *end of the world?*." Jesus then recites a whole list of "end-things"-- the last of which is the coming of the Son of Man in judgment. Then he says, "This generation will not pass, til all these things are fulfilled." Let no one tell you the word "generation" in this place means a "dispensation," for that is just not true.

If you do not have a fairly good understanding of Apocalypticism in the Bible this can be confusing.

A small insight into the growth of the apocalyptic thinking of the early Church before the New Testament was completed may be gained by carefully comparing Mt. 24 and Mk. 13, for Matthew 24 is an "expanded" version of Mark 13. This "end of the world"

question is not in Mark (v. 4b). Also, "world" should be translated "age," as the RSV properly does.

Mk. 13--called "The Little Apocalypse" by Bible scholars--was inserted in between the accounts of the "life of Jesus" and the "death of Jesus." There is evidence that this was, in its original form, a small apocalyptic pamphlet which was distributed among the Jerusalem Christians, warning them not to make the mistake of identifying with the Jews in a last-ditch stand against the Romans when they destroyed that city in A.D. 60, and attributed to Jesus.

Much more should be said about this--and the part Apocalypticism played in the early Christian community and the writing of the N.T., but I must conclude this far too brief explanation with the simple answer, Jesus did not say anything about the end of the world.

I wonder why the laity are kept in the dark about what the Bible really says?

75

The Bible Says...

By Floyd Hale

Question: Was John the Baptist "Elijah" who was to come?

Answer: Matthew and Luke (relying on Mark as their source) present John the Baptist as "Elijah," the forerunner of the Messiah-- even Jesus is (mis)quoted as saying he was (Mt. 9:14). But in the Gospel of John (1:21) John the Baptist himself denies that he is Elijah.

First of all this contradiction must be admitted as such. To understand the Bible, its contents must be dealt with honestly. Any trying to deny such contradictions in the Bible is a smoke screen hiding the facts--and hindering the true method of finding the real message in the Scriptures.

The reader should know that the author of John had complete literary freedom in composing his very unique Gospel. He is building a "Theology of Christ," not writing a biography of the real Jesus. John had a "good reason" for showing that the Baptist was a "nobody"-- announcing a "somebody." The Gospel writers had a big problem to overcome--why was Jesus baptized by John? Did this not make the baptizer more important that the baptizee? (John is even careful not to say the Baptist baptized Jesus.)

They all quote from their "Scripture" (the Old Testament) to "prove" that John the Baptist was the "fulfillment of prophecy" as the *forerunner* of the Messiah, not his superior. There was a tradition circulating at the time that Elijah would return and set the stage for God's takeover. But look at the "prophecy" they misquote. Isaiah 40:3 says, "A voice cries: 'In the wilderness prepare the way of the Lord'," (RSV), not "A voice crying in the wildreness. . ." Isiah was talking about something else altogether which applied to his time.

The Gospel writers' thought they had to be "biblical" (with the O. T.) in telling the story of Jesus. He in character and action could stand on his own--he didn't need all that "proving from the Scriptures" anyway.

This also passed on into Christian tradition what is actually an erroneous method of interpreting Scripture, called "midrash."

76

The Bible Says...

By Floyd Hale

Question: Will Christ someday return from heaven riding on a white horse, smite the nations with a sword, rule them with an iron rod, reign over them for a thousand years, and then let Satan loose to lead the whole world in another war against his saints?

Answer: The main body of the book of Revelation (an Apocalypse) is made up of *seven* major visions. The above question is an outline of the first five scenes of the *seventh* vision. Scene six is the resurrection of the dead and Judgment. This is usually thought to be "the end," but there is another scene in this *seventh* vision, in which God comes down to earth to "make all things new." This last scene is ignored by those who treat Revelation like it foretells the end of the world.

The person interested in what "the Bible says" should learn how to interpret this apocalyptic jargon, otherwise he/she never knows whether anyone else's interpretation is true or not. Realizing that my interpretation may be considered just one more preacher's opinion, I'm going to tell you what the above means.

This *seventh* vision, briefly highlighted above, summarizes what has been going on throughout this book--from the time the rider on the white horse rode out in the first scene of the *first* vision-- "conquering and to conquer." The "sword" which issues out of Jesus' mouth is his "gospel," GOD IS IN CHARGE, which is preached and *practiced* by the faithful servants of Christ, until the persecution put on by the "Beast" (Roman Government) is broken. That being "the end" of that, the Church ("Holy City") will be free but thoroughly disciplined to continue its mission of "healing the nations." Nations are "healed" when God's justice (what's right) produces and permeates government. Not a bad hope.

This book was written to a group facing most severe times in first century--not for people twenty centuries later.

LETTERS TO THE EDITOR

Dear Editor:

Regarding the articles by Floyd Hale, I feel you are doing a disservice to your readers by publishing his articles, especially to the newborn Christians, who are not yet familiar with "WHAT THE BIBLE REALLY SAYS."

You convey the idea you even believe he went too far in your column of Feb. 16. But it slipped by you and now there is no alternative, but to go ahead and publish his answers.

If he does not believe in the virgin birth of Jesus, that he does not believe arose from the grave the third day, and that he now sits at the right hand of God, what does he believe? (His remarks on Feb.9)

That is the difference between Christianity and the other religions. He could qualify as a Sadducee, they say there is no resurrection (Mk. 12:18, Acts 23:8). So they are, or will be SAD-U-C.

Jesus is the Son of God! Isaiah was a prophet, and Amos 3:7 says "Surely the Sovereign Lord does nothing without revealing his plan to his servants the prophets." Is. 7:14 does apply to Jesus and Matt. 1:20-23 fulfills the prophecy.

Mr. Hale, not Revered. I find 'reverend' only one time in the KJV, and than it applies to God, keeps saying

Matthew is not an Aopostle, doesn't he believe Mark was aware who they were? Mark 3:13-19 lists the twelve.

Mr. Hale reserved more space to qualify his unbeliefs to questions, the damage has been done, and he failed to justify his unbelief of the virgin birth of Jesus. I hope all who read his column of Feb. 9th will search the scripture for the real truth of "What the Bible says."

God loves you, and so does the virgin birth Jesus, the Son of God.

A Reader

Editor's note: Thanks for your thoughtful letter. Something good usually comes from about anything and I hope this holds true with these columns. They should make people think and study. D.B.

j

The Bible Says...

By Floyd Hale

Question: Did Jesus say "You must be born again"?

Answer: No. But before you say I am flatly contradicting what "the Bible says," let me explain.

The Fourth Gospel, in which this statement appears (John 3:7), was not "just another life of Jesus." Whether intended or not it put Paul's gospel into a Gospel form, for the Greeks (where Paul had founded the churches). The red-letter words are the words of John, not Jesus'.

The Gnostic thinking at the time was, the "soul" (spirit) came "from above" (the spirit world), and got imprisoned here in a physical "body of death." If it were "made alive from above," it would return "home" when the "evil" body died. Paul had presented Jesus to these Gentiles as God's Savior "come from above" to rescue them "from this evil world," that they may "go to be with their Savior--forever."

When Jesus told Nicodemus he must be born "*anothen,*" that Greek word had a double meaning--*from above* and *again.* John gave Nicodemus the latter meaning--how a man could go back into his mother's womb when he was old and be born "a second time," so Jesus could give it the right meaning, "from above." The KJV translators had no English word with the double meaning of *anothen,* so they chose "again," which in a sense was right, but Nicodemus had already said that. (The New RSV translated it "anew.") Anyway, the Gnostic "from above" is lost to the modern reader.

One of John's purposes in writing was to counter a lot of the Gnostic thinking in the Church, but he retained its "spiritual" emphasis. This comes out in this line (which he has Jesus saying), "You must be born again." John's Gospel became the popular Gospel of traditional Christianity, and his "3:16" became for many the "Golden Text of the Bible."

In the first (older) three Gospels one "entered (lived in) the kingdom of God" by doing God's will. That could be tough, which is why, I think, having a "spiritual experience" is the more desirable way. It can all be kept very private, where the former involves public action.

The Bible Says...

By Floyd Hale

Question: What does it mean to be saved by the grace of God?

Answer: It means exactly what it says--by nothing more nor nothing less than the grace of God. Grace is unconditional--or it is not grace. This means everyone is "already saved"--many just may not know it yet. *God accepts everyone--including sinners.* It is when a person "experiences" this acceptance that grace "works" in his/her life. This is what we usually call "getting saved."

Fear of God--afraid of being punished by Him--can not bring about *positive* change in a person, regardless of how much "being sorry" is done. This is why God has called off all punishment (He never was a wrathful God anyway) and decided "from the beginning" to depend entirely on His love and mercy. God has "gambled" all on GRACE. It is the greatest force for personality and character change in the world. Its main handicap is, it is just too good to believe-- and it is kept a secret.

You will find a lot in the Bible to contradict about all I have just said, but that is only because much of the Bible is mistaken about God-- and Jesus.

Saul--who later became the great Apostle Paul-- sought (as few other people ever have) through righteousness to be accepted by God, but only because of "Jesus Christ" did he find that acceptance--as a sinner. That was such a revolutionary experience in his life that he said others "must accept Christ also" (the way he did) to find God's grace. But when this experience shaped his gospel, it became the basic dogma of the Church (by his writings becoming Christian Scripture). That put a "condition" on grace and *unwittingly* changed Jesus' real image as "Lord" (to be followed) to "Savior" (to be believed in). The former has to do with saving the world-- out in the world; the latter has to do with saving oneself--in church.

It is important that a person experience God's grace--to make them gracious. But Jesus should not be "used up" in this, for that leaves the real Jesus as Lord of life out of Christian disipleship.

The Bible Says...

By Floyd Hale

Question: If God saves everyone by unconditional grace, why should I be concerned about how I live? Wouldn't this promote a "do your own thing" life style?

Answer: God accepts everyone as his children. He always has and always will. This says nothing about their character, morals, etc. He doesn't even discriminate between the good ones and the bad ones, Mt. 5:45, a "scripture" overlooked by the doctrine makers.

If this allows you to "do your own thing with your life," that might show how little you appreciate God's grace--and how little you value your life--and others. The heavy burden of unconditional grace on one's conscience is not as "liberating" as you might think.

This kind of grace is what motivates real positive change (Rom. 2:4). I believe your thinking (like that of most of us) has been conditioned too much by the negative in traditional religion--fear of God's punishment, hell, etc. Since there's lots of that in the Bible, that's what makes it so bad when people take that stuff as God's Word. Fear can change one's behavior to conform to a so-called Christian standard, but only God's grace can change ones' disposition to love.

Unconditional grace pulls the rug from under the believer. One then has nothing to seek in order to "be saved." Realizing that, one may see what Jesus was all about and chose to follow him. Or he/she may not. If one does chose to, it will not be from a self-centered motive--like saving oneself, or being blest.

Jesus wanted people to be so concerned about the welfare of others that they would do something about it. People need to be told they are "saved"--safe. That would give them a chance to experience the real grace of God. That works--a lot better than believing a bunch of doctrines about Jesus

Our task is not to take literally what the early Christians said about Jesus in eulogy, but to learn how to see the real Jesus through all this. That's what the Gospels are for.

The main reason the grace of God is not believed is it's too good to believe.

The Bible Says...

By Floyd Hale

Question: Why do the different Gospels report differing sayings of Jesus from the cross?

Answer: The "seven sayings from the cross" contained in the four Gospels are all traditionally attributed to Jesus. But none of Jesus followers were close enough to have heard Jesus if he said anything. (John's Gospel, in which Jesus "says" the most from the cross, is not a factual account of what happened.) A close reading of most of these separate accounts shows that various Old Testament scriptures were used as source material in shaping these stories.

Mark, the first to report this event, saw Psalm 22 as a good description of Jesus in his agony. The first line, "My God, my God, why. . .?" represents the whole of that Psalm--which has a positive ending. Those who say this was God's leaving Jesus "alone" to bear the full burden of sin press this too far. Neither was Jesus (as some have said) disappointed, because he was "playing the suffering servant"--believing God would rescue him at the last minute.

Matthew follows Mark and adds no "saying" of his own.

Luke as a whole portrays a more positive image of Jesus. He softens the negative "mockeries" by the two thieves (in Mark) by having Jesus promise "Paradise" to one of them. This expressed Jesus' view of "sinners" which runs throughout Luke. "Father, forgive them" perfectly fits the character of Jesus. (This line does not appear in some of the ancient copies of this Gospel.)

John differs most from the others: Jesus' committal of his mother into John's care is not factual; it is add support to John's being the author of this Gospel--"the one whom Jesus loved." "I thirst" comes from Psalm 69, and sets up their offering him the vinegar drink.

"It is finished" is John saying Jesus "completed the work the Father gave him to do"--which has been called "the plan of salvation."

Whether Jesus said these sayings or not from the cross they say something very meaningful about him.

81

The Bible Says...

By Floyd Hale

Question: Does the Bible say, "Beat your plowshares in to swords, and your pruning hooks into spears"?

Answer: I didn't switch this around, the Bible says this--in Joel 3:10. In Isaiah 2:4 the Bible says (what you probably had in mind), "They shall beat their swords into plowshares, and their spears into pruning hooks." (You see why I call this column "The Bible Says"?)

This "prophecy" of Isaiah was a *hope* founded in faith, not a *foretelling*. But hope is not hope unless it is lived out. Thus Joel was telling the nations not to live out Isaiah's "prophecy." Isaiah preached when Judah was still a nation, with a Davidic monarch. Joel lived about four centuries later, after Judah had lost its independence--had no king or self-rule. This helped account for them being two different kinds of "prophets"--if Joel can even be properly called a prophet.

Isaiah preached justice; Joel preached vengeance. Isaiah preached peace; Joel was an avid promoter of the first Zionist movement-- "fight the nations that keep the kingdom of Israel from being restored." Isaiah believed "The Day of the Lord" was when God's will would be done by the king and people. Joel believed "The Day of the Lord" was apocalyptic--God would do it in military fashion. Isaiah-- and the other Pre-Exilic (before Babylonian Captivity) prophets-- promoted doing what was right, often ridiculing the temple-centered religion of Israel. Joel--and the other Post-Exilic (after the return from Babylon) prophets-- promoted the practices of the revived temple-centered cult.

The Pre-exilic prophets (of which Isaiah was the "Prince") were "real prophets;" the Post-exilic prophets (of which Joel was not the greatest) were "just preachers." One reason for this was the latter by then had a "Bible" (The Law)-- which limited them to "tradition." The former had no "Scripture"--they depended on God's direct inspiration.

Which of these "poems" (RSV) would you say was God's Word? How could they both be?

The Bible Says...

By Floyd Hale

Question; What do you have to believe to be a Christian?

In the early Church's rush to "promote beliefs about Jesus," the real Jesus got unwittingly left behind. He asked people only to "believe in" his gospel--"God is in charge" (the kingdom--rule--of God). This was not creedal--just believing THAT God is in charge. Believing IN is experiencing what is believed--God takes over the believer, or there is no real religious believing.

This may sound radical, but that was Jesus. Jesus didn't ask people to believe in him--or his teachings. Jesus did not push religion per se, for that tempts people to "seek to be righteous," rather than "seek God's rule."

Seeking God's rule is more than "getting into the kingdom;" it is doing in life the will of the Ruler over life. It is living "as though" God were in charge of this world (which He actually is--it's His, not ours).

Done Jesus' way this is revolutionary, for this is the way God will "take over" the world--through the faithfulness of his servants (agents). This is why Jesus' teachings majored on "obedience," not "piety."

Believing a bunch of stuff ABOUT Jesus can be the "religious" way of ignoring Jesus' call to discipleship. Following the leader is none other than doing what the leader does. Jesus was one preacher who practiced what he preached--"God is in charge." That's why they said he was "anointed of God." ("anointed" is pronounced "messiah" in Hebrew.)

As far as discipleship was concerned, Jesus said that was a "losing" affair, not a "saving" one--as his own life and death illustrated. But it worked. Because Jesus lived it--faithfully, God's will is much, much more being done in human affairs today than it was then, and the end is not yet.

The title "Christian" literally means "one who imitates Christ"--does what Jesus did. This "name" is not for one who just believes certain things about Jesus and the Bible, stays out of trouble, and leaves God's ruling up to Jesus--when he returns.

83

The Bible Says...

By Floyd Hale

Question: What do you think of the escapades of Sampson in the Bible?

Answer: Fantastic! This is a good example of how some Bible writers used "wonder stories" about their cultic heroes in promoting their national pride. The Sampson legend is found in Judges, chapters 13-16.

Besides his exploits among the foreign fairer sex, he killed a lion with his bare hands, tore the huge gates off a city entrance, and slew a thousand Philistines with the jaw bone of an ass. But most people remember the foxy way he burned the enemy's grain fields and destroyed a building full of "the uncircumcised."

The last two feats are told in the fine art of Hebrew storytelling. He catches three hundred foxes (how?) and ties their tails together in pairs. Then he sets their tails on fire and sends them off through the enemy's grain fields.

At last, blind and captive, but secretly regaining his strength (his hair had grown out again), he is taken to his captors' temple (which doubled as a sports arena) to put on his strong man act for them. He gets a little boy to lead him to the main roof supports, where he literally brings the house down, killing about three thousand pagan spectators-- and himself.

The real Sampson was most likely a heavyweight who had shown courage in resisting domination by the Philistines, but what he actually did and what he is credited with doing in the Bible are two different things. Hebrew stories like this were told to fantasize "great heroes of the past." It was hoped this would inspire much needed heroes in the present--and future. How much these stories were embellished as they were handed down is hard to say, but centuries later they gained Sampson a seat with Israel's ancient Judges.

One indication that these tales evolved out of folklore instead of real events is that they do not tell of meaningful or realistic deeds; they fantasize revenge by the oppressed on their enemies (as does the whole book of Esther).

If there is any moral in this story of Sampson, it might be: "Don't sleep with foreign women" (16:1,4,13f)--for which he was not condemned.

The Bible Says...

By Floyd Hale

Question: What became of the saints mentioned in Matthew 27:52-53 who came out of their tombs when Jesus was crucified? Did they eventually die again?

Answer: The apocalyptic explained Jesus as the (mythical) "Son of Man" who was to "come on the clouds" (from heaven), effect Judgment, and establish God's rule (kingdom) on earth, in the "end-time." Even as a martyr he was given "power" to accomplish the cause for which he died. This is why the disciples "affirmed" that "God *raised* Jesus to His right hand of *Power.*" The popular belief in the resurrection at the time ("life after death") gave form to the stories of Jesus' "resurrection-ascension," which resulted from that *apocalyptic* affirmation. It ought to be obvious that these are "stories."

"In the last days" (an apocalyptic phrase) it was believed the "saints" (meaning martyrs) would "come back from the dust" and be rewarded (Daniel--an Apocalypse--12:2). Since to Matthew the "resurrection" of Jesus was an apocalyptic "event," this report was a "scriptural" effort to support that affirmation. If this is confusing it is because the popular apocalyptic expression form, incorporated into the first three Gospels, has been taken literally, obscuring the real Jesus.

Matthew would not try to explain to us moderns what happened to the dead saints who were "seen alive," anymore than he would try to explain how Jesus "walked on water." He might apologize for having to use apocalyptic, saying it was the only "faith language" at the time which explained the meaning of Jesus' death. The problem is we have failed to learn how to interpret apocalyptic. It is not just a symbolic description of what's going to take place someday.

Until we understand this great book of Revelation we turn it over to nuts like Hal Lindsay and David Karesh, leaving most everyone else unaware of what it really "says." What it says to us is the "cross" is the way God is saving the world. That's not an exclusive vocation of Jesus. He asked his followers to carry one too.

85

The Bible Says...

By Floyd Hale

Question: Would you please explain in your weekly column how a Bible reader like me is able to know by his own reading of the Bible what is true and what is false?

Answer: I am taking for granted that a "Bible reader like you" has been born and bred on the generally held view that the Bible is to be taken literally--as true. Most of what I write is a reaction against this view, for I believe it sets people up to misunderstand the Bible as a whole--and its more important parts in particular--such as the Gospels.

In every article where I quote some scripture which "I don't believe" (as you say in your letter), I go on to tell why, and explain the deeper meaning those passages had for their authors and original readers. But I think my explanations get overlooked by some who remember only "what I don't believe."

"True" and "false" are not proper categories into which the Bible is to be arbitrarily divided. The story of Jonah (which you mention), is a perfect illustration of this. It is literally "false," but a "true" teaching when treated as a parable dealing with the hatred of "foreigners" (in a 4th century B.C. situation).

It takes some real disciplined study to gain a knowledge of Bible background. I think the Church is delinquent in providing its members this learning experience. Just "read the Book and believe what it says" does not get the job done--it only confuses it.

I am going to make another statement which may be the only thing remembered from this article by some: The Bible is not Truth--it is not God. *It is the only sacred physical instrument the Christian has which points to the Truth beyond itself.*

I would think its sacredness alone would demand that those who "believes in it" open up their minds to research its origin and development. Finding out what each book meant to its original readers is the first step in the modern reader's learning what's "true" in it for her/him today.

The Bible Says...

By Floyd Hale

Question: Where in the Old Testament is the Messiah mentioned? I can't find it in my Bible.

Answer: You are probably not looking in the King James Version--the one America grew up on.

In it "Messiah" is mentioned in Daniel 9:25 and 26. The Hebrew word means "(an) anointed (one)," and is translated as such in every other place. The KJV is not consistent by translating it "Messiah" in these two verses only (even capitalizing it). Why? Because at the time (1611) the Church was sure this foretold Jesus' coming and his death.

Traditionally the Jews considered those filling a "high office" in God's kingdom "appointed by God." At first it was the kings. To show this an "anointing" was a part of their coronation ceremony. After 588 B.C. (Captivity), no more kings, the priesthood became the "high office" of the Jewish community. When Daniel was written (165 B.C.) priests were commonly called "anointed ones" (as a minister is now called "Reverend").

"Foretelling" in Daniel is actually a recitation of past history in an apocalyptic ("futuristic") writing style. "Messiah" in Daniel 9:25 and 26 (properly translated "an anointed one" in the RSV) refers to two specific priests. The author knew that this first "anointed one" was Joshua ben Jozadak, the priest who came back from Babylon with the first returnees to "restore" the temple cult in Jerusalem in 538 B.C. After "62 weeks" (434 years by Daniel's "hebdomad" symbol) "an anointed one shall be cut off." The first readers of Daniel knew this was the High Priest Onias III, who was assassinated in their time (when Daniel was written).

This whole confused subject of the "Messiah" in the Bible deserves a lengthy study, but I can not teach Bible lessons in this short column. I can only state a few of the *facts about the Bible* from week to week which demand that a whole new look at our Bible be taken. I encourage those interested to take it from here. Facts about the Bible can't hurt it--only help it.

The Bible Says...

By Floyd Hale

Question: Where in Jeremiah is the prophecy that a potter's field would be bought with Judas' thirty pieces of silver? I can't seem to find it.

Answer: That's because it's not there.

It is mentioned in Jer. 32:6-15 that a piece of land was purchased for seventeen shekels, but this deal was made by the prophet (in the 6th century B.C.) to "prophesy" the Jewish captives would return to Jerusalem--"where property would once again be bought and sold."

In Zechariah 11:13 "thirty pieces of silver" is paid a shepherd for his wages. That money was then "cast into the treasury" (RSV). In Hebrew the word "potter" was spelled almost the same as "treasury" and by mistake replaced it in this Old Testament text--that's how come it to be in the King James Version. There would be no pottery shop in the temple.

Combine all this with Jeremiah 18:1-2, where the prophet is ordered to "go down to the potter's house," and you have the "scriptures" from which Matthew midrashed this story (he's the only one reporting it).

It is believed by some that Matthew relied on a list of "fulfilled prophecies" in writing his Gospel. The first Christians felt under heavy pressure to defend their claim that Jesus was the "promised Messiah." Being Jewish Biblicists, the way to do this was for them to "prove from the Scriptures" (our Old Testament was their Bible) that Jesus and what he did had been foretold.

Two important insights may be gained from this. First, although this was a popular way of interpreting the scripture at the time, called "midrash," it was unnecessary. Who Jesus was and what he did could stand on its own--even better--without it.

Second, the way "fulfilled prophecy" is handled in Matthew is a good lesson--right from the Bible--in how we should not use our Bible today. This gets right to the heart of a need for a "new" approach to Bible study. This does no damage whatsoever to the truth in the Bible; it is the only way that commodity is identified.

The Bible Says...

By Floyd Hale

Question: Does Jesus ever contradict himself in the Gospels?

Answer: Mk. 8:11-13 and Mt. 12:38-40 are the same confrontation by the scribes and Pharisees, in which they ask Jesus for a "sign from heaven" (to prove his divine authority). In the former he says very strongly, "NO SIGN shall be given to this generation." While in the latter he says, "No sign . . . EXCEPT the sign of the prophet Jonah. All the double talk trying to harmonizing these is in vain--Jesus just didn't say both. Then which did he say?

Since Mark was the first Gospel written, we begin by assuming Jesus said "No sign"--period. Since Matthew was written years later it can only mean "need" arose in the Church for an exception to what Jesus said in Mark. That "need" was support for the emphasis being given to the "resurrection tradition." What better than the "three days and nights" of Jonah in the fish as a "sign"? Since Matthew edited Mark in a number of places, here was a good place to do it again.

If "Jonah sayings" were going around in Mark's day--and there is evidence that they were--the nature of Mark's saying argues even more for its authenticity. The nearer you get back to the historical Jesus the less there are signs and wonders attributed to him. This "no sign" helps affirm this.

This was not a matter of Matthew "changing Scripture," for Mark was not considered "Holy Writ" until over a century later. This is one more illustration of how the "beliefs about Jesus" grew up in that first century--right in the Gospels.

Rather than criticize Matthew's doing this, I am glad he did. For by comparing the whole of Matthew with the whole of Mark, we can gain a truer picture of the real Jesus and what he said, and how Jesus was soon transformed into a Superman.

To make such a study *we must loosen up on our view of the authority of the Bible.* For some this is like losing one's faith (it was for me), but it must be done for the sake of the Truth in the Christian Faith.

It is to this end that I point out "contradictions in the Word." I think I do it in a way even a blind man could see them.

The Bible Says...

By Floyd Hale

Question: Why do Matthew (19:17) and Mark (10:18) differ on what Jesus told the man who asked him about how he might gain eternal life?

Answer: Few Bible readers would compare these two passages. Those who did might not notice the difference, or think both said the same thing a different way. But a close look at these two parallel passages raises a serious question; for the difference between the two is of major significance.

In Mark (the older of these two Gospels) the man addresses Jesus as "GOOD TEACHER, what must I do. . ?" But in Matthew he addresses Jesus only as "Teacher," with the "good" going over into his question--"What GOOD DEED must I do. .?" This get's more complicated in Jesus' answer. In Mark Jesus says, "Why do you call me good? No one is good but God alone." In Matthew Jesus says, "Why do you ask me about what is good? One there is who is good." You don't have to look too closely to see that the word "good" gets shifted around and the text confused.

Since Jesus' response in Matthew doesn't quite make sense ("Why do you ask me about what is good? One there is who is good."), this suggests the author of Matthew did the shifting. And, since Matthew used Mark as his main source, it is easy to conclude that Matthew was "offended" by Jesus' being "offended" at being called "Good."

When Matthew was written, the tradition that Jesus was more than just a man was growing, and this registers that emphasis. This is not just a cultural accommodation on Matthew's part, but a theological revision. When this is placed with the several other similar editings of Mark by Matthew, one can see how the doctrines about Christ evolved rapidly out in the early Gentile Church, while the Gospels were being written.

The reason I point out things like this in the Scriptures is not to find fault with the Bible, but to show that there is a real need for Christians to understand their one and only sacred Textbook--the Truth depends on it.

90

The Bible Says...

By Floyd Hale

Question: Did Jesus cleanse the temple once or twice?

Answer: The first three Gospels report him cleansing it at the end of his ministry. The Fourth Gospel says he did this at the very beginning. Any explanation of this which does not first admit one or the other writer is "mistaken," is not treating the Scriptures honestly.

The uniqueness of John's Gospel must first be understood. I put "mistake" in quotes, because John intentionally moved the temple cleaning to the beginning of Jesus' ministry for at least two reasons. At the beginning it would show that Jesus--right from the start--had divine authority over Israel's religious system. And he wanted the raising of Lazarus to be Jesus' final act, bringing the authorities down on him.

In Matthew (21:46) it is the cleansing of the temple and teaching therein daily that initiates Jesus' arrest. In John it is the raising of Lazarus which leads directly to his destruction (read all of chapter 11). The theme of this last Gospel is *Life* ("abundant life," "eternal life," etc.), and John wants Jesus rejected and killed as the "Life-Bringer." John is writing for the Greeks, and this is Greek drama at its best.

John has complete literary freedom in scripting his "Gospel," for it is not "just another Gospel." It is his own theological treatise on the God-like "Christ" who comes down from heaven to bring *Life*--now! The seven "I Am" lectures (all only in this Gospel) are John's own teachings put on the lips of Jesus, the last one being "I AM the resurrection and the *life*" (for which he fabricated this "action parable" about Lazarus). Even though John ends his "life of Jesus" with the story of his resurrection (similar to the first Three), in his main theme he says Jesus "IS" the resurrection--while he was yet alive.

The uniqueness of this Fourth Gospel should be understood, for it reveals many changes in the beliefs about Jesus during the last half of the first century. For instance in it the emphasis on "following Jesus" in the older Gospels has changed to just "believing that Jesus is the Christ."

The Bible Says...

By Floyd Hale

Question: What is the purpose of baptism and who should be baptized?

Answer: The only purpose of baptism is to fulfill the requirements of most churches (except the Quakers and the Salvation of Army). It is explained as the symbol of the "washing away of sins." Jesus would certainly be opposed to any ritual or ceremony being made necessary to salvation. (Mark 16:16 is not the words of Jesus.) Even though he was baptized by John, Jesus did not baptize his followers--or anyone else.

Baptism was the mark of John's ministry--that's why he was called "the Baptizer." Paul evidently gave little if any significance to baptism (I Cor. 1:14-17). Jesus said the baptism he recommended was *not with water*, but with the Spirit. It was natural that the traditional Church went with the water one--calling it "Christian"--while neglecting the Spirit one.

We may think it rather silly that the Jews required circumcision as their mark of kingdom citizenship, but with Christians it depends on being dunked in water. At least the dunking lets females in on it. Speaking of circumcision, the Fundamentalists (by midrashing the Scriptures) say God, about A.D. 33, decided to change His method of adoption from circumcision to water baptism (less painful I guess). But--according to the literalists--God changed his mind about a lot of things throughout Bible times.

There used to be strong word-battles between some Christian preachers on this subject--public debates which drew large crowds. A few denominations were founded with baptism the main plank in their doctrinal platform. The major Protestant one in America even has it as its name. I am glad all the fuss over this has stopped. In fact--with a few exceptions-- baptism is in the fine print, off in the footnotes of faith. This tells me that someday it might be dropped altogether. But tradition (that great democracy in which the dead vote) doesn't give up its popular superstitions too easily.

92

The Bible Says...

By Floyd Hale

Question: Who is going to be the Antichrist? When?

Answer: "Antichrist" is mentioned (as such) only in I John 2:18-22; 4:3-7 and II John 1:7. This language comes from the dominant apocalyptic jargon of the day, in which "Messiah" was to be opposed by an "anti-Messiah"--or by many "false-Messiahs" posing as the real thing (Mk. 13:22). Paul (II Thes. 2:3-4) mentions this figure as "the man of lawlessness, the son of perdition" who poses as God (not as Christ). In Revelation it is the "red dragon" who was kicked out of heaven for leading a rebellion, cast down to earth as Satan. You see, the image of this rascal differs from author to author in the New Testament. The literalists just try to put them all together into one person--yet to come.

I and II John simply mention this personage and say, in essence, let's quit making such a mystery out of this--*it is anyone who is against Christ.* And he says there are several of them all over the place. Since antichrist was to come in the "last hour"--and the Christians then believed they were "living in the last hour"--we who live nineteen centuries later should be able to forget about him, but the Fundamentalists won't let us.

The second century opened up on a mad scramble to decide what was Christian and what was not ("what was not" being heresy). The Church did not begin as "one" and merely spread its orthodoxy out over the Greek world. It was different (if only slightly) in most places, depending on the different leaders and the local pagan religious thinking of converts.

Gnostics in the Church, who by declaring the human body inherently evil, disturbed those who had said Jesus came in the flesh (I Jn. 4:1-3). There was heated debate about this; the Gnostic Christians lost out, and we have the Doctrine of the Incarnation as a result.

In spite of all this furor, the author of the John books was really wanting to make sure the Christian emphasis on the love of God which was demonstrated in the life of Jesus was primary and to be emulated.

93

The Bible Says...

By Floyd Hale

Question: Where in the Bible does it say Cain and Abel married their sisters? There were no other available females.

Question: It doesn't say that. The confusion comes when the "stories" in the first eleven chapters of the book of Genesis are taken as literally true--history.

Anyone reading that God and the first man on earth held a conversation; a woman was made because none of the "other" animals were "fit to be the man's helper"; a snake talked to this woman--and she talked back to it; the snake lost his legs because he tempted the woman to eat the forbidden fruit; one of their sons went off into the land of Nod, and not only married there but built a city; and God flooded the whole world and confused the languages; should be convinced that he or she is not exactly reading about real happenings.

Your friend (you mention) probably argues that Cain took one of his sisters with him to Nod as his bride, on the only grounds that the Bible does not say he didn't. All kinds of things can be read into this story, but why not leave it as its author wrote it? Even if he did marry his sister, who were all the people who were going to populate that new city he was building to be named after his son Enoch? And I guess Enoch married his sister?

Who were all those people to threaten Cain out in the world where he was to wonder? And how would they know not to kill him because there was a "mark" on him?

The author of this myth (a legitimate teaching tool--Jesus used it in telling parables) was trying to make a religious point I guess; but I fail to get it. One thing is for sure, when it is taken to be literally true this really fouls up one's view of the Scriptures. My advice is, forget everything in those first eleven chapters of Genesis except the first Creation Story--and don't take it literally.

In saying things like this I get accused of "destroying the Bible," but in my many years of ministry I have found most people appreciate it.

The Bible Says...

By Floyd Hale

Question: How many sisters and brothers did Jesus have?

Answer: In Mt. 13:56 sisters are mentioned, but nothing is said of brothers. You can't count too much on John's mention of Jesus' family.

In Mt. 12:46-50 Jesus' mother and *brothers* go to where he is meeting with some folks, to take him home--and put him in a home. When told they are there, instead of going out to them, he turns to his disciples and says, "Whoever does the will of my Father in heaven is my brother, and sister, and mother." There's no way of knowing exactly how many siblings Jesus had.

To have Jesus be the only child of Mary, some suggest that the "brothers and sisters" were Joseph's children by an earlier marriage. Very unlikely. (Or cousins.)

The most authentic evidence that Jesus had at least one brother is in Paul's letter to the Galatians (1:19), where he mentions meeting in Jerusalem with "James the Lord's brother." This gives us some information about the Disciples we do not have otherwise.

James (the brother of Jesus) and not Peter took over as leader of the followers of Jesus in Jerusalem. Peter's martyrdom in Rome (not a proven fact) made it very convenient for him to be considered by the Roman Church as the first "vicar of Christ"--the leaders (bishops) of Rome following him (in apostolic succession).

It is doubtful if this James had such a radical "conversion" after Jesus' death. He must have already been a strong influence in the corps, for he could not have muscled his way into such a group so quickly. Jesus' movement, *by its very nature,* was not to depend on some "official" leader. The strong "family" tradition is probably what placed James in charge. Furthermore Paul mentions him as an "apostle," showing that this title had a much looser meaning to begin with than just "the twelve."

You didn't ask for all this but I thought I'd fill up the allotted space with some related guesses on my part.

95

The Bible Says...

By Floyd Hale

Question: Does the Bible teach there is a hell?

Answer: In the first place the Bible is not a "teacher." It is a very complicated literary source for understanding the origin, development and practice of the Jewish and Christian religions. To pick out a few--or many--texts from it, and say this is what "the Bible teaches" is to misuse--even abuse--the Bible.

One thing "the Bible teaches" is that Hell is the invention of the Christians. It was not in the Jewish Scriptures, our Old Testament. Just prior to the Christian era the Apocalyptist had invented a place where their God was going to burn their enemies--for ever and ever. It was called "Gehenna." The Greeks spoke of a place where the dead went, "Hades," but nothing took place there (this was similar to the Jewish "Sheol" in the O.T.) The language of the early Christians was full of the names of both these places, Gehenna and Hades, both translated "Hell" in the King James Bible. The Revised Standard Version carries "hades" over into the English, and leaves "gehenna" (the hot one) "hell."

Quoting the places where Jesus mentioned hell (mainly in Matthew) does not prove it exists--or that he believed it did. For what he said about it is not all that certain; and if he did use the term, it could have been as an apocalyptic "figure of speech"--which it actually is.

It ought to be obvious that no one actually believes there is a Hell--where people will burn forever. This is why the Church soon invented Purgatory--a place "this side of Hell" where all unconfessed sin could be cooked out before the Resurrection. (This became a good fund-raiser, for the rich could buy out an ornery relative.) There was "scripture" in the Christian Bible at the time which could be midrashed into supporting this (II Maccabees 12:43-46).

This subject is one more of the many which demand that we gain an understanding of the real authority of the Bible, what the Bible really is and is not--and not just what it "says."

The Bible Says...

By Floyd Hale

100

As I opened my file to prepare this week's article I noticed it would be the 100th appearance of "The Bible Says. . ." in the Benton Evening News. (What else is new?)

Since I don't have a question in hand to answer this week, I thought about reminiscing about the past two years--for it has been a most interesting time in my life. After working on and rewording a summary of "what it's been like," I decided it could best be done by simply passing on (as space allows) some of the various comments I have received in letters from the readers.

"We sure enjoy your well written articles in the paper."

"You don't plan on staying in Benton very long do you?"

"In the past weeks as I read your answers I just laughed at them and felt sorry for those who believed what you said."

"Good work--keep it up."

"Do you know Christ as your personal Saviour?"

"I believe you are using the wrong Bible."

"I hope something can be done about this (stopping the articles) before too many people are misled or confused."

"I think your articles are pretty sound from the standpoint of Bible scholarship, cleverly written, and certainly provocative for this part of the country."

"May God have mercy on your soul."

"Why is it you never have anything good to say about the Bible?"

"I read your column every week. I can't say that I agree with you, but I read it."

"If you don't believe the Bible, why don't you get out of the church?"

"Thinking 'The Bible Says' was another religious column of stale piety I read right past it. But thanks to your critics I discovered the column last year and now look forward to it each week."

"Please forgive me for writing to the Editor about you?" (This party should have written this to the editor.)

As I said, it's been interesting. Keep those cards and letters coming in folks.

The Bible Says...

By Floyd Hale

Question: Why was Jesus called a glutton and a drunkard?

Answer: One reason for this was--as this passage in Mt. 11:19 shows--he was also "a friend of sinners." Don't pass over this too quickly, concluding that this was his way of trying to get them to repent of their sins. He accepted them and associated with them as friends.

Jesus' life style was far from that of the "holiness people" of our day. He certainly did not "keep himself unspotted from the world" (a part of James' definition of being religious, 1:27). Jesus was disgusted with religious people trying to be so pious while ignoring the needs of the poor, sick, and oppressed. Jesus believed his heavenly Fathers' primary desire for his children (everyone) was that they enjoy life--that's why he created it--and them. It was the handicap those in control--the rich and religious (which was about the same crowd)--placed on the good life for others, which disgusted Jesus.

Jesus enjoyed life. This was at the root of his compassion on those who could not. It's a trademark of "sinners" that they enjoy life. That's why Jesus joined with them in the celebration of life. This is what got him rejected by the religious leaders. After that they saw no good in him.

Jesus measured religious behavior by doing what was right--regardless of what anybody says. We have turned that around and made it "doing nothing that's wrong"--which can be doing nothing at all. As long as there is anyone in this world--anywhere--who is being denied the kind of life that can be enjoyed, doing something about that is the Christian's task.

It can be said that this was an extreme criticism of Jesus, being "a glutton and a drunkard," was only a criticism of him, but his followers would not have passed this on about their Lord if there had not be good reason for it. If a Christian is to be "Christ like" (is what he name "Christian" means) there should be more effort placed on discovering what Jesus was really like.

The popular image of him--he was a holy Joe and died for our sins--misses it a mile.

The Bible Says...

By Floyd Hale

Question: Does the Bible say when God created the world?

Answer: You may be surprised to know that the King James Version used to carry that date--exactly 4004 B.C. It appeared at the top of the center marginal notes column on the first page of Genesis. That would be exactly 6,000 years ago (at this writing, 1994`).

Someone may say, "Man put that date there--the Bible doesn't say that." But when all the years ascribed to the generations listed in the Old Testament genealogies are added up, back to Adam, this is the sum. This would make Adam and Eve's birth date January 6, 4004 B.C., would it not?

Genealogies were not kept until late in Jewish history; but even if they were accurate back to Abraham, the twenty old timers (and some of them were really old) on back to Adam were strictly fictional characters. To be accurate this information would have to have been revealed to the author of Genesis. (But a Biblicist wouldn't have any trouble believing this.) If so, Luke wasn't paying close attention to the Revealer; he added (by mistake) the name of Cainan (it didn't belong after Arphaxad (Arpachshad)--according to Genesis 11).

The Literalists do a grand job of quoting scripture by the yard, to prove their favorite doctrines, but they seem to never see what the Bible literally says. Since a knowledge of Bible background wasn't handed down with the Bible (what a shame). It's being "Scripture" was thought to made this "unnecessary." We have for centuries built up a strong tradition of being told what "the Bible says"--we rarely read it ourselves. When we do it is either to find an encouraging word or as a pious act.

I don't know what it is going to take to get us understanding our Bibles. In the meantime we are going to be willing victims of all kinds of silly "Bible doctrines" which hide from us the real Truth in the Bible. I started to say I was just one small voice crying in the wilderness, but I'm not. I am one of the sheep in the fold doing a little bleating once a while.

The Bible Says...

By Floyd Hale

Question: Did Jesus come back to life?

Answer: I'd say he didn't "come back to life."

I am going to be so bold (foolish, some would say) as to ask some questions about this as reported in the Gospels. How could one who came "back to life" leave a tomb before it was opened? How could he talk with two of his closest friends without them recognizing him?-- then suddenly make himself just disappear? Or enter a room without opening the door? Or eat fish if he didn't have a physical body? Why in one account did Jesus allow the women to touch him, while in another he told them not to? Why were the disciples told to go up into Galilee where Jesus would meet them there, and were also told in another account to remain in Jerusalem?

These are not idle questions posed for the purpose of causing doubt or destroying the Scriptures. They demonstrate that these accounts are about something other than a Jesus "coming back to life."

Remove the mythical characters, angels, from these Resurrection Stories, and you have no stories. All this ought to tell us we are not here dealing with a physical happening, *but with the "faith language" of certain people in a certain situation who continued to experience the "presence" of a certain man's "life" after he was dead.* If that life (and death) is to effect us as it did the disciples, and we are to learn the obedience they were taught, we must first understand their *apocalyptic affirmation* that "God raised (exalted) Jesus (as Son of Man) to his right hand of *Power*." You can see how the "Ascension" story also grew out of this. From this basic affirmation--the *true* foundation of the Christian Faith--the various Resurrection Stories at the end of the Gospels developed in a few years (before the Gospels were composed). Then they were soon taken literally.

The "resurrection" of Jesus is at the heart of the Christian Faith, and we should have all along been following the scholars who point out what this meant to his disciples. Instead we have gone for the popular (traditional) view that all this means is we too will "come back to life" someday.

The Bible Says...

By Floyd Hale

Question: Who is Babylon that's mentioned in Rev.18? Also who is that great whore?

Answer: Babylon symbolized Rome in this Apocalypse (Revelation). That's not hard to see. Ever since the Babylonians took the Judeans into captivity in 587 B.C., every oppressing nation or empire was labeled "Babylon" by the Jews.

Revelation is written in Jewish apocalyptic style to the Churches in Asia Minor, whose Faith had just been outlawed by the government. Christians had become "enemies of the state," because they would not recognize the Emperor as "Lord"--take the pledge.

Babylon in Revelation is also referred to as the "great mother of all harlots." ("Harlot" and "whore" are the same word in John's language.) She rules over many people ("waters") from atop "seven hills" (Rome is situated on seven hills).

"She" has led the nations of the Empire into "fornication" with her"-- commerce that splurged in all kinds of refinements and sensualism. "She has become drunk on the blood of the martyrs," and for this she is to be judged. John saw God using the ten nations ("kings" from Daniel) under her control rising up in rebellion and "destroying" her.

The whole 18th chapter is a number of funeral dirges that John delights in chanting over this doomed sex symbol. The 19th chapter opens with "Hallelujah" and "Praise the Lord," for "our God the Almighty reigns!" You can imagine the good feelings enjoyed by the fearful Christians as this was read to them, hiding away in a secret place of worship. I doubted if it inspired any "love of enemy."

Right when evil was on the throne John declared "God is in charge!" That is the faith that overcomes the world. Instead of falling away, the Christians remained faithful (at least enough of them did)--unto death--that their number grew. In feeding them to the lions the Romans finally got sick at their conscience, and in 323 the persecution was officially lifted by the Emperor, Constantine, who accepted Christian baptism. This was the "end" John invisioned.

The Bible Says...

By Floyd Hale

Question: Did the Disciples go back to Galilee after Jesus' crucifixion, or remain in Jerusalem?

Answer: According to Matthew they go back to Galilee, where Jesus meets with them--and promises to "remain with them always." But in Luke they stay in Jerusalem, where he meets with them--and then ascends.

If you have any doubt about this check it out. In Matthew the women are told by an angel to tell the Disciples to go back to Galilee--and they went. There is no way to read into this a meeting of Jesus with them in Jerusalem. Jesus then reveals himself to the women at the tomb and *repeats* the instruction for his men--"Tell them to go up into Galilee--there they will see me."

In Luke, on that "very day"--the "third day" after his crucifixion--Jesus appeared to two of his discouraged followers leaving the city. They go back to town and find that he has already "appeared" to Peter. Immediately he appears among the whole group, gives some brief instruction, walks out to Bethany and ascends (on the same day he was "raised").

They could not then have gone up into Galilee, for Jesus told them to stay in Jerusalem--and they did (according to Luke).

When the Fundamentalists tell you that these two separate accounts can be harmonized--"giving *for you* the full account of all that happened"--and you believe them, it just shows how much they have kept you from understanding your Bible.

The four Resurrection Stories contradict each other in many other ways (myths--being "myths"--don't have to agree literally). In this and the above I am not tearing down the Bible; I *am* trying to destroy (week by week) the high thick wall of Literalism around it which has kept us from learning about the very foundation of our Faith.

It (our Faith) was first expressed by the disciples in their *apocalyptic affirmation* : "God has raised (exalted) the Son of man to His right hand of Power"-- from which each of the four different "resurrection stories" resulted.

The Bible Says...

By Floyd Hale

Question: Please explain how there can be three Gods in one?

Answer: I won't try to explain it, for there is no such Deity.

Did you ever wonder why the Jews B.C. had no "Doctrine of the Duality"? They spoke of God (up in heaven) and the Holy Spirit (down here) without them being two persons in Yahweh. It was because the Jews, being Asiatics, could deal with the metaphysical without having to reduce it to an exact science. The Greeks, being Westerners, could not. It was this "scientific" controversy in the early (Western) Church which arose over the nature of Jesus--God or man?, which ended up giving both him and the Holy Spirit divine personhood.

By the time Matthew was written verse 7 was injected into the 5th chapter of I John (KJV), giving us the only "scripture" which specifically describes a trinity. The RSV properly leaves that verse out of the text.

A person, to be a person, must have an independent personality. To think that three persons could be one is a contradiction in terms and reality. To simply say that God, being God, could pull this off is to put the blame on God for thinking up this whole stupid idea. If God is Spirit, and everywhere-- even in Jesus, wouldn't that make a "Trinity" unnecessary?

From what I observe as the character of Jesus, it was no accident that his followers "saw God" in him. But for those later (who had not seen Jesus) to "quote them" as proving Jesus was God, is to miss the all-important *experience* of those first followers. That involved commitment to "doing the will of the God they saw in Jesus"--the way Jesus did it. This is where the Holy Spirit comes in as the "power" in the doing of that will in life.

To take the religious language in the above paragraph (which I will admit is imperfectly phrased) and manufacture a Doctrine of the Trinity out of it, is to inject a superstition into faith. It seems to me Jesus wanted his followers to pass on their experience "of him" to others in the doing of God's will, rather than in a creed about a three-headed God.

The Bible Says...

By Floyd Hale

Question: Was Peter mistaken in saying Psalm 16:10 foretold Jesus' resurrection (Acts 2:25-31)?

Answer: Quoting a long list of other scriptures which speak of Jesus' resurrection does not "prove" Psalm 16:10 foretold it. And, each quotation must be understood in its particular context. This text illustrates that.

The KJV translators of this Psalm (in the 17th century) worded it to agree with the Acts 2:25-31 interpretation of it. The RSV gives us the original Hebrew version: "Therefore my heart is glad, and my soul rejoices; for thou dost not give me up to Sheol, or let thy godly one see the Pit. *Thou dost show me the path of life.*" You can see that the Psalmist is poetically celebrating his own hope in God. Death, symbolized by "sheol" (that big "pit" under the earth where dead people went), does not threaten his faith.

Since it was obvious the Psalmist was speaking of himself, Luke ("Peter") has to argue that David (still in his tomb) was referring to the "resurrection of Christ." But David was neither a "prophet" (foretelling the future) nor the author of this Psalm. The "promise" in Acts 2:30 is that one of his sons would follow him as king and his dynasty continue (as Ps. 132:11-12 plainly shows).

The book of Acts is a late reconstruction of the history of the beginning of the Church. There is no way its author, sixty years later, could have had access literally to the many speeches he quotes. (To say God revealed all this to him is to beg the issue.) To show that these are Luke's words, they are from the Greek translation of the Jewish Scriptures (the Septuagint)-- the Gentile Christian's Bible. Peter, being a Palestinian Jew, would have quoted the Hebrew version of this Psalm.

Actually, Peter would not have quoted this Psalm at all, for it is the testimony of the Psalmist about himself. (The KJV translated to make it support Acts 2:25f.) This was the Church's way later of proving its doctrines were true--because they were "Scriptural." This practice is called "midrash"--and several preachers yet do it with finesse.

The Bible Says...

By Floyd Hale

Question: Is Mark 16:9-20 supposed to be in the Bible?

Answer: Who says what's supposed to be in the Bible and what's not? That has always depended on the religious council forming their own canon of Scripture. When the Church of England came out with the King James Bible the scholars in charge believed this twelve verse ending on Mark belonged in the Bible-- for it was in all the old copies they were using.

Most of the critical research in the ancient manuscripts has been done after the KJV came out (1611). Most of the oldest and best copies have been discovered since then, and they do not contain these twelve verses. Evidence points to them being added sometime in the 2nd century by some fanatical sect.

It is easy to see how someone back then, looking at Matthew and Luke (written after Mark) would think Mark had lost its ending. So, they took parts of Matthew and Luke's endings and made up one for Mark. This (what is called "internal evidence") confirmed that these twelve verses were not on the original copy of Mark's Gospel. (My judgment, for whatever it's worth, is that Jesus would not have made the crazy statement credited to him in verses 17 and 18 anyway.)

Some conservative scholars have built quite a case for these verses belonging in the Bible, quoting some of the early Church Fathers who are supposed to have been "closer to the original situation," but their bias shows up stronger than their scholarship.

Since the doctrine that "God inspired every word of the Scriptures" became a dogma during the period when the KJV was the only authorized version of the Scriptures of which Americans were aware, this passage being removed would punch a hole in that belief.

Some "Baptists" don't want to give up this "scripture" because it's the only place in the Gospels where Jesus is credited with making water baptism necessary to salvation (v. 16).

Removing these last verses of Mark illustrates what I sometimes call "cleaning up the Bible."

The Bible Says...

By Floyd Hale

Question: What ought to be done to the Islamic terrorists, who, in the name of their God, kill innocent people in Israel?

Answer: I would in no way excuse or defend these ungodly acts, but before we condemn we should take a look at the God of the people they are killing. In the Jewish Scriptures (in our Christian Bible) Jehovah told the Israelites to take the land of the original Palestinians by killing ALL the men in war and slaughtering EVERY woman and child--down to the last ox and sheep. The religion of Islam originated in the 6th century A.D. and inherited its concept of God *directly* from the Jewish Scriptures.

As the early Christians (almost all Gentile, in the 2nd century) began to think seriously about creating a Bible of their own, an influential leader in the Church, one Marcion, wanted to replace the Jewish Bible they had inherited as their only Scriptures, with one made up only of Christian writings. One of the very good reasons Marcion gave for this was the Jewish God Jehovah had a lot of mean characteristics when compared with the Christian "God" Jesus.

But the conservatives made such a loud protest, that the project was aborted--with brother Marcion "sentenced to hell." A pamphlet was circulated at the time, in which their Scriptures (our Old Testament) were defended as "inspired by God." To gain acceptance for this pamphlet (II Timothy), it was written in the name of the Apostle Paul, who had been long time deceased. (Oddly enough, when the "new" Christian writings were finally added onto the "old" Jewish ones, II Timothy was included.)

As Christians help send millions of dollars to Israel to pay for fighting these Islamic terrorists, we should also clean up our Bible--in which terrorism was not only condoned but divinely commanded.

Don't tell me--or anybody else--the God whom Jesus called his heavenly Father ordered any brutal acts on anybody (even in the name of justice). He is a merciful God--thank God!

106

LETTERS TO THE EDITOR

Dear D. (Editor):

I don't usually read columns in any newspapers, but after so many letters pro and con regarding Mr. Hale, I started to read his. I must say that I admire his great knowledge of the scriptures and ancient history. That has taken a lot of research.

Our young minister doesn't take the scriptures literally either.

A Reader
(from out of town)

Editor;s note: Mrs. G. I appreciate your letter regarding Rev, Hale. Have had several people tell me they appreciate his articles, but they do not write letters. D.B.

To the Editor:

I have a complaint. I am very upset that our hometown newspaper would print the answers to Bible questions that Mr. Hale has. Why would anyone want to be called a preacher of the Gospel if they do not believe anything in the Bible is true? As a Christian, I am very offended by his remarks that the word of God is not true.

A Reader

To the Editor:

In many ways Mr, Hale's opinions in "The Bible Says" are different from mine, but I do not plan canceling my subscription to the newspaper.

If any action is taken where Pastor Hale is concerned, I believe it should be in prayer. God's ways are higher than our ways. so perhaps God is working through these articles.

However, I hasten to say that while Pastor Hale has obviously spent many years in gathering the "knowledge" he has, there is a whole other side to this "coin"--a spiritual side. It seems Pastor Hale is a bit one-sided. I will continue to read his articles however, because it is good to have different views presented where the truth is sought. Perhaps this man is using reverse psychology. It's a known fact that when man's views and beliefs are challenged, it causes him to look more intently at why he feels and believes the way he does.

Getting back to facts, they are fine as far as they go; but they are very cold. indifferent, and empty. Facts in no way impart life to man, the Lord said, " I am come that they might have life, and that they might have it more abundantly." (St. John 10:10)

A Reader

k

The Bible Says...

By Floyd Hale

Question: What is the difference between the Catholic Bible and the Protestant Bible?

Answer: My answer will be almost a repeat of March 16 "The Bible Says" ("Have any books been removed from the Bible?"), but maybe I can touch on some things not in that response.

In 504 the great Bible scholar Jerome translated the Christian Scriptures into Latin. His product was called the "Vulgate." Since the common ("vulgar") language of the people was no longer Greek this was necessary. He knew the Greek Old Testament used by the Church, called the Septuagint, contained fourteen (give or take one or two) more books than in the older Hebrew text (used mainly by the Jews in and around Jerusalem). Since the Church grew up on the Septuagint version, Jerome left these in--scattered throughout the O.T., as yet in the Catholic Bible; but he did mention in his preface that these were not in the older Hebrew text.

Martin Luther, in the 16th century, didn't like some of these books in question, for they supported a priestly hierarchy and favored some of the "doctrines" about which Luther contended with the Pope. Knowing that Jerome (10 centuries earlier) had said these were not in the Hebrew Bible, Luther left them (all fourteen, to be consistent) out of the main text of his German translation. But he did place them in an appendix, under the title "Apocrypha" ("of doubtful authenticity").

When the Protestants in England came out with their King James Version soon after (1611), they followed Luther's suit with the Apocrypha thing. In their next edition a few years later, they left it out altogether.

Whether these books should be in or out of the Bible is a big issue only for those who hold a narrow view of the authority of the Scriptures. Personally, I think it is good to know what's in those "Catholic" books. In one of them a passage can be misconstrued to suggest Purgatory. (Frankly, I like Purgatory better than flat out hellfire forever.)

The Bible Says...

By Floyd Hale

Question: Did Jesus ascend to heaven on the day of his Resurrection, or forty days later?

Answer: "The Bible says" he did both--and in the words of the same author (Lu. 24:1-53 and Acts 1:1-11). In his Gospel Luke puts it late on the night of that first Easter Sunday. Later on he expanded it into forty days, to use that event in the introduction to his "History of the Church" (Acts).

Some who refuse to see the contradiction here will say "some of the details left out of the Gospel account were merely added later in Acts, to give us the full scriptural report." But these accounts were not written for "us," and this is being dishonest about what the Bible says. It was either one day or forty. (Actually it was neither.)

All the resurrection and ascension accounts of Jesus in the Bible are the "stories" which developed out of the first apocalyptic *affirmation* that "God *raised* the Son of Man to His right hand of *Power*." This completes the Son of Man apocalyptic "cycle" (returning to from whence he came).

The Church developed its doctrines out in the Gentile world where the Jewish apocalyptic way of saying things got taken literally. This, plus Paul's belief in the "resurrection of the body"-- long before he was a Christian--corrupted the phrasing of this Christian Doctrine. And, all this happened while the four Gospels were yet being composed.

The term "raised" (by God) naturally includes ascension as well as resurrection. With Jesus "ascending" he had to be "resurrected," and vice versa. All this was to get the Son of Man (not the physical body of Jesus) to his ruling position--"in the heavens." In the apocalyptic mythology this "Son of Man" symbolized the Kingdom of God (or Kingdom of Heaven). Since Jesus completely identified himself with that Kingdom, this symbol was laid on him. This speaks the truth of his Lordship and the nature of discipleship.

This is all mixed up in the first three Gospels, and requires a good understanding of the apocalyptic expression form, instead of just taking it all literally.

The Bible Says...

By Floyd Hale

Question: Was Jesus optimistic (Mk. 9:40) or pessimistic (Mt 12:30)?

Answer: If both of these are the authentic words of Jesus, it reflects a serious flaw in his disposition.

Mark says Jesus said, "Those who are not against us are for us," while Matthew has Jesus saying something just the opposite, "He that is not with me is against me." Even though each of these appears in a different situational context, this does not mean they are both proper. To propose that these two sayings are compatible-- each supplementing the other--is to miss discovering the "Christian" attitude in these scriptures.

Matthew was published later than Mark, and in a very "churchy" situation. It was written to (and for) a "Synagogue" which was trying to become a "Church." You can imagine the conflict going on within that fellowship. Change in fundamental religious views is not easy or swift, and fence-straddlers always make up the silent majority in any group. Matthew sees these "neutrals" as aiding the opposition, which accounts for his "what Jesus would say about them." (This was a common practice with the Gospel writers, for Jesus had to be the authority on any current issue which arose.)

Mark's account being the older is strong evidence that it is what Jesus actually said. And, what is convincing for me, the optimism in it reflects more the attitude of Jesus. He took the long view, and was patient with opposition--it would prove to be a force for good in the end. This is why he told his disciples they should tolerate mistreatment--turn the other cheek, return good for bad. That takes optimism plus.

There is a sense in which the pessimistic view is true, but within a Christian context that's another thing. It tends to treat as enemies those who may be your friends. This is a form of paranoia--worse than pessimism.

Some one has said if you don't learn to love your enemies, you won't long be able to tolerate your friends.

109

The Bible Says...

By Floyd Hale

Question: Does it matter how a person is baptized (sprinkled, poured or totally immersed), and what is the purpose of baptism?

Answer: It doesn't matter how a person is baptized; for Baptism--even explained as symbolical--is unimportant anyway. It is one more practice of formal religion which places spiritual value on a ritual. I believe Jesus would turn over in his tomb if he knew it is required for membership in the great Church which bears his name. Jesus paid a high price for condemning the ritualistic, ceremony promoting, incense burning pomp of his native Faith.

I know there is a list of "scriptures" as long as your arm which supports, if not requires this, but the author of every one of those "scriptures" was a baptized Christian. I will pay attention to those who say "we are to follow Jesus in baptism," when they start following him in all the other things he told his followers to do.

Water Baptism was carried over into the Church because Christianity was a breakaway from the first "Baptist" movement. A lot of good can come out of a Baptist Revival, and Jesus is one of them; but those who make much out of Jesus' baptism should go on and declare that we should thus all be followers of John the Baptist--Jesus was not.

The "Baptists" remained and grew into a large group rivaling the early Christian movement for a while. One purpose in the writing of the last Gospel (John), was--in a most subtle way--to try to get the "Baptists" to follow their leader in claiming Jesus as the Christ. In keeping with this carefully worded appeal it is no accident that there is no explicit statement of John actually baptizing Jesus in that Fourth Gospel (check it out).

It very explicit in all four Gospels: "John baptized with water, *but (please note that 'but')* BUT Jesus will baptize you with the Holy Spirit" (Mt. 3:11, Mk. 1:8, Lu. 3:16, Jn. 1:33, and even Acts 1:5). Now we are talking Christian Baptism.

The Bible Says...

By Floyd Hale

Question: Did the boy David really slay the giant Goliath?

Answer: You may be surprised to know that one Elhanan also gets credit for this. "The Bible says" both did it (II Sam. 21:19 and I Sam. 17:51).

The History of Israel, Samuel-Kings, was compiled from a number of sources, long after the fact. Since the Hebrew "historians" continually edited their past to make it speak to their present--and future, King David's reputation is one of the things which got improved on in the process-- and it certainly needed it. In an older source there was a story about one Elhanan killing a Philistinian giant named Goliath (II Sam. 21:19). This was the source for a very embellished story years later about the boy David's killing this giant (I Sam. 17-19). Those putting Samuel-Kings together included both these accounts, although they didn't agree.

But long after the Samuel-Kings "History" was composed, someone rewrote the whole of Jewish history, I and II Chronicles. One of the Chronicler's objectives in doing so (ca. 300 B.C.) was to further clean up the character of "the great King David." He had by then become their patron Saint-- strictly because he established for them their original "empire."

The Chronicler saw the contradiction in these two stories, and eliminated it in his version by saying it was "the brother of" Goliath that Elhanan slew (I Chr. 20:5). Later on both of these "Histories" were included in the Jewish Bible--side by side.

Stay with me, this gets even better. Centuries later when the King James Version was being composed, they saw this contradiction in Samuel and inserted *"the brother of"* into Sam. 21:19 (as had the Chronicler in his "version" at 20:5), making it agree with the Chronicler. This left David the sole giant killer.

At least the KJV people were honest about this, by putting "the brother of" in italics (as above) showing it was their editing. The RSV leaves the contradiction as was. I think it's obvious who slew the big guy--and who got the credit.

The Bible Says...

By Floyd Hale

Question: What is the Baptism of the Holy Spirit?

Answer: John Wesley was right when he saw that the Baptism of the Holy Spirit was something more than a (first) work of grace--"being saved." But he was mistaken about it being a "second work of grace," relating it to one's salvation (by being "made holy").

You can not see in the gospels the "Baptism of the Holy Spirit" in the behavior of the disciples, for by the time Jesus got killed they were hardly catching onto its relevance. But they had caught his "spirit," and not long after his death they courageously took off--in *radical obedience to God's will--* out in life. They soon got into trouble, in and out of jail. Read the first five chapters of Acts and you will see the behavior of those first *faithful followers* of Jesus--without him there doing it for them.

As you read--slowly, see if you can identify the following: 1) The four times they *publicly protest* the "unlawful killing of their leader by the authorities." The open practice of 2) *freedom of religion* and 3) their *right of free speech--* even when court-ordered to remain silent. (They once held a prayer meeting in which they prayed, not for protection, but for *boldness* to keep on speaking out--and the Holy Spirit zapped 'em again.)

The "God in charge revolution" was off and running. It soon simmered down--became completely dormant--under a lot of ecclesiastical regulations, but another *Protest* movement about fifteen centuries later got it back on track (halfway). It was the nations influenced by that Reformation which peopled America- right at the time of its borning.

By the way, did you notice in your reading of Acts who are "given the Holy Spirit"? It is they who *"obey God"* (5:32)? Not before, but *in* their obedience. The disciples were *obeying* at much risk just by remaining in Jerusalem when they were "baptized" (actually "filled" the first time).

All four gospels report this as the *one* "Christian baptism."

The Bible Says...

By Floyd Hale

Question: Can a person be righteous without being religious?

Answer: Tradition says "No." What did Jesus say about this?

In the only story he told about Judgment Day, he said it would be like "separating sheep from goats." It is obvious the sheep--on the right (I wish he had said "left")--had not been religious, for they were surprised they were considered "righteous." What had they done? They had done the simple humanistic thing of caring about and for their needy neighbors.

The goats--on the left (I wish Jesus had said "right")--were just as surprised, for they were sure their religiosity would get them through the pearly gates. Their rabbis had told them many times they could not work their way to heaven--"it's not what you do, but what you believe that saves you." The Judge told them to go straight to hell (Mt. 25:41). Jesus sure had a way of turning a phrase.

What made those goats "cursed"? It wasn't what they did; it was what they didn't do--while being very religious. They didn't care about and for their neighbors in need. Their rabbis had no doubt also told them Humanism was of the devil. It looks to me as though Jesus put a special blessing on secular humanitarianism.

Another story Jesus told, called The Good Samaritan, helps answer your question. There was no way anyone hearing Jesus tell this story would consider a half-breed Samaritan a righteous person. (With some of us the fact that he carried alcoholic beverage in his saddlebag would make him an evil person.)

Yet this traveling salesman met the "one most important requirement of religion" by keeping the "second one"--caring about and for another person in need. Jesus credits this to his humane "compassion" (Lu. 10:33), not to his religious beliefs.

Where would you look for Jesus today? I grew up being told you found Jesus in Church. He didn't even say he would be found out with the needy and oppressed--he said *he would be them.*

113

The Bible Says...

By Floyd Hale

Question: Could Daniel really interpret dreams and foretell the future?

Answer: Daniel could not only interpret King Nebuchadnezzar's dream, he could tell him what he dreamed. The traditional view of the Bible causes some to believe this was true of the young hero of the Apocalypse we call the book of Daniel.

The apocalyptic was a way-out kind of *expression form* which gave its author the freedom to say just about anything he wanted to--any way he wanted to--to get his very important message across to his oppressed audience. The "message" in Daniel was to the Jews in Jerusalem to "remain faithful to the Law" (their Scripture) during the Antiochan Persecution (171-164 B.C.)--which was the Syrian King's violent effort to wipe out the Jewish religion.

An Apocalypse promised the "end" (Judgment) was "soon" coming on the oppressor, so hang in there. All kinds of details about the "end-time" of tribulation, during which the author was actually writing, is "revealed" to him--in dreams and visions. The author of Daniel wrote as though he lived over four centuries earlier (during Babylonian Captivity), "foretelling" what was going to happen right down to the "end-time," during which his book was to be "unsealed"--made public. He was not very accurate on his "ancient" history, but he had a good knowledge of the few years just prior to the "end" (during which time he was actually writing).

One does not have to read far into Daniel to see that history is not the subject matter. It is important to know all about this book, for two reasons: First, its "prophecy" is the popular and erroneous kind-- foretelling the future. Second, getting this Old Testament book straight is a big help to understanding the book of Revelation in the New Testament; for John used it and several other Apocalypses (the woods were full of 'em at the time) as sources for getting his message of hope to his persecuted brethren at the beginning of the Roman Persecution, ca. A.D. 90.

The Bible Says...

By Floyd Hale

Question: How did Judas take his life after betraying Jesus?

Answer: The scripture record leaves a quite a bit of mystery around Judas and his betrayal of Jesus. One illustration of this is the confusion about how he took his life. The two different accounts of it do not agree.

In Matthew Judas repents of his dastardly deed, takes the money he was paid for it back to the high priests, and "hangs himself." The priests take the money and buy a burial ground. None of the other Gospels mention this (beyond the original betrayal deal). In the opening chapter of Acts, where Judas' replacement in "the twelve" is elected, he is reported as buying the burial ground himself, and "falling headlong (evidently over a cliff) bursting open with his bowels gushing out."

There is no need of trying to harmonize these two accounts with a lot of double talk, such as the rope broke and Judas fell on jagged rocks. Those who would try to explain away the contradiction just refuse to see what the Bible literally says. Interesting that these same people claim the Bible is literally true.

I imagine there were other stories about Judas' death which circulated-- some wilder than these two, relating how mean he was, and how bloody was his end. You can sense the feelings of the authors in these two.

I have no explanation for this contradiction--I don't need any. I've learned to take the Bible like it is, and then try to find out what is important in it. Its Truth is not in its print. It goes far beyond that. And each person who wants to know It, must find It for him or herself.

Instead of dictating to others what "the Bible says," and quoting a long list of favorite verses (all out of context) to prove "God said it," those who are educated in this field should help others learn how the Bible is to be used intelligently. This is a rich and rewarding exercise in faith, but in the process a person may have his or her doctrinal playhouse torn down.

(Adults have no business living in playhouses anyway.)

The Bible Says...

By Floyd Hale

Question: Were Jesus and John the Baptist related?

Answer: In Luke's birth story, John's mother Elizabeth is mentioned as Mary's "cousin" (KJV). The RSV translates this "kinswoman." This would have made John and Jesus at least members of the same larger "family."

In the Fourth Gospel John Baptist, upon seeing Jesus come to him for baptism, said he had no prior knowledge of who Jesus was. It is hard to think John and Jesus grew up relatives but strangers.

John's Gospel is not a documentary on the life of Jesus--far from it. To learn anything about the real Jesus this Gospel should not be used. I don't have space here to explain this, just to say John has all the legitimate literary freedom to say anything he wants to in relating "Christ" (not Jesus) to the spiritual life of the Greek Christians. He probably has the Baptizer saying he doesn't know Jesus personally, to add to the "divine inspiration" of his exclamation (upon seeing Jesus coming to him for baptism): "Behold the Lamb of God, who takes away the sins of the world!"

As to Jesus and John being relatives, this is in Luke's Nativity Story. It ought to be common knowledge by now that this is a "Story," not the reporting of facts--about Jesus or John. If you compare the two stories, that of John's birth and that of Isaac's in the Old Testament, you can see that Luke relied heavily on that story to script the birth of John. Luke wants Jesus' "forerunner" to have at least a half-miraculous birth also.

In the lengthy account of Zechariah and Elizabeth's birthing John, there are many marks of myth, making it obvious to the reader that more "Hebrew* storytelling" is going on here. But having been taught as children that all the O. T. stories are "true," this one gets accepted the same way. I was one of those children, and it made it very hard for me to gain a realistic view of the Bible when I was preparing for the ministry. The Bible is heavy theology--all of it. We need to know that none of it was written for a "Children's Storybook."

116

The Bible Says...

By Floyd Hale

Question: Did Jesus really send a bunch of evil spirits into a herd of hogs?

Answer: This story is in Mark 5. (Matthew and Luke relied on Mark as their source for this story, so they can not be quoted as verifying the authenticity of this event.) The possessed man lives in a cemetery (how?). He can break chains to pieces by which he was bound (how?). Without an introduction to Jesus this demoniac recognizes him as the "Son of the Most High God"--and worships him,

Jesus commands the unclean spirit to come out of him (not knowing there were several in him?). Jesus asks his name, and is told it is "Legion." This tells Jesus there are about 2,000 of them. It just so happens that there are enough swine grazing nearby for each demon to possess his own pig; so Jesus sends them into the swine, and they all run into a lake and drown.

The contents of this piece of fiction can be explained from the culture of that time and place. If this story were read in any other book, it would readily be recognized for what it is, a myth. But it's being in the Bible, and especially about something Jesus is reported to have done, the Literalists declare it to be true. They would say, "If Jesus did not do this, how can we believe he did any of the other miracles? And if he did not perform miracles he was not the Son of God-- and we are all going to hell." This kind of crazy reasoning is the Fundamentalists keep the uninformed masses from understanding the Bible.

There is nothing wrong with this story being fiction. Demon possession is not only a questionable phenomenon, but for one man to be inhabited by 2,000 of them? Evil spirits talking to Jesus-- and him talking back? They knew more about him than he did them? And there probably were not that many hogs in the whole Middle East, for pork was not a common food of the other Semites of the area (this included the Arabs).

This "action parable," similar to the feeding of the five thousand, was a legitimate way at that time for Mark to claim Jesus was God's man. And I agree with Mark.

117

LETTERS TO THE EDITOR

To the Editor:

In response to Mr. Hale's column of May 8; I realize I'm not as well educated as Mr, Hale, but I am reminded of Romans 1:22 that says, "Professing themselves to be wise, they become as fools."

Be that as it may, I do feel sorry for him since I know that eventually he will answer for his false teaching and the people he has misled.

Mr. Hale wonders how the possessed man can live in the cemetery. My Bible says he also lived in the mountains. It doesn't say he never left the cemetery. He wonders how he breaks the chains. Doesn't he think if demons have control of his body they would use their own strength? Why does Mr. Hale insist on applying human limits to supernatural events? Doesn't he think demons would recognize Jesus without being introduced? After all, Jesus was there when they were kicked out of Heaven. Who says Jesus didn't know how many there were? Jesus asked his name, not how many. Maybe that was for the benefit of those that were with him. And what of faith? What of I Cor. 2:5 which says "that your faith should not be in the wisdom of men, but in the power of God." Is your faith in the wisdom of men or that Jesus is who he says he is? How much faith can a person have with all that doubt and unbelief?

                                A Reader

Editors note: I don't remember where it is in the Bible, but the person asks to be helped for his unbelief. Bible writers put things in the Bible that were messages for those people under their conditions and cannot always be applied to all situations for all time.

Thanks for writing, It's good to know people are studying and thinking. D.B.

I

The Bible Says...

By Floyd Hale

Question: What does it mean to be a Christian?

Answer: The first followers of Jesus lived Jesus' way--the way he lived. Because of this they were known for a while as people of "The Way." Then up at Antioch, which was out in the Greek world, they were "for the first time *called* Christians" (Acts 11:26). This was not by their own profession; the word "called" in this passage shows it was a name laid on them in derision--"Christ imitators." Like nicknames--especially those made in ridicule--the title stuck. While trying to turn the world right side up, they were accused of turning it upside down (Acts 17:6).

By the time the Apostle Paul wrote and the last Gospel (John) was composed, a "fundamental" Christian Faith was taking shape. Its teachings, shaped by the combination of the Jewish Apocalyptic and Greek Gnostic religious precepts, were "theological interpretations of the Christ." Much of this had little to do with the man Jesus--who he actually was and what he really did. Even the story of Jesus--which is found only in the first three Gospels--was colored by these doctrines.

Christianity was such a good religion, having had a positive effect on the growing Western culture, makes it seem unnecessary that we rediscover (for the first time?) the real Jesus. But that need is real; and if the contribution he made to the "salvation of the world" is to be understood and realized--and continued--the present "quest of the historical Jesus" must be taken seriously.

It was the *impression* Jesus made on his first followers which got this great institution we call the Church started. Regardless of all the doctrines *about* him which developed, it is what inspired those first disciples which is to be identified and then recaptured by modern would be "followers" of Jesus.

Although this may change some of our traditional beliefs, it must be done--"in the name of the Kingdom" Jesus died promoting.

118

The Bible Says...

By Floyd Hale

Question: Did God actually turn the Devil loose on Job?

Answer: The Bible says He did--and that answers this question for the Biblicists. But what kind of God would do such a thing? To say that God could do this if He so chose, or did it for Job's good--or to teach us all a lesson--is no proof that God did it. That kind of defense of Scripture misses what the author of this "story" is saying.

God, Satan, Job and his three "friends" are all characters in this poetic drama. It plays out the question (and its answer) in staged dialogue, "Why do bad things happen to good people?" It is as modern as Broadway--in fact it played on Broadway a few years ago as "JB."

Job was written to refute the "law of retribution" which was popularly believed at the time (and yet pesters the minds of many people). In Satan's discussion with God about Job's good fortune, he says Job would forsake his righteous ways if he suffered. So God let Satan take away everything Job had--except his life (and his wife, who becomes a part of his misery). Fortune gone, his children all die, and his body is covered with sores, and his three friends try to get him to confess his sin, but Job does not break. He admits his faults but asserts his innocence. Job has the audacity to say God is unjust if he is being punished.

Although the problem of suffering is not solved in this book, Job keeps his faith and trust in God. This is the point the author is making. It is a good one, but the "poetic happy ending"-- meant to convince the reader that the law of retribution doesn't work-- actually supports the opposite when taken literally. God not only restored Job's health and his family, but "twice as much wealth as he had before"-- twenty two thousand sheep, camels, oxen and she-asses. (These figures--to make an emphasis--alone should tell you this is fiction.) And best of all, he lived to a ripe old age.

Treating this story as something which actually happened, you not only miss its important truth, but accept a very mistaken image of God.

119

The Bible Says...

By Floyd Hale

Question: What Old Testament prophet said he would go naked and wail like an ostrich?

Answer: One of the greatest poets in all Israel--or of all time, as for that matter--Micah of Moresheth. (Everyone knows where Moresheth is.)

Had Micah felt challenged by the "streaking" his distinguished colleague had just pulled off in Jerusalem (Is. 20:3)? Was he just spicing up his poetry so it would sell (1:8)? Did he carry through on his promise?

If you read only the KJV you wouldn't know that this is poetry. And, reading only the KJV you wouldn't know that the bird he was going to imitate was an ostrich either. The KJV translators probably didn't know that an ostrich let out a mournful wail, so they translated it "owl." This is typical of the inconsistency of the KJV, for they translated this same word "ostrich" in another place. But back to Micah's vulgarity. . .

The question of whether he did or not is mute when this is seen as a line in a poem. Micah was not above such a thing, if it made a point for God, but he was merely picturing his disgust and contempt for the injustices his government allowed if not inflicted directly. The poor were being run en masse through the gristmills of the rich; the common people were slaves in God's country rather than citizens.

You owe it to Micah to read his small book of poems--only seven or eight pages. His contribution to the Judeo-Christian traditions eventually helped shape the free America you enjoy. His message is as modern as civil rights--in fact that was his message.

His writing style is super. You'll discover the source of the line, "Tell it not in Gath," and you will see that it was he who summarized all "preaching" in these words: "O man, what does the Lord require of you but to work for justice, be compassionate, and walk in humility with your God."

The "rending (removing) one's garments" in public was the show of complete humility, sometimes disgust, in Old Tsetament times.

120

The Bible Says...

Question: Did a prophet ever "streak" in Israel?

Answer: Yes, and he did it the most embarrassing way, by walking. And to add pain to humility he did it barefooted--for three long years. Why?

The Assyrian Empire was pushing westward toward Egypt in its move to rule the whole world. Judah, the "southern kingdom," lay in between. The king wanted to do something about it--as all political leaders are bent (or pushed) in a crisis. Isaiah believed that to join with Egypt--as the majority party wanted--in resistance would be suicide.

Judah was a small barren mountainous lot, and not of real value to a potential invader. He figured the Assyrians would bypass them on their way to Egypt. He tried to convince the king that if he would not get into a "foreign entangling alliance," and would take care of God's business in his own country, God would see to their national security. Isaiah knew this would involve paying tribute but he was for "peace at any price."

If Assyria had to "teach Judah a lesson" in international politics it would mean bondage. To drum up support for his views he dressed as a "slave"--which was no dress at all--and "campaigned" through the whole area in and around Jerusalem for three years, telling the people that's the way they would become--slaves to a foreign power.

Isaiah's self inflicted humiliation was the price he would willingly pay for "God's cause." The high respect in which he was held by all, including those of the king's court, added to the scandal of his demonstration.

When Isaiah found out the king had already (secretly) made a pact with Assyria, he was so disgusted he went into "retirement" for several years.

When Babylon inherited Judah from the Assyrians they placed a stooge king, Manasseh, in charge, whose first official action was to have the great prophet put to death. Isaiah's disciples (the Prophetic Party) went underground and produced the first written document to reach the status of "semi-scripture," the book of Deuteronomy.

The Bible Says...

By Floyd Hale

Question: What is this new Quest of the Historical Jesus movement among the Bible scholars today all about?

Answer: It is "the thing" right now in New Testament studies, although it's not new. With the introduction of the critical method applied to Bible study about two centuries ago, who Jesus was and what he said came up for open investigation. This can only be for the good.

The New Testament writings are the creation of the Church (which saved those that served its purpose). By the time the Gospels were composed Pauline (Gentile) Christianity was already going strong. Although many sayings of Jesus had been handed down, some had been shaped into doctrinal statements by his followers; this was only natural. The Gospels were shaped to be used for evangelism.

Early Christianity was a Spirit movement. Those who had the "Spirit of Jesus" felt they could speak for him-- making his "word" relevant. The Fourth Gospel goes even beyond this; the author gives his own interpretation of the Christ as though Jesus is explaining himself.

But where's the real Jesus who inspired all this? The Church should not only welcome but lead in this "quest" of him.

Once scholars are free to make educated guesses you can expect some wild speculation. Right now we are going through this "new" and confusing process, but this will eventually correct itself. Truth will stand the test of open investigation.

I can already see some of the resulting new insights coming together in a more accurate picture of Jesus than we now have.

Under critical scrutiny the Gospels reveal one thing which I think is indisputable. The Church, mainly through the Apostle Paul's preaching out in the gnostic-thinking world, presented Jesus as a "personal" Savior, when he (Jesus) was actually one who taught--and practiced-- a radical doing of the "will (rule) of God" in life. *Isn't this exactly what the world needs?*

The Bible Says...

By Floyd Hale

Question: What does the Bible say about paying taxes? Should we send money to a government that is corrupt and does evil things?

Answer: Your questions tend to assume the Bible is an answer book, spelling out the right solutions to all of life's problems. Jesus seemed to think it was a hypocrite who asked him about paying taxes (Mk. 12:15). Instead of a pat answer, which you seem to think your question has, Jesus suggested the asker figure this out for himself: "Render to Caesar the things that are his, and to God the things that are God's."

It would be stretching any scripture too far to say it is the task of government (and I assume you mean the U.S.) to do only holy things with its revenue, but taxes go to the many services rendered for and to the people--which can only be done by a government. In our country taxes are not "tribute" paid to a foreign colonizer (as they were in Jesus' day). It was "paying tribute" without having a vote which helped inspire our independence

I believe our government spends a lot of our tax money getting God's business done-- not only in our country, but around the world. The person who feels the government is evil, to the extent of not deserving of his/her financial support, has the right of conscience (I suppose) of not paying their taxes. But if you take this route, you should have a very good lawyer or be willing to take the consequences--or both.

The Apostle Paul advised the Christians to pay their taxes. He said the government was God-appointed, and was a terror only to wrong-doers (Rom. 13:1-7). When his government turned on him and had his head removed, I wonder if he thought about having said this.

He wasn't writing Scripture anyway. And when this was finally included in the Bible, it was not to become a "law." The Jews made this bad mistake when they canonized their "Teachings of Moses" (Torah). They were then politicized into a national religion and forced on all citizens as the "Law."

The Bible Says...

By Floyd Hale

Question: If the Bible is mostly myth, what part of it can we believe?

Answer: The first part of your question is hypothetical, making the last part unanswerable in a correct way. "Myth" can not be applied to the Bible in some general way ("mostly myth"), dividing the Scriptures into "true" and "untrue" categories. As I have pointed out occasionally in this column, there are myths in the Bible. This was an ancient--and excellent--teaching tool. A Myth is literally untrue, but often teaching something very true.

The first creation story is an example (Gen. 1:1-2:4a). This story, being a Creation Myth, is not literally true. For example God did not create "days and nights" on the first day and then create the sun three days later "to separate the day from the night." This story was not written to explain that the world was created in six days, but to teach that life is sacred ("good"), and is to be treated that way. The author used the seven days cycle to put the emphasis on Sabbath ("holy"), the central theme of the priestly religion of Judaism. To say this story is a Myth does in no way deny God being the Creator.

The Fundamentalists who want a "day" in this story treated "as a thousand years" refuse to see what the story says, for God didn't create the sun to divide historic periods into "light and darkness." Let the story stand as a myth, and then its truth may be learned. Take a myth literally and you can only get a false teaching out of it.

Classic, I think, in understanding some of the Bible writers use of myth, is the story in II Samuel 12:1-4 where Nathan confronts King David about his affair with Bethsheba. Nathan makes up this story about "the one ewe lamb." It was literally untrue, but Nathan made it so believable that it tricked David into passing judgment on himself (read on down through verse 10).

To identify myth in the Bible one must forget the traditional literalism which has been forced on the Bible, and understand it the way it was originally written.

The word "myth" has more than one meaning. I think your question suggests the *myth* that I believe the Bible is "mostly myth."

The Bible Says...

By Floyd Hale

Question: Did Matthew and Luke really just copy what Mark wrote about Jesus and leave out or add what they wanted?

Answer: Students of the Bible know that Matthew and Luke used Mark's Gospel as their primary source in writing their own. That they "just" did this and added what they "wanted" suggests frivolity. Examining what they left out, added, and changed helps one better understand the Gospels.

A critical comparison of these three Gospels reveals that each author had his own purpose in mind as he told "The Story of Jesus." It sure was not to "fill in" what the others "left out," to provide a "full account," for this doesn't explain the contradictions. I have often wondered how each of these Evangelists would have written if he had known his manuscript was going to be included with the others in the Scriptures--and then centuries later be treated as literally true.

In this column I have often pointed out various differences between these Gospel accounts. This is not to "find fault" with the Scriptures, but to demonstrate that a more realistic approach needs to be taken to the study of Jesus and his teachings--for the sake of Jesus and his teachings. Just saying there is this need gets brushed aside by the traditional view of Jesus which disregards much of what "the Bible says" about him.

The first Gospel writer's saying Jesus said, "Why call me good? There is no one good but God" (Mk. 10:17,18), and another Gospel writer later changing this to "Why do you ask me about what is good?" (Mt. 19:16,17), makes me want to know why, and know more about Jesus' real view of himself. When one Gospel says Jesus went "immediately" after his baptism into the wilderness, staying there for forty days (Mk.1:12,13), and another says he was up at a wedding in Galilee "three days later" (Jn. 1:35-2:2), I have a right to know a little bit about how these men wrote their Gospels.

This is not an exercise in wild speculation on the part of "atheistic and agnostic university professors." It is the only way we can get back to the real Jesus about whom these Gospels were written.

The Bible Says...

By Floyd Hale

Question: Is Jesus of Nazareth the Christ that is foretold in the Old Testament?

Answer: You seem to take it for granted that Christ is foretold in the Old Testament. I would have to look closely at each of the particular passages you might point out as "foretelling Christ."

Ever since the Babylonian Captivity there was a strong Zionist desire that the great and glorious Davidic Kingdom would be restored. Anyone leading to the accomplishment of that would be "another (son of) David." This was strictly nationalistic. The God of their religion was used as the one who had "promised" this--and would make it happen

When Jesus came to be looked upon as the Messiah (Christ) this title, "Son of David," was laid on him. To support this the two birth stories have him born in Bethlehem--the city of David. But the "prophecy" quoted (Mt. 2:1-6) as foretelling this, was actually Micah's poetical review of David's rise to power (Micah 5:2), not about Jesus. What ought to make it clear that Jesus was not the Son of David Messiah is that he never "sat on the throne of his father David."

"Messiah" (with a small "m") is the Hebrew word translated "an anointed one." It signified *anyone* who was recognized as working for God's cause. Since Jesus did a magnificent job of this, you can see how the small "m" soon became capitalized when applied to him. But all the Messianic hopes (and there were others beside the "Son of David" one) never applied to Jesus.

It was what Jesus did and said--and died for--which inspired his followers to say of him he was "anointed of God." Our task is to try to see in him what his disciples saw--per chance we too might be *inspired to follow him.*

This call of discipleship has been *silenced* by the Biblicists--taking all kinds of passages from the Old Testament (out of their context) and faith statements in the New Testament, and forming fundamental creeds about "Jesus Christ," to be *believed in order to be saved.*

Have you never wondered why Jesus didn't quote any of these "prophecies" about himself?

126

The Bible Says...

By Floyd Hale

Question: Is there a Church organization mentioned in the New Testament?

Answer: The disciples in Jerusalem never considered themselves starting a new religion. Jesus never had anything like our traditional church in mind. I'm sure he would have seen his cause--the kingdom of God--being limited by it.

To quote from the New Testament about the church, one should remember *the church wrote the Gospels--* long after the fact. The author of the Gospel of Matthew (ca. 80) has Jesus founding the church--on Peter (Mark was unaware of this). Luke, writing after Matthew (ca. 90), saw the birthday of the church as the first Pentecost after Jesus' death. The author of Ephesians (a bishop of ca. 95) affirmed that Jesus "died for the church."

Again let me remind you, these are all efforts to read the church back into "the beginning." This was not to foster a hoax; it was just similar to the way the first Christians read Jesus back into the Old Testament.

The Christian Church took shape out in the Gentile world, where the situation forced it to exist and grow only as an institution. Because many "different churches" evolved, the Emperor Constantine (in 325), for political reasons, "forced" them to become catholic ("one"). Nicea, the place to which the emperor called that "first world Christian conference," gave its name to the creed the bishops agreed on there-- after lengthy and hot debate (with the few dissenters finally being banished).

All kinds of quoting from the New Testament can "prove" what the church is, but the traditional church (including those who think they are "New Testament") was actually formed on the "doctrines about Jesus" by the Apostle Paul, and not on Jesus and his teachings. There's a world of difference. So much so that Jesus would not recognize our creeds about him.

The church is the best *organization* in the world, I believe. I would not want to see its demise. I'd just like to see it be rid of its silly false doctrines, and recognize fully--and only--the one whose Name it bears.

The Bible Says...

By Floyd Hale

Question: Why does Chronicles disagree with Samuel-Kings, when they both are histories of the same period?

Answer: II Sam. (8:4) reports David's taking 1,700 horsemen from King Hadadezer, and I Chronicles (18:4) says it was only 7,000. II Sam. (24:9) says in the census Joab took there were 800,000 valiant men in Israel and 5,000 in Judah. I Chr. (21:5) ups this to 1,100,000 in Israel and 470,000 in Judah.

I have picked out just a few of the differences in the numbers, for this is the easiest way of seeing the obvious contradictions. Most Old Testament writers (and those who later revised their reports) embellished their accounts by using larger numbers--all completely unrealistic.

It takes a closer comparison of Chronicles with Samuel-Kings to see the editing the Chronicler did to the older account, Samuel-Kings. When examined, a pattern becomes clear revealing why the latter "improved on" the former. By the time the last edition of Samuel-Kings came out, about five centuries after David's reign, his character had been improved on a lot. This was mainly because he had given them their first kingdom--practically an empire at the time. Because of this Judaism had elevated him to the status of patron saint. God even promised(?) his dynasty would last forever (something written down after Israel was no more.)

When the history of Israel was revised by the Chronicler about three centuries later, that great kingdom of David was just memory, and they were wanting another ("son of") David to restore it. This called for cleaning up the character of David even further. That's why he in Chronicles has become all saint--not even a wart. The best illustration of this, to the Chronicler Bethsheba never existed.`

This gives you a pretty good idea of how to take the stories about Abraham, Jacob, Joseph, Moses, and the Exodus. These went through almost a thousand years of retelling before reaching their present form. Each time revised to say something about the current situation--and the future.

The Bible Says...

By Floyd Hale

Question: What did Paul mean when he wrote, "Imitate me, just as I also imitate Christ"?

Answer: I don't want to bore you with word meanings, but the RSV says "imitate," which has a slightly different meaning than "follow" (in the KJV). This is probably because "follow me" in Jesus' invitation to discipleship is a bit different than Paul's "imitate me."

Paul was not one of the original "followers" of Jesus--living with him--"his way." Paul went out to establish a "Christian Religion," which was something different, and for this he was ostracized by the Jerusalem disciples (the actual "imitators of Jesus").

What did Paul mean when he asked the Corinthians to imitate him? The first step in understanding any biblical passage is to look at it in its context. This appeal by Paul comes right in the middle of his giving them advice on a number of things. He tells them to try and not offend anyone--for their sake. *Do it like I do--the way Jesus did* (I Cor. 11:1).

Then Paul goes on to advise those Gentile converts to keep some Jewish traditions he was passing on, dealing primarily with gender in the fellowship. He begins by asserting firmly that just as "Christ" (not Jesus) is head of the Church, the husband is head of the woman.

Men, he says, should leave their hats off when they pray or preach, but women who pray or preach should don their bonnets--otherwise they might as well have their heads shaved. Then he says man--with his bared head--is the image and glory of God. A woman is the glory of her husband, for women were made for men, not men for women.

I'm trying to understand just how Paul is "imitating" Jesus with this kind of thinking, when Jesus seemed to delight in shooting down silly "sacred religious traditions" like these.

Too bad Paul could not have spent some time with Jesus. If he had Christianity would have been a whole different religion. But if Paul had been with Jesus--and really imitated him--he would not have gone out and started a Gentile Church.

But now I am raising more questions than I am answering.

The Bible Says...

By Floyd Hale

Question: Why is Higher Criticism called "hostile" by some Bible traditionalists?

Answer: Higher Criticism is the modern application of literary science to the Bible writings. Its purpose is to learn and share the truth *about* the Scriptures--when, where, why, to whom, by whom, and in what literary form each of them was originally composed. It goes as far as it can into determining what the original text was--and which of the older remaining copies is to be chosen for use as "scripture."

The term "criticism" in this title can be misunderstood. The "critics" of this approach to the Bible give it a negative meaning (as I just used the term). It is not aimed at "finding out what's wrong" with the Scriptures. The scholars in this field do not force a "religious" evaluation on their findings--they would not be true critics if they did.

If they were "against religion" as they worked, they would have a biased approach--and it would show up in their conclusions. The same applies to those who defend a religious belief even though it is proven baseless.

I think you can understand why this has been a slow science to be accepted--yet rejected by many. A religious tradition like "God wrote the Bible" doesn't give way quickly-- nor easily

It is a foolish thing to think that the Bible needs a biased defense. It is its own best defense when all the facts *about it* are known. The literary scientists in this field are careful to note any unsureness they might have about a particular text. They sometimes make "educated guesses," and when they do they say so. Researching anything ancient-- especially literature--very seldom reveals clear evidence. But when there is a whole lot of evidence pointing in a certain direction, you have to go with it.

Scientific (unbiased and scholarly) Criticism is a necessary part of a civilized culture. We would not dare reject it in all the other areas of the humanities. It shows a lack of open-mindedness to condemn a Bible scholar by simply calling him or her a "Bible critic."

The Bible Says...

By Floyd Hale

Question: To me there are people who have accepted Jesus as Savior and have been baptized! Where will they go?

Answer: From your letter I take it you mean after they die?

They go nowhere. Their "lives"--what they lived--will go on in life. A person's "life" and not his/her "ego self" is what's immortal.

It is the kingdom of God that goes on. We finite mortals have the rare and holy privilege of contributing our "lives" to that glorious enterprise. If we do this we won't have to worry about--even believe in--an afterlife. (Believing in heaven doesn't make it so anyway.)

Bringing the hereafter into this does one of two things. As a figure of speech heaven can help prick the mind open to go on quest of the meaning of "evelasting life;" or it can cause the week-minded to fantasize another life "up there"--and miss the purpose of the one down here.

Religion, which was meant to help people discover the will of the Creator and do it, also tempts good people to get their eyes on a "next world." But I have noticed those who yield to this temptation usually keep one eye firmly fixed on this one, causing them to become somewhat cockeyed. This world is not a prison from which to escape. It is where the Creator is doing His creating (kingdom work) for the good of all.

I believe Jesus lived his life the most meaningful way possible, by giving himself unreservedly to the doing of his heavenly Father's will--in life--for the good of others. Because this took his whole life--mind, body and soul--he became the most immortal person who ever lived. History, I believe, attests to this; and the book of Revelation, when understood, explains this very clearly (e.g. 19:11-15, 20:4).

Instead of asking people to believe in him as Savior and be baptized, Jesus called them to help him enlarge God's "kingdom (rule)" over the world. But he warned those who went about it right, they'd run into opposition--mainly from religious folk (Mt. 10:17).

131

The Bible Says...

By Floyd Hale

Question: Why did Abraham lie about his wife being his sister?

Answer: So the story goes, in his foreign travels Abraham was afraid some man might kill him to get his wife Sarah. So he convinced her that posing as his "sister" would be the best thing for her--because it would keep her dear husband alive.

Sure enough, on one of their trips to Egypt her beauty (at age 65?) won her into the heart--and house-- of the Pharaoh (Gen. 12:10-20). This seemed not to bother either Abraham or Sarah, but it did God, for he sent plagues on the estate of Pharaoh. It is rather odd that God was not displeased with Abraham's conniving, but with Pharaoh's philandering. It is odd also how the plagues revealed to Pharaoh that Sarah was Abraham's wife. Even odder yet is the pagan Pharaoh's having a better conscience than God's man Abe.

Those who have researched the literature of the Old Testament believe this tale was first told on Isaac and Rebekah (Gen. 26) and then later (during oral transmission) moved back onto the Father of all Faith. There is even another version of this brother-sister act in Gen. 20, but there Sarah turns out to be only half-sister. (I guess in this case Abraham told only a "half truth."

Why did the authors of Genesis mix fiction in with history? There are lengthy answers to this which I can not go into here, but the main one was to continually support current claims by scripting past promises. You will notice running throughout these accounts that God gave the land of Canaan to Abraham and his descendants--long before the Exodus. Abe's other son Ishmael (by Sarah's despised maid Hagar) accounts for the Arab nation--"a wild ass bunch whose hand shall be against every man" (16:12). The two nations which gave the Israelites the most trouble were Moab and Ammon, founded by Lot's two sons by incest (Gen. 19:37-38).

All of this was good propaganda for the Jews, but it certainly is not the Word of God for us.

When the Christians got their "New" Bible together they should have left their "Old" one out.

The Bible Says...

By Floyd Hale

Question: Without the Bible, what would be our standard of morality?

Answer: The Bible, directly and indirectly through the dominance of the Christian Faith in Western civilization, has been the greatest and positive influence on morality in America, thank God. But our situation in this great land is unique. Our nation was founded at the time the new "Protestant Bible-centered revival" was at its peak. This continent was virgin territory (if we can forget the Indians--and we did) in which there were no other rival religions--not even a traditional Christianity. In fact the coming of the original immigrants was to get away from "traditional Christianity"--for which we praise them.

I think all this--and more--causes your question to infer that without the Bible there would be "no" moral standard. All cultures have their moral standards, and they are not all bad, but that's a whole other issue.

It is because I am very concerned about the future of the "Bible standard" in our land--and the world-- that I write in this column. Conservative Christianity tends to believe the Bible should be "God's law of the land," and if the Christian Coalition had there way it would be. I am very much for the Christian ethic influencing the lawmakers of the U. S.--and our culture in general--but "religious laws" are for the religious only (if they want to live that way).

We should learn from the "Bible" that when the Jews canonized their Torah ("Teachings of Moses") into Scripture,' treated it as "God's revealed Word," and then went on to make it their "Law," their Bible literalism squelched the *prophetic faith*--which resulted in the rejection and killing of Jesus of Nazareth.

The Bible is to have its influence, not by being pushed as God's revealed moral "law" for everyone, but through a "Christian witness" *which uses its Bible properly.*

There is some bad "morality" in the Bible which should stay in there-- not get out--some of it even credited to God.

The Bible Says...

By Floyd Hale

Question: How are the books Nahum and Lamentations alike yet very different?

Answer: The book of Nahum *celebrates* the fall and destruction of Nineveth. The book of Lamentations *laments* the fall and destruction of Jerusalem which followed in just a few short years.

Nahum was a very gifted writer and sang with exuberance and glee his funeral dirge over the smitten tyrant Nineveth. Some scholars believe this small volume of poetry was composed as a pageant and performed in the temple courtyard. Assyria (often called by its capital's name,"Nineveth") had been a world dominating demon. She was known for wiping out the ethnic identity of her conquered foes. She annihilated the northern ten tribes of Israel, and probably would have done the same to Judah if the Babylonians had not interrupted her world parade.

Then just one generation later the Babylonians took Judah captive and carried away her talented and elite to help build a world culture in Babylon. When a foolish rebellion broke out by the few left back in Jerusalem, they returned to completely destroy the city. Someone who must have witnessed that terrible drama composed Lamentations.

The style of language in this heart-rending poetry suggests very strongly that the author was a Levite who served in the temple. To included this document in the Sacred Writings its authorship was credited to Jeremiah--who also lived through those awful days.

The little book of Nahum was included in the twelve "Minor Prophets" because the people loved it--in it their God of wrath had finally vented His full vengeance on their old enemy Nineveth.

Nahum and Lamentations. . . similar books, yet very different, illustrate how many of the books were included in the Jewish Bible.

If you have a question about the Bible, why not send it in to this newspaper. You don't need to sign your name to it if you'd rather not.

The Bible Says...

By Floyd Hale

Question: What was the difference between what Peter taught and what Paul taught?

Answer: This question gets directly into the issue raised by the title of this column, "The Bible Says." To take what the Bible says in I and II Peter and the first few chapters in Acts is not to quote Peter. We do not have any of the words of Peter in our New Testament. As troubling as this may sound to some, we don't have any of the writings of the original "Twelve" (if they wrote anything). I sure wish we did.

The two books bearing Peter's name were written years after he was dead (the second one nearly a century) and reflect the thinking of Paul--for the Church was founded and grew up on the ministry and writings of that one "Apostle."

Acts is not a documentary; it is a doctrinal treatise reading the "teachings" of the Church back into its beginnings. (This is the way the Old Testament "historians" wrote.) Thus "Peter's sermons" in Acts are primarily Pauline in doctrine. One purpose of its author was to smooth over the personal differences between Paul and Peter.

You may think this was a very unethical way of writing, but it was legitimate in the religious standards of that day. Knowing this simply means we must be informed on what "the Bible says."

That Mark wrote his Gospel from "first hand information about Jesus" he gained from Peter is a highly questionable tradition.

We do know what Paul taught, for his writings we now have date close to the original. But we should not take everything he wrote as his "teachings." Most of it was personal advice to specific addressees. To quote Paul as "what the Bible teaches"--giving it the Word of God authority--is to claim something for Paul he was certainly unaware of.

Paul did write one letter, Romans, the nearest to his formal "teachings" on the Christian Faith.

I very much wish I had the answer to the question you raise. It would solve a great mystery.

The Bible Says...

By Floyd Hale

Question: What does the author of Matthew mean when he says--repeatedly--"This was to fulfill what the Lord had spoken by the prophet . . ."?

Answer: Taken literally this very dogmatically says that the incident cited had been foretold and was now (then) taking place. But a little research in how most of the New Testament writers wrote, shows that this method of interpreting the Scriptures (in this case the Old Testament) is called "midrash." To prove a chosen point, it claimed a second and hidden meaning in a certain text.

Isaiah 7:14 is cited as foretelling the virgin birth of Jesus, when it actually had to to with a child born of a "young woman" in Isaiah's day. Hosea 11:1 is quoted as foretelling that Jesus would return from Egypt (being taken their as an infant by his parents), but that passage is clearly talking about the Exodus centuries earlier. Rachel in Ramah wept for her children (the lost tribes of Israel), and Matthew wants to say this foretold the slaying of the infants in Bethlehem by Herod (which didn't actually happen).

No "prophecy" can be found for Jesus coming from Nazareth, and "Nazarene" was a title for someone other than an inhabitant of that town. John the Baptist's preaching "in the wilderness" is predicted by Isaiah (40:3), but in that passage it is a voice crying "make straight in the desert a highway for our God," which shows that it was a prophet (not Isaiah) calling for the exiles to return home from Babylon.

In Jeremiah it was seventeen pieces of silver and not thirty, and it had nothing to do a potter's field. Zechariah is the only prophet speaking of thirty pieces of silver cast into the treasury, but that was a certain man's wages for a day, and "treasury" should have been translated "pottery,"

This is not being destructive or dishonest with Matthew's Gospel. It is a serious effort to help us see how the early Christians unwittingly misused their Scriptures, that we might stop doing the same to ours.

136

The Bible Says...

By Floyd Hale

Question: Does the Bible say God repented?

Answer: Yes, in a number of places. The Revised Standard Version translates this "God changed His mind." You may say God--being God--has the prerogative of changing His mind, but does this not make Him unstable?--even untrustworthy? I'm not questioning God; I'm questioning the ones who wrote these "scriptures."

In one place the Bible says God "repented that He had created the human race," and to show it He drowned them all (except one righteous family). In another place God said He was going to destroy the Ninevites, but "repented of the evil" he was going to do, and let them live.

When taken literally, what does this do to one's concept of God? What does it do to one's own disposition, for one is supposed to become like the God he/she worships?

The Bible word translated "repentance" or "change of mind" means a deep change in thinking and disposition--a complete turnaround. I believe God is stable minded, normal--otherwise He could not be trusted.

The story of the Flood in Genesis 6 is myth--pure myth. It doesn't even have a "moral" to it, except that God stopped violence and wickedness one time by performing the most wicked act of violence imaginable (which He didn't actually do). Have you never noticed that those who are the loudest for capital punishment are usually the strongest believers in the Bible?

In changing His mind about burning the Ninevites, God is one of the "characters" in a parable, the little book of Jonah. This means the one telling the story may have "God" doing whatever he chooses for Him to do *to make a point*--in this case a very good point is made.

The most ridiculous change for God is yet ahead, according to the Fundamentalists. The God of *grace* is going to change back into a God of wrath. This is taking apocalyptic in the Bible literally--strictly a no no.

God never changes. You can count on that.

The Bible Says...

By Floyd Hale

Question: Were all the laws just that God gave to Moses?

Answer: Whoever wrote these laws seems to have had a hangup related to gender and sex. It was an "abomination" for men and women to wear each others clothing (Deut. 22:5). A man and his wife who "lay together" were considered "unclean" until sundown (Lev. 15:18). If a man were to "lie with" a beast, not only he but the beast also was to be put to death (Lev. 20:15). Adultery was a capital crime for both the man and "his neighbor's wife" (Lev. 20:10). If a brother and sister "see the nakedness" of each other, they both shall be cut off from their family (Lev. 20:17).

A bride charged by the groom and found guilty of not being virgin, "shall be stoned to death--*with stones*" (Deut. 22:21). A man with bruised testicles was no longer a member of the assembly (Deut. 23:1). Speaking of testicles, if a woman grabbed a man by his "private parts" who was beating up on her husband, she was to have her hand cut off--"show her no pity" (Deut. 25:11,12). Pity the husband who would go along with this.

Those defending this as "Holy Writ" say this was the Law, and we are no longer under the Law (the first five books of the Old Testament). Then why do we retain it in our Christian Scriptures?

To say that God had a different standard for people back then is another way of double-talking this issue away. Any defense of such stuff being the "Word of God"--then or now--is nonsense.

The Law of Moses as a whole was a great step forward in the cause of justice. I like God's getting the credit for it. But to force on intelligent people the dogma that the Bible is the perfect and complete revelation of God's will for humanity is to do injustice to the cause of justice it promotes.

Jesus had a high regard for the Law (his Scripture), but he saw its being treated literally and legalistically, rather than the source of edification and inspiration, as neglecting the "more important matters of justice and mercy . . ." Notice that justice is to be balanced with mercy.

The Bible Says...

By Floyd Hale

Question: Is baptism essential for salvation? And did the Holy Ghost ascend like a dove, or in the form of a dove, at Jesus baptism?

Answer: An individual's salvation is by grace. All one needs to do to experience that is to accept it--it's free. There can be no conditions or requirements put on God's grace--even baptism--or it is not grace. Since the Christian Church was a "break-off" from the "Baptist" movement, they took baptism with them. Most churches require it as a public sign of the inward work of "grace." Jesus didn't. He didn't seem to think much of religious ceremonies. Maybe that's why he didn't baptize his followers.

While a lot of scriptures can be quoted to "prove" water baptism is required, let me quote a little scripture also. In all four of the Gospels it says: "John came baptizing with water, *but* Jesus came to baptize with the Holy Spirit." The Church seems to have retained the former, calling it "Christian," while neglecting the later.

Mark says John, upon baptizing Jesus, "saw. . . the *Spirit* descending upon him like a dove." Matthew, using Mark's account as his source, rephrases this a bit: John "saw the *Spirit of God* descending like a dove, and alighting on him (Jesus)." Luke, also relying on Mark as his source for this, rewords this: As Jesus "was praying, . . the *Holy Spirit* descended upon him in bodily form, as a dove." In the Fourth Gospel the actual baptism of Jesus is very subtly omitted by the author (for a special reason); but as Jesus approaches John at the Jordan, the Baptizer says he "saw the *Spirit* descend as a dove, . . and it remained on him (Jesus)."

The wording of this "story" should not be pressed into its literalness, for it is the "religious way" the Gospel writers (not John the Baptist) had of claiming Jesus' life and work had the special anointing of God.

To say that we are to "follow Jesus in baptism" can be a way of substituting a *religious ceremony* for "following Jesus in the doing of God's will" (which is what he called his followers to do).

139

The Bible Says...

By Floyd Hale

Question: What happened to Christ between the temple incident at age 12 and his baptism?

Answer: He probably worked as a carpenter in Nazareth.

Question: I would like you to explain where and by whom the first marriage was performed?

Answer: Marriage was a rather established habit long before the Bible was written. I know of nothing in the Scriptures which would answer your question.

Question: Why is the Gospel of John looked down on by some Bible scholars?

Answer: I know of no Bible scholar who "looks down on" this Gospel. Many point out that it is not just another Gospel; it is a "Christology," written in Gospel form. It is a theological interpretation of the "Spirit of Christ."

The criticism of scholars comes from those who are threatened by the idea of not taking any part of the Bible (i.e. John's Gospel) literally, historically true about Jesus.

Question: Just where were the pastures in which the boy David shepherded his father's sheep?

Answer: They must have been near Bethlehem.

Question: I would like to know what the Bible says about a person claiming to be a Christian and sin ever day, and don't treat no one right?

Answer: I'd say that person anin't no Christian.

The Bible Says...

By Floyd Hale

Question: Who took Christ out of Christmas?

Answer: It has not been primarily the commercial gift selling and secular Santa Claus and Christmas trees-- nor the Communists. It is the way traditional Christianity *unwittingly* celebrates the Christmas Myth. (Before you jump on this word "Myth," please hear me out.) The baby Jesus in a manger, his virgin mother sitting near by, and the shepherds and wise men standing around have nothing to do with "Christ."

The Birth Stories in Matthew and Luke were composed to help point out the *kind of person Jesus had been* and *what he lived and died for* not to provide statistical data on *how and where he was born.* Mythology was a perfectly legitimate way of doing this, but when the story is treated as factual--as it soon was-- the Myth replaces the Christ.

At Christmas time each year the Church repeats its "programing" of children's minds with an unreal image of Jesus, while hoping the kids will grow up with a proper view of the real Jesus. The beauty in this pageantry helps make this mental switch all the more impossible.

It is easy to see that these two Birth Stories disagree at several points when their literary composition is closely compared. Then, if the "wonders" of the angels and the star were removed, there would be no story left.

I am not for removing the Birth Stories from the Bible, far from it, but the traditional Christmas pageants have done the most in taking Christ out of Christmas.

I am for the proper understanding of this story and its purpose. This has to begin with the "child" that's in the adult--"born" there by the Christmas Myth. This may not be an easy process for the traditional Christian, but Christians by profession are supposed to be seekers after the truth.

Preserving and defending the Christmas symbols can be a substitute for bearing witness to the Christ of Christmas.

I am sure there'll be letters to the editor about this one, especially by those who insist that "every word in the Bible is the Word of God." But these are the very people who complain most about "Christ not being in Christmas anymore."

The Bible Says...

By Floyd Hale

Question: Did a woman write the book of Ruth in the Bible?

Answer: I wouldn't be surprised, for it was a bold plea for women's rights--the rights of "foreign" women no less. It was so revolutionary that its message had to be couched in the form of a historic novel.

When the Hebrew Scriptures were translated into Greek, this little book was placed back between the "Law" and the "Prophets," because Ruth lived in that period, giving it the appearance of history. But it was actually eight centuries later that this powerful piece of propaganda was penned

When Ezra brought the "Law" (Genesis-Exodus-Leviticus-Numbers-Deutreronomy) back from Babylon and got it adopted as the first Jewish Bible (ca. 400 B.C.), it was mainly for the purpose of ridding the Jerusalem community of non-Jews. That "ethnic cleansing" fell almost entirely on the necks of foreign women. Many were torn from their families and driven out of the country. Although the "Law" (Deut. 32:3) demanded this, the author of this little book placed "what's right" above "Scripture."

Very shrewdly the author (ca. 375 B.C.) built this very convincing "love story" on the fact that Boaz's wife, Ruth, had been a "foreigner"--a Moabite (the worst kind). In this little pamphlet Ruth's non-Jewishness is repeatedly stressed, yet she is fully accepted in the "community of God's people" for being such a lovely person. Then after its "they lived happily ever after" ending was this post script: "Boaz (by his wife Ruth) begat Jesse, and Jesse begat DAVID."

How could the first readers keep from pondering, "What if the foreign wife Ruth had been chased out back then? There would have been no "great King David--who gave us our great Kingdom." Since the people at the time this was written were longing for "another (son) of David" to come and "restore the kingdom to Israel," would not they also ask, "By running off these foreign wives now might we not be 'cutting off Messiah'?"

This is another example of how only by knowing the literary form of a Bible book can one get it's message.

The Bible Says...

By Floyd Hale

Question: Does the Bible pronounce a blessing on those who would dash little children against a rock?

Answer: The author of Psalm 137 (last verse) praises this sick kind of violence. It would be "poetic vengeance" on the Edomites--blood relatives of the Israelites--who had joined with the Babylonians in the destruction of Jerusalem in 586 B.C. Being neighbors they continued to vandalize at will the defenseless Judeans not taken away into Captivity.

Before we hastily condemn the sanction of such inhumane treatment of innocent children, we should remind ourselves that "Christian America" dropped an atomic "rock" on the city of Hiroshima (Aug. 6, 1945), "bashing" thousands of innocent Japanese children--some of which lived to suffer the burning and cancer. Amazing, what can be justified when it's done to the "enemy."

The late doings of Brother Jimmie Carter in the area of reconciliation makes me wonder what would have happened if President Truman had sent General Marshall to Tokyo on August 1, 1945, to tell the Japanese what we were going to do immediately if they did not surrender? But that would have been no way to "Remember Pearl Harbor (Jerusalem!)."

On a subject like this it is hard to take Jesus ("who loved the little children") seriously when he said, "Love your enemies."

Then what in our Bible should we take seriously? Those who take it all literally as the Word of God could quote Psalm 137:9 as justifying our incinerating the Japanese children in Hiroshima--the Bible blesses the doing to your enemy's little ones. Most people don't know how to take the Bible-- as a whole--because they've never had it intelligently explained to them.

A small step forward in understanding how to take the Bible would be to know-- what can plainly be seen-- this Psalm was composed by someone after Jerusalem was destroyed, and not four centuries earlier by King David.

In all the devotional books full of the Psalms I have never seen one with the 137th in it.

143

The Bible Says...

By Floyd Hale

Question: I would like to know your views on Heaven and Hell?

Answer: Since your other questions also relate to this, maybe my one answer will cover them all. In this space I can only be brief--far too brief for an answer to such a provocative question.

To begin with it should be realized that there was a people who had the ten commandments and God's just laws to live by, without an "afterlife" playing any part in it. It was only after they failed to bring their "community" on earth up to God's just standard, that "another world" began to come into the picture.

"Heaven" began as a figure of speech, the "place" where God was "completely in charge." (This also helped explain his absence.) In the prayer Jesus gave his followers to pray--*and thus live by*--is this petition: "God, be in charge here on earth-- just like You are in heaven." This is not giving God the permission to take over; it is committing oneself to helping make it happen. The easiest way to evade this calling--and remain religious--is to get oneself ready to "go to heaven." But I have never seen any one yet who wanted to go there until he/she was dead.

I might add, believing there is a heaven doesn't make it so.

"Hell," the one where people burn for ever and ever, was invented during the intertestamental period, by some of the Jews for those who persecuted them. I can think of no worse crime than torturing good people; but Jesus, rather than damning the persecutors, said there was a way good people could "take it," and turn that into a world redeeming force. He called that "cross bearing." (And he knew what he was talking about.)

There is something very psychological about believing in Heaven and Hell (as these are commonly thought of) being the creation of religious people for themselves and sinners-- respectively.

You asked how you could get a copy of my book. Since you live away from here, I'll send you one in which I have a full chapter on this subject.

144

The Bible Says...

By Floyd Hale

Question: What is Fundamentalism?

Answer: Like every "ism" it is a mixed bag. I grew up in it and on it, and was loyal to its cause until I learned better some years after entering the ministry. I've been accused of switching to be popular, but the Fundamentalists preach the "popular gospel"--some in the raw, some intellectualize it into a "spiritual self-help exercise."

I think all Fundamentalists would agree that the Apostles' Creed (although it did not come from the Apostles) states their faith--"the one and only true Faith." The loudest of these good people claim that the Bible is "inerrant and infallible," which is just not true (as I point out almost every week in this space).

From the beginning the Christians, being Jews, inherited a narrow view of the authority of Scripture--it was somehow "breathed by God." But it was not until the birth of Fundamentalism in the last century that this came to mean "God dictated every word of it."

When the Waldenses (a lay order of monks in the 12th century) started teaching the Bible to the common people, a papal edict resulted which literally denied the laity's reading the Bible. In the following century the Church of England put to death one of its first Bible scholars for translating it into the language of the people.

Fundamentalism places much emphasis on the Bible, while really not wanting people to understand it. For if people really understood it, rather than accepting a bunch of its scattered verses thrown at them as "Doctrines," they'd tell the Fundamentalists to go suck on a dead fish.

My gripe with the Fundies is not primarily because they are wrong, but because two or three of them stand at the door of almost every Church and refuse to let anyone in who wants to do a little thinking for him or herself. Thinkers are let in only if they keep their thoughts to themselves.

I'd say the biggest error of Fundamentalism is its believing the traditional gospel, instead of finding out what Jesus' gospel really was. There is a difference between the two, you know-- or did you know?

LETTERS TO THE EDITOR

Dear D. (Editor):

I have a copy of a letter from another newspaper regarding Fundamentalism that Rev. Hale should see. I don't want the readers of Rev. Hale's column to miss this man's opinion, so I am enclosing the clipping.

Holmme Letter: Beware of Fundamentalism

The tragic murder of the doctor and friend in Florida by a former fundamentalist minister is yet another reminder the truth needs to be told about the danger of fundamentalists. As a former Old Testament professor of mine expressed it, "One can not understand fundamentalism until you recognize it is not a theological position but a psychological problem."

The psychological problems vary with the individual. Fear, doubt, anger, anxiety, unhealthy self-esteem uncomfortableness with ambiguity and questioning, and most of all, the dangerous "need to be right." I am certain that anyone who is against more things than they are for, or who lives in fear more than hope, is not exactly emotionally healthy.

The emerging power of the religious right is very scary for anyone, deeply spiritual or not, for any group of folks who "know they are right" will be all too quick to prove that You are wrong.

I believe if one begins to examine some of the bizarre behavior and pronouncements of fundamentalists, one can begin to see some of the various psychological disorders they have. (Rev, Dave R. Holmes, Omaha, Nebraska)

An (out of town) Reader

Editor's note: To my mind comes the role of women as defined by literal Bible teaching, that the man is the head of the house. I believe women are people, and God looks upon them as equal.

m

The Bible Says...

By Floyd Hale

Question: Rev. Hale, why don't you believe the Bible?

Answer: This is a fair question. And I am sure you--and some others who read this column--may feel that in my pointing out errors, contradictions and inconsistencies in the Bible I am treating the Scriptures with disrespect.

I think it could be said that the Bible teaches "honesty is the best policy." The best way I can preach you a sermon on "telling the truth" is to begin by applying this to the Bible itself. It can not only take it, it comes out much better as a guide to faith and Truth if this is done.

One of my purposes in writing this column is to show the need--a real need--among Christians to understand their Scriptures. This is not as simple as reading them to see what they "say." For instance, if you looked therein for advice on how to treat a fool, you'd probably begin in the book of Proverbs--for it says more about "fools" than all the rest of the Bible books combined.

What do you find there? It says (in the 26th chapter) to "answer *not* a fool according to his folly," and then it goes on in the very next verse to say, "answer a fool according to his folly" (vv. 4 and 5). I would be a fool for pointing this out if it were not to encourage readers to open-mindedly search the scriptures for Truth.

My summary of Truth in the Bible is that God accepts and loves us all (even us sinners) and wants us to work at getting His will done in life, for the good of the poor, hungry, sick and oppressed. In my reading of the Gospels I find this is what Jesus did. The One he called Father is a just God, who not only asks people to be just, but to promote justice in this His world. Does this sound like I don't believe the Bible?

Several years ago I was asked to have the funeral of a man whom I did not know. His wife (whom I also did not know until she requested this) said he had gained back his faith in the Bible through reading my column, "The Bible Says."

I think my column is taken about the way most things are: people tend to find what they are looking for.

The Bible Says...

By Floyd Hale

Question: Where in the Bible does it say a king was driven out to live with the wild beasts for seven years, eating grass like a cow?

Answer: In the book of Daniel it is reported that this happened to the Babylonian King, Nebuchadnezzar, to teach him that the Most High God is in charge of this world (4:28-35).

In Babylonian Captivity (as the story goes) a promising Hebrew lad was chosen to sit on the pagan king's "counsel of wise men" which advised him in all his affairs. This young man, Daniel, sticking strictly to a kosher diet, exceeded the "Chaldeans" in wisdom. He could not only interpret the king's dreams, he could tell him what he had dreamed.

Stories like these about Daniel (in the first six chapters of this book) were handed down and told to Jewish youth to keep them adhering strictly to the holy ordinances of their ancestors. This was especially important to the Jews because "pagan" cultures continually pressed in upon them. At the time this book was written (ca. 165 B.C.) the Greek ("Western") culture was being driven down their throats by the Syrian governor, Antiochus IV. Their resistance to this brought the Syrian army into Jerusalem, where it tried savagely to wipe out the Faith of Israel.

By the time the reader of this document got to the seventh chapter he/she was convinced Daniel was wise enough to foretell the outcome of their present "tribulation"--which he did. The remaining six chapters make up four Apocalyptic Cycles, each foretelling the "end" (of the beastly Syrian governor and the desolation of the Temple)--in "three and a half years."

This book got the credit for inspiring the success of the Maccabean Revolt (164 B.C.), causing the Apocalyptic to be the popular mode of religious thinking in Jesus' day. This makes it necessary that the student of the Bible understand how to interpret this unique literary form-- for it permeates the first three Gospels, and Revelation is a complete Apocalypse.

147

The Bible Says...

By Floyd Hale

Question: Does God really love everybody?

Answer: I believe I am safe in saying there is not one Christian who would give a "no" answer to this question. Yet I wonder how many understand how far that love reaches. The Bible is confusing at this point.

God's nature is defined in only two places in the Scriptures, one as Spirit, and the other in I John 4:8, "God IS love." I could quote a lot from the Old Testament that God's love is "everlasting"-- that's a long time. Paul said "love never ends"--that's even longer.

There are also many scriptures which say God is a God of wrath--or He will change his disposition someday back to showing wrath toward a good percent of us ("the others," of course). To say this is in keeping with His love is just not true. All this about an end to the "day of grace" is to misunderstand grace. Grace is God's *unconditional acceptance* of sinners (that's all of us). Grace that comes to an end is not grace--hasn't worked.

This does not mean God likes or condones our sinning. But instead of eternal punishment (after its too late to change anything), He's got a better way; and it would work a lot better if all people knew about it.

The God who created us in freedom has "gambled" everything on his love and grace. I think He knows that's the only way positive change can be motivated in a person--in the long run. And God has plenty time; we don't.

Punishment, hell and all the rest God is "going to do to sinners" in the Bible is there because its writers read too much of their own human (religious?) nature into God's nature.

When Jesus said God makes the rain to fall and the sun to shine "on the just and unjust alike," he was not talking about rain and sunshine. He was undercutting the religious dogma of his time (if not all time) that said God, to be just, must punish sinners. *Consequences of sin*--most of which fall on the innocent (even far into the future)--is what we should be concerned about, not about who's going to catch what after they are dead.

It may be hard to believe that God loves with no "if's" attached. But He does

148

The Bible Says...

By Floyd Hale

Questions: Was it believed in Bible times that the seat of the conscience was in the kidneys?

Answer: In the Hebrew culture this was true. The Jewish Talmud (Berakhoth 61a) says one kidney prompts man to do good, the other to do evil. Even in the prescription for preparing the burnt offerings, the kidneys of the sacrificial animal were to get special attention (Lev. 3:3-5).

In the Western culture the heart won out as the seat of morality and the kidneys no longer made sense, and would most certainly appear foolish in the English Scriptures (knowing what we do now about the function of the kidneys). So the King James translators set to correcting this. For "kidneys" they chose the word "reins," from the Latin "renes" ("kidneys"), but meaning the region of the kidneys in the body, the "loins." Yet where it is obviously referring to the organs, as in Leviticus, they translated the same Hebrew word "kidneys."

The Revised Standard Version went all the way and "westernized" this into "heart." But this caused a conflict in passages where both heart and kidneys were mentioned together--as they often are. To remedy(?) this they changed heart--already in that passage--into "mind" or "soul" (e.g. Ps. 7:9, 26:2, Jer. 11:20, etc.). Why they didn't go ahead and translate it "conscience" I don't know. If you just replace the word "reins" in the KJV with "conscience" you will have the original meaning of the Bible writers. Notice what that would do for Ps. 73:21 and Lam. 3:13 in the KJV.

Well, the kidneys in the Bible didn't make it, but this is just a small lesson in how the Bible language developed. The Bible writers chose their words from current customs and beliefs--and so did the translators.

In that Volume of human words one may find, if intelligently pursued, the Word of God. If all the words are treated as God's words, there's no telling what you'll end up believing.

I'd say, in good old Hebrew phraseology, as you read the Bible let your kidneys be your guide.

The Bible Says...

By Floyd Hale

Question: How reliable is the accuracy of the Old Testament Bible from the original texts until today?

Answer: There is no way of knowing this, for we do not have any of the original texts with which to compare later copies. Copies can be compared only with *older* copies, and none of them (so far) date near the originals.

For a long time the Jews had a sacred tradition which contributed to this literary gap. When a new copy of a Scripture was made, the older one was to be disposed of (similar to our custom of destroying a soiled flag).

Up until the Dead Sea Scrolls find (1948), the oldest copy of the book of Isaiah in existence dated in the 8th century A.D. Among those Scrolls was a copy of Isaiah which dated about 200 B.C. This bridged the literary gap of about a thousand years. There were several minor differences in the two, yet none which altered the basic message of the text.

Once an O.T. document became recognized as "Scripture"--which was always centuries after it was written--little if any editing was done to it. It was *before* it was canonized that major changes were made.

The classic example of this is right in the Bible itself. The history in I and II Chronicles is a 3rd century B.C. "radical revision" of the *same history* covered in Samuel-Kings (which was compiled in the 6th century B.C. from many yet earlier "revised" sources). When the two are compared, many of the "facts" do not agree. *Samuel-Kings was not yet Scripture at the time the Chronicler wrote*--and he was certainly unaware that both his and the earlier "history" would someday be included side by side in "Holy Writ."

There never was any such thing as an original "five books of Moses" anyway. The many different sources used in putting that ("first Jewish Bible") together show clear evidence of having been "revised" many times prior to that 5th century B.C. compilation. (Moses lived in the 12th.)

We have close to the original texts (we're close enough), but to say that no changes were made in them from there on back is wistful thinking.

The Bible Says...

By Floyd Hale

Question: How reliable is the accuracy of the New Testament Bible from the original texts until today?

Answer: In the first place we don't have any of the original texts to compare with our present copies. In the second place most folks don't realize the books now in our New Testament were widely distributed and many times recopied, several years before they were ever considered "Scripture." It was during that period that most of the changes in the texts were made. Two brief examples: Verse 5:4 in the Fourth Gospel (KJV) was added after it left the authors hands, as was also verse 5:7 in the First Epistle of John (KJV). The RSV properly deletes these.

Because the N.T. books were written in a more advanced culture and closer together in time than were the O.T. scrolls, our copies are much nearer to the original texts. Literary analysts tell us we are closer to Paul's original words than we are to Shakesphere's. The question is not "Did Paul actually say it?," but "What words of Paul are the Word of God?"

When it comes to the Gospels, we are dealing with a whole different kind of literature. Even if we had accurate copies of the original Gospels (which for all practical purposes we do), that does not mean all the "words of Jesus" in them are "original (authentic)."

The first Gospel, Mark, was composed much like the "five books of Moses," from traditions which circulated widely and sometimes amended, until unified (and thus further edited) into "The Story of Jesus." Mark was the first to do this, and that was about forty years after Jesus' death. Matthew and Luke used his Gospel (long before it was considered "Scripture") as their primary source, often changing what he reported.

The many years of researching this subject has led me to conclude: Those dogmatically proclaiming our Scriptures to be the "accurate accounts of the men God inspired to write them"--along with the so-called "scholars" they quote to support this--are either very uninformed, or they take advantage of the ignorance of people to hold the Bible as "God" over them.

151

The Bible Says...

By Floyd Hale

Question: In II Cor. 15:29, please explain those who are baptized for the dead?

Answer: All we know about this practice is from this one reference to it (in I Corinthians). It illustrates the confusion caused by the belief in the Resurrection in the early Church--and the importance of Baptism.

The apocalyptic form of expression which dominated the language of the first Jewish Christians--which spoke of the "resurrection of the body," was soon taken literally. In its original symbology it represented the continuing revolutionary influence in and on society of the "lives" of the followers of Jesus who were martyred--as though they came back to life and "ruled forever with Christ." This is clearly explained in Revelation--for those who take the trouble to understand the expression form in which that book is written.

Although Paul was not an Apocalyptist who believed this literally, he used its rhetoric in proclaiming the "resurrection from the dead." In its popular sense Resurrection said death was a "sleep" in between this life and the next one--so if you die in a state of grace death is not to be feared. The doctrine of Resurrection was not new to Paul; as a Pharisee he believed in it before he was converted. He just added a Christian spin to it.

Since the resurrection (to Paul) was the believer's final salvation, and baptism was becoming required for those being saved, the question arose, what happens to the faithful who died without having been dunked? Evidently the solution for some was, why couldn't it be done by proxy? (This makes as much sense as any other kind of Baptism anyway.)

I doubt if Paul would have accepted this as orthodox, but it came in handy as a left-handed "proof" of the resurrection. Paul's apocalyptic "resurrection of the body" phraseology offended the Gnostics in the church at Corinth, who believed the physical body was inherently evil. Paul got around this by telling them they'd be resurrected in a "spiritual body" (but spirits don'e have bodies).

The Bible Says...

By Floyd Hale

Question: Is the coming of Christ foretold in Daniel 9:25?

Answer: Because the Church in the 17th century believed that Daniel 9:25 foretold Christ's coming, the King James Version translated "an anointed one" in that verse "Messiah"-- even giving it a capital "M."

In Israel anyone (prophet, king, priest, etc.) doing a job or filling an office considered important in God's kingdom was referred to as "an anointed one." At the time of the writing of Daniel (165 B.C.) the priests were commonly referred to as "anointed ones"--the way a minister today is called "Reverend." The Hebrew word was pronounced "messiah." So after Jesus was considered "The Messiah," this became a favorite passage midrashed into "foretelling" his coming (and his death in verse 26).

To come up with this "prophecy" the author of Daniel midrashed Jeremiah's "70 years" (25:12) to make it fit into his "70 weeks of years" he needed, by multiplying it by the good apocalyptic number "7" (an angel told him to). The whole of chapter 9 is a recitation of the period of history from Babylonian Captivity down to the Maccabean Revolt (167-165 B.C.) as though the author lived back at its beginning and was foretelling it as yet in the future. Apocalyptic writers were "free" to write like this.

When the KJV came out (1611) very little was understood about the apocalyptic in the Bible. But the modern Bible scholars have researched it thoroughly. So the RSV properly leaves this "an anointed one" in these two places in Daniel. The KJV was not only mistaken but inconsistent in its translating it "Messiah," because in every other place in the Old Testament they left it "an anointed one."

The first "anointed one" (v. 25) was the *priest* who came back with the first returnees in 530 B.C. The second one (v.26) was the High *Priest* Onias III who had just been assassinated ("cut off") in 171 B.C., during the lifetime of the first readers of Daniel. This is the way this book told them they were living "in the last days"--of the Antiochan Persecution.

The Bible Says...

By Floyd Hale

Question: When the Apostle Paul quoted the figure in Numbers 25:9, why did he miss it by a thousand (I Cor. 10:8)?

Answer: Paul says 23,000 of the Israelites died--"in a single day;" while his source for this, the book of Numbers, reports it was 24,000. If Paul had upped the figure, I would say he was doing so to give emphasis to his point, as was the habit with some Bible writers. But since he didn't, I can only conclude this was a mistake on Paul's part. He was human, you know.

While the Israelites were camped in Moab on their way to the Promised Land, the "daughters of Moab" (harlots) carried on a thriving business among the male pilgrims. This led the Hebrew men to worship the idols of their "foreign girlfriends"--this went along with "sacred" prostitution in those days. This made God very mad (according to Numbers) and he right off had Moses hang all the chiefs--heads of family clans, "that the fierce anger of the Lord might be turned away from Israel" (v.4).

The judges were to order the slaying of all the men who had "gone after the gods of Baal and Peor." While everyone was weeping, a man was brought in with one of these foreign women--right in front of Moses and the whole congregation. One Phinehas rose to the occasion and stuck his spear right through this man and woman, and this stopped God's killing at 24,000. God said: "Phinehas has turned back my wrath from the people of Israel. . . so that I did not consume them (all) in my jealously." Paul probably believed God really said this and was that kind of God--after all, it was in his Bible.

This chapter in Numbers was most likely written in Babylon or afterward. This kind of "stories" was told by the priests to dissuade the men from marrying the local "foreign" women. Kosher blood could not be mixed.

Your question caused me to once again research the origin of the book of Numbers. In doing so I became more than ever convinced that God's ways are far above the thinking of a lot of the Old Testament writers.

The Bible Says...

By Floyd Hale

Question: Would you please explain the severe warning in Revelation 22:18-19?

Answer: It reads: "I (John) warn everyone who hears the words of the prophecy (message) of this book: if any one adds to them, God will add to him the plagues described in this book, and if any one takes away from the words of the book of this prophecy, God will take away his share in the tree of life and in the holy city, which are described in this book."

This warning has often been quoted as applying to the whole Bible, but "this book" is Revelation--the one John was sending out to the churches. It did not become a part of the Bible ("Scripture") for several decades, and so those quoting it and recopying it many times over--during that period might feel that they could add some helpful material or leave something puzzling out--as was done regularly to many manuscripts.

Those writing Apocalypses (of which Revelation is one) edited and borrowed from other Apocalypses freely. John was very aware of this (for traces of over twenty sources can be found in his), and he did not want his changed one iota, for it might foul up what he was saying to his brethren who were undergoing tribulation--the Roman Persecution was just setting in (ca. A.D. 90).

This bombastic warning is in good apocalyptic style, and the copyists who "heard" this document read to them knew what its author meant--without believing its literalness. (Can you imagine all the plagues mentioned in Revelation being put on one person?)

This awful sounding warning is a good illustration of how we need to know how to interpret the apocalyptic material in the Bible. It is not just a bunch of wild symbols, it is a whole view of how a "militant" God is going to save the world. It was completely foreign to Jewish thinking--completely contradictory to the message of the prophets--until the book of Daniel (the first Jewish Apocalypse) became popular just before Jesus's time.

Why is this not taught people in Bible Study groups?

The Bible Says...

By Floyd Hale

Question: Why do Christians think Humanism is bad?

Answer: I'd like to change your question to "Why do *some* Christians think Humanism is bad?" I have read some literature put out by a right-wing Christian group condemning Humanism for its being a "secular religion replacing Christianity." If Humanism is for the good of humanity they are "not against us" (Jesus would say). It is narrow thinking to suppose that God has his blessings only on anything wearing the Christian label. Traditional religion can get so turned in on its own religiosity that things human lose their divine relevance.

Compassion was a--if not the--key word in Jesus' ministry. The only story he told with a Judgment Day setting, the dividing "right and left" of the "sheep and the goats," was about humanitarianism (Mt. 25). I like to think of the sheep being to the "left," for they were the liberals. They were so liberal that they made it into heaven without being "religious."

You've heard it said "there's going to be a lot of surprises on that Day." Well, in Jesus' story the sheep and the goats were both surprised. The goats (who must have looked upon themselves as righteous) thought they were sheep, but didn't pass--they were even to be punished--forever (Mt. 25:46). In not caring about and for the needs of humanity they really didn't care about their God. What they "believed" is not even mentioned.

The sheep were just as surprised, for they did not know that their humanistic concerns were considered "righteousness" by the Judge. I don't think I am doing a bit of damage to this text by saying that their being rewarded with "eternal life" simply meant they knew what life in the long run was all about--and it does have a way of running a long time.

It just might be God is raising up Humanism to teach Christians what their religion is all about, not saving themselves but the world--which is full of human beings who need to be treated like they were human.

The Bible Says...

By Floyd Hale

Question: Was Peter the first Pope?

Answer: There is "scripture" to support this, Mt. 16:17-19, but here is where the Bible scholars come to our rescue. It doesn't really take a scholar to compare this with its parallel passage in Mark 8: 27-30, and find it not in Mark. If you are interested I would ask you to give close attention to these two accounts. Draw a pencil line around these three verses in Matthew--block them off. Since Mark is older than Matthew and the author of Matthew used Mark as his main source, it is obvious that these three verses 17-19 were "added." Why? There had to be a reason.

In that time and place the tradition was that a "legitimate" cause had to have a proper successor in command, or it just was not legitimate. By the time Matthew was composed, the tradition of Peter's being "Christ's vicar" (representative left in charge) on earth was beginning to take shape in the Church (although this violated a principal teaching of Jesus). Thus this "tradition" was *edited into* this Gospel "in the words of Jesus." It is a very superficial view of Scripture which forces one to defend these as the words of Jesus, and go on to explain their meaning as acceptable in some way.

Notice, when Matthew's interpolation (verses 17-19) is removed, it reads exactly as Mark's account. Matthew does this kind of "editing" Mark in a number of places; and when he does he usually leaves a telltale literary blunder. The "blessing" (in Matthew) Jesus puts on Peter in this place is completely incompatible with his immediately calling him "Satan."

The above is not anti-Catholic, nor an effort to destroy Matthew's authority as a Gospel. It is the result of unbiased analysis of the text (applying all relevant historical data). It is called Higher Criticism and gives the believer the information needed to understand this passage in his or her Scriptures.

This should convince a person that there are other "words of Jesus"--all of them in fact--in the Gospels that need to be examined for authenticity. This doesn't hurt--actually helps--the image of Jesus in the Bible.

157

The Bible Says...

By Floyd Hale

Question: Is it wrong for a Christian to "swear" to tell the truth in a court of law?

Answer: Administering the oath to "tell the truth on the stand" is the courts way of warning the witness he or she may be legally charged for any false testimony given. In ancient times it was to call on God to curse (damn) oneself if one lied. Now, instead of asking God to "damn me" if I lie, at the end of my promise to tell only the truth, I simply say "I will, so help me God." I have a notion this milder ending came because of Jesus' words about swearing.

The purpose of this oath is to make one legally responsible for his testimony.

This injunction by Jesus didn't have to do with testimony given in court. The more pious people of Jesus' day would swear by almost anything--all the way from heaven down to their own heads (off), to impress people that they would keep their word. This was not only vain but revealed that they applied a double standard to truth-telling. Jesus told his followers to cut through all that malarkey, and let their word stand undefended-- "Yes" or "No." Did you ever hear a person make a long speech before saying "No"?

I think one can get the broad truth in what Jesus said about this, without making his statement literally a "law of conscience." There are a lot of more important things in our culture which need our conscientious attention. To make a big issue out of "swearing (or not to swear) in (or out of) court" can be a substitute for getting involved with the "weightier matters" of truth.

I'd like to call attention to this section in Matthew (5:27:39) where Jesus mentions a number of things "You have heard it said of old." This was a very clever way of "quoting" (actually paraphrasing) some of their Scriptures. In this Jesus demonstrates that he was a critic of his Bible--and this was not because he had some kind of divine authority. Taking the "Law" (their Bible) literally as God's Word caused them to miss God's Word in what Jesus said and did. We have much to learn from him on this, for in "quoting Paul" we have caused Jesus's call to discipleship to go unheard-- and thus unheeded.

The Bible Says...

By Floyd Hale

Question: How can some say the Bible is "inerrant and infallible"?

Answer: This claim is made by Fundamentalists. A leading figure in that camp has defended this indefensible dogma against various "liberals" on TV shows a number of times in the last few years.

This claim is the unrealistic extreme to which some are driven, to support the Scriptures as the source of God's Wisdom. But it need not be done. In fact it makes a lot in the Bible "divine wisdom" which is far from it.

It is much better to learn what the Bible really is (which the conservatives resist doing), and then apply ordinary education methods in teaching the literature in this great Book. God's Truth can defend itself--if its promoters are open and honest in their promoting it.

Some think I am too critical and negative in my continually pointing out "what's wrong" with the Bible. But this is because too long we have been subject to the tradition that the "Truth" is synonymous with everything "the Bible says." Since it is the determined effort of a few to keep the rest of you from even being exposed to the truth about the Bible, I feel that I must bypass their office. They operate mainly out of fear, by threatening believers that to question the Bible is to lose one's faith."

A whole denomination-- the largest Protestant Church in America--has recently been taken over by a few of these "inerrant and infallible" prophets. They have a majority support, but to hold their place of power they must keep that majority uninformed in Bible. They have gone on a purge of their denominationally controlled colleges and universities, to expel the "liberal" professors. Even in "liberal education" liberal has become a bad word.

It is that vast uninformed good people which must begin to become informed, if the Bible continues to have the influence it has enjoyed in the past. The hard part in this is seeing the need. I try to illustrate--repeatedly-- this NEED, from right within the Bible itself.

159

The Bible Says...

By Floyd Hale

Question: What is prophecy?

Answer: Its pure meaning is "a message of divine truth relevant to the now time." The popular (and corrupt) meaning of this term is "something in the future foretold." It is used both ways in the Bible. The later is more popular for it suggests mystery, a glass ball and divine revelation.

This term is used in its pure sense all seven times in the book of Revelation--a book which is mistakenly considered foretelling the future--"right down to the end of time."

To defend their new Faith as legitimate, the fulfillment of "prophecy," the New Testament authors quoted extensively from the Old Testament--their Scriptures. Matthew again and again says such and such was "to fulfill that which was spoken by the prophet" so and so. This usually led to a midrash (loose) treatment of an O. T. passage. A choice example of this is Mt. 3:3:

"For this is he (John the Baptist) who was spoken of by the prophet Isaiah when he said, 'The voice of one crying in the wilderness: *Prepare the way of the Lord, make his paths straight'.*"

But when you look at that passage in Isaiah (40:3), it reads like this:

"A voice cries:'*In the wilderness prepare the way of the Lord, make straight in the desert (wilderness) a highway for our God'.*"

The English translation makes it clear that Matthew simply midrashed Isaiah by moving the semicolon from after "cries" on down to just after "wilderness." Compare the two texts above very closely. The Isaish passage was trying to poetically inspire the Jews in exile at the time to return to their homeland--across a desert (wilderness) on a highway their God would build. That's the language of inspiration.

To say this also has a second and hidden meaning in it for centuries later is simply not to be honest with Scripture.

John the Baptist--and Jesus--did not need this kind of "fulfillment of prophecy." Some people, when told this does not foretell John and Jesus, think this denies them their roles in God's cause. This should teach us something, right in the Bible, about how to use--and not use--our Scriptures.

160

The Bible Says...

By Floyd Hale

Question: Dear brother in the Lord. . . Have you never felt that God would be somewhat grieved over your articles in the newspaper?

Answer: I doubt that He reads them. He's got better things to do.

Many times in my articles I have come to God's defense, against a lot of the bad press some of the Bible writers give Him. For instance that he drowned all the people on earth (except one family) one time--with all the innocent little children, because they were all bad. Even if He had, why all the animals (except two each)? They were not wicked.

I think God appreciates someone standing up on his hind legs and saying--even shouting, "He didn't do it!"

I have to say that an angel of God is not going to someday put in a sickle and gather the people of earth "into the great wine press of the wrath of God," out of which "blood will flow four feet deep for 200 miles from that place." You can't convince me the God whom Jesus called his Heavenly Father would have any part in such a brutal affair.

If God is grieved, I believe it is over those who declare all this kind of stuff is "God's Word"--and have no other explanation for it.

I can understand how you might be disturbed at my style in writing, but I try to make it obvious that this is one way for people to get a better understanding of the Bible.

It is because I believe God's Word is in the Bible that I want people to know how to find it--and that's by treating the Bible realistically. The Bible is a great story of faith, but we don't have to tell that story in the same terms those a thousand years B.C. did.

Men wrote the Bible. I believe most of them were inspired by God; but that does not mean their concept of God was perfect--or that he dictated what they wrote.

I invite you to point out one thing I have said about the Bible which is not true. I can be corrected.

161

The Bible Says...

By Floyd Hale

Question: Did Jesus actually tell his disciples that one of them was a Devil?

Answer: In the Gospel of Mark (8:33) Jesus addressed Peter figuratively as Satan. That was because of the satanic temptation Peter was unwittingly laying on Jesus, to not go all out by exposing himself to the authorities in Jerusalem (Mk. 8:33). But in another place he actually tells his disciples, right at the start, one of them is a Devil. "Jesus said this" in John (6:70), but that is not Jesus speaking. That is the Fourth Gospel's way of telling the "Story of Jesus" to make it express the author's own "Doctrine of Christ."

The Gospel of John is not just another Gospel. It is more of a historic novel, where a historical character is given all kinds of characteristic actions and sayings to produce the author's own "novel" effect. By the time John wrote, the Church had fully accepted Paul's gospel about Jesus, which made him into a heavenly personage who came to earth to die to save people from their sins.

It doesn't take a Bible scholar to see that the Jesus in John is nothing like the humble son of man of the first three Gospels.

Since Jesus had been eternally with God--actually was God (according to John)--he walked the earth "knowing everything." He knew all about Nathanael as they first met (1:47). He knew how many ex-husbands the Samaritan woman at the well had--and that she was living with a possible sixth one (4:18). He knew all men and what was in them (2:25). He knew who of his followers would not believe and who would betray him (6:64). At the Last Supper he repeats that he knows who will hand him over, and tells Judas, "Go ahead and get it over with" (13:11).

Yet when people tell what Jesus was like, they almost always quote from John, for therein Jesus "describes himself" (the way we like him--none of that radical discipleship in Matthew, Mark and Luke). He succeeded in his purpose--giving Paul's gospel a Gospel form--but little did he suspect that his and the other three would all appear side by side in the Bible--and all be claimed later as "literally true."

162

The Bible Says...

By Floyd Hale

Question: Did Jesus institute the Lord's Supper in his own memory?

Answer: Jesus was down on religious ceremonies; they soon become a substitute for what they symbolized--as "the bread and wine" did. Scholarly literary analysis point to the early Church as the originator of this Christian Feast, not Jesus.

The first meal of the Disciples together after Jesus' crucifixion (especially if it were days later) must have been a bonding experience for them. Their "table grace" surely would have included thanks for Jesus' giving his life. The customary meal for those away from home was dry "bread" and some cheap "wine" (easily carried with them), which would naturally make this a remembrance ritual--a Seder. To me the wording of Mt. 26:26 could easily have come from a "blood covenant" made by the Disciples to continue their following of the Master.

It was the custom of religious folk then and there to come together on the eve of their Sabbath Day--which began at sundown the day before. They first celebrated "around the table"--the closest kind of fellowship. The first Christians surely would have celebrated the death of their Leader. They might have made the "bread and wine" a separate part, at the beginning of the meal--a memorial. Putting sayings on the lips of Jesus which "belonged" there, was a custom of the first Christian prophets (preachers).

If this was a "Love Feast" Paul certainly didn't find any love in the way the Corinthians went about it (Cor. 11:17-34).

When the Lord's Supper became the primary "means of grace" it really lost Jesus' blessing. "Hocus-pocus" is a loose pronunciation of the Latin words, "This is my body," recited by the priest in the dedication of the "Elements," at which time they became the actual "body and blood" of Jesus.

The Protestants haven't done much better in their serving "Holy Communion" ("to your comfort"?). It emotionally deceives people into to "receiving Jesus" as the sacrifice for their sins; replacing their sacrificial witnessing to him as Lord.

I'll no longer serve it-- nor receive it.

163

The Bible Says...

By Floyd Hale

Question: Why did the Apostle Paul say some of the Christians at Corinth were becoming ill and dying because they were eating the Lord's Supper in the wrong manner?

Answer: This is very puzzling. I'd like to think the author of the last verses of Mark's Gospel (in the KJV) inserted this scathing rebuke into Paul's letter also (I Cor. 11:17-34).

This raises some very serious questions. Unless they took Communion the wrong way intentionally how could they be guilty of such a crime? Paul could get pretty nasty, but this doesn't seem like him at all. He never says he instructed them on how to do it. (In all his correspondence with the other Churches Paul never mentions the Lord's Supper.)

Did he really believe that some of the illnesses and deaths among them were the results of their "eating the bread or drinking the cup of the Lord in an unworthily manner?" Pardon my language, but this seems like pure voodoo to me.

Paul says what they were doing wrong was leaving love out of their "Love Feast." It was a potluck meal but each ate out of his own pot (and drank out of his own bottle), and the poor brought no pot (nor bottle). Paul said (and I paraphrase verse 20), "If this is the Lord's Supper, He sure wasn't invited."

The Christians got together on the first day of the week, which began on the evening before. This was a time of "feasting." A meal together was a very bonding experience--the total acceptance of each other. Paul founded this Church, and I can't imagine it getting this far off track. If it had been then like it is now, the poor wouldn't even have been there to get slighted.

The word "unworthily" (a bad choice of word by the translators) has registered fear in some humble people who will not take communion because they don't feel they are good enough. Back when I served Communion, I told those people (if any of them were present) that this meal was for the unworthy. I not only don't serve it any more, I don't take it. You'll probably say this will get Paul's whammy put on me.

164

The Bible Says...

By Floyd Hale

Question: Was Jesus foretold by the Old Testament prophets?

Answer: The first Christians were Jews, and therefore very "scriptural" in their views. This meant they were forced (they thought) to prove every aspect of their new Faith was "Biblical"--a product of, or foretold in the old Faith. Since they proclaimed that Jesus was the Messiah (Christ) they had to show (they thought) how he--and just about everything about him--had been foretold in their Scriptures (our Old Testament).

Matthew's Gospel is a good place to see how this way of treating the Scriptures is obsolete. Look in Matthew at the "fulfilled prophecies" about Jesus' birth, why he was taken to Egypt as an infant (he wasn't actually), brought back out of Egypt (thus could not have been), grew up in Nazareth, introduced by John, taught in parables, rode into Jerusalem (on two donkeys), rejected, arrested, and betrayed by Judas.

And then when you look at the "prophecies" quoted as foretelling all that, you can see that *none of them fit.* The second one mentioned above, and it is typical of all,

quotes from Hosea 11. It is obvious Hosea is talking about Israel, "God's son," whom He brought out of Egypt (in the Exodus). To say that this passage has a hidden and second meaning, applied to a later time, is to further practice this old erroneous way of interpreting the Scriptures, called "midrash."

In the first place Jesus did not have to be foretold by Scripture. All he needs is to be understood for what he so courageously said and did. So much of our traditional "faith" has been based on fulfilled prophecies about Jesus instead of just "believing" Jesus was right.

When all the creeds "about Jesus" are cleared away, and he is left standing tall as a revealer of God's love snd will, then we are getting to the roots of our faith.

But I have to add, in prophetic sarcasm, it might be to evade the clear challenge of Jesus that we have perpetuated the ancient practice of Biblicism, which ends up replacing God's Word with what "the Bible says."

The Bible Says...

By Floyd Hale

Question: What is sin?

Answer: There is no end that could be made of a list of "sins." But however scriptural that list, the sin which is the mother of all other sins could yet be missed.

Jesus answered this question indirectly by recommending obeying the "first" commandment, "Love God with all your heart, soul, mind and strength." To break this commandment would therefore be the "greatest sin"--I would think. But this left a loophole for the righteous folk, who believed this commandment could be kept by "doing nothing wrong"--not sinning, so Jesus very cleverly explained this commandment with a "second" one--*like the first* (Jesus had a way of bringing religion down to earth): "Love your neighbor as yourself." Simply stated then, not loving others is *not caring.* Love that does not care is not love.

Not caring is a "sin of omission," which makes it indefinable. It is easy to Love God ("in your heart") and remain inactive. But loving one's neighbor requires doing something--according to Jesus. He illustrated keeping this commandment of "caring" by telling about the Samaritan who did for the victim by the roadside exactly what he would have wanted done for himself. (The key word in that story is "compassion".) Religion can get in the way of what it is really all about.

There was nothing "religious" in what that Samaritan did, yet without even knowing it he kept the "great commandment" (Lu.10:25f). Samaritans were considered bad sinners by those to whom Jesus told this story.

Jesus told another story about some folks who "cared" for their needy neighbors, and were surprised on "Judgment Day" that they were "righteous" (Mt. 25:31f). Jesus said "treating others like you want to be treated sums up all the Scriptures" (Mt. 22:40). That takes in all of them about sin.

Why should we concentrate so much on all those awful sins of the sinners, and pay no attention to the main one which is so easily committed by religious folk, that of "being good"--for nothing?

166

The Bible Says...

By Floyd Hale

Question: Did Paul and Jesus preach the same Gospel?

Answer: Jesus preached the gospel of the Kingdom (Rule) of God--"God IS in charge." Paul preached a gospel about Jesus--"He died so God could forgive our sins." There is a lot of difference between the two.

Jesus *taught* a lot about the "kingdom of God"--how God rules, but he never *preached* "about it"--he preached "IT." That is, he proclaimed the kingdom (rule) of God TO BE--right then--always (Mr. 1:14,15). He called on people to believe in his gospel, which was to live "as though" God were in charge. "Believing IN" meant doing God's will in the world--that the world might be saved. Paul asked sinners to "have faith in Jesus Christ as their Savior"--for their own salvation.

"God is in charge" was "good news" to those who were not in charge (of anything)--and that was about ninety percent of the people at that time. But it was "bad news" to those in charge--the few who were running the traditional religion and government-- and to be rid of his message they had to get rid of the messenger.

It was obvious to his followers Jesus' death was sacrificial, for his life was lived that way, and so it was given a Levitical interpretation. Paul--who "never met Jesus personally" (and was rejected by the Jerusalem disciples), made "Christ's atonement for sin" the theme of his message. Because of this--and Paul's evangelistic zeal--his gospel gained a vast number of converts across the Roman Empire. Thus his missionary work and writings established the "doctrines" of the newly forming Church--of which we are direct descendants.

The last Gospel written, John, gave Paul's gospel a Gospel form (it's not a biography of Jesus).

This difference in Jesus' and Paul's gospels should be looked into, but chances are it won't be--the main reason being we (like those of old) like Paul's gospel better than Jesus'.

Traditional theologians have gone to great length working that gospel into the doctrines of the Church, while ignoring Jesus' gospel.

The Bible Says...

By Floyd Hale

Question: Has the persecution of the Jews been because they crucified Jesus?

Answer: In Matthew 27:25, following Pilate's ceremonial washing his hands of the blood of Jesus, it says, "All the people answered, 'His blood be on us and our children'." By edict the Roman Church has held the Jews guilty of Diocide ("God-killers") up until after World War II. This "scripture" helped justify centuries of anti-Semitism. It condoned or ignored their abuse, including the death of six million by the Nazis in modern times. What a shame.

Then why is it in the Bible? Here is where an understanding of Bible background, a knowledge of why and how the Bible documents were originally written, becomes so important. When Matthew wrote, the Jews were making it hard on the Christians-- who were just breaking away as a sect of Judaism, claiming to be the "true Israel." Their boast was they had accepted Christ (the promised Messiah), whom "the Jews" had rejected and condemned to death. You can understand the bitter feud that went on, causing Matthew to place this statement (Mt. 27:25) on the lips of those rallying for Jesus' execution.

It ought to be obvious that the statement is spurious. It would have been insinuating their guilt for them to have said "and upon our children." It is obvious those words were phrased by a Christian years later to justify treating the "children" vengefully.

Even if some of "the Jews" had said this at Jesus' crucifixion, that does not mean its consequences had God's blessing. Before any passage in the Bible is taken as the Word of God, it should be run by the spirit and mind of Jesus for scrutiny. (He is quoted as saying, "Forgive them.")

The last Gospel written, John, is highly anti-Semitic.

Just because something is "scripture" does not mean it has the authority of God back of it. The hard drive to establish and defend Bible morality has unwittingly produced a form of idolatry known as Biblicism. This confuses and distorts the open search for God's Truth in the Bible.

168

The Bible Says...

By Floyd Hale

Question: How many times are the nations destroyed in Revelation?

Answer: A third of the world's population was killed in the 9th chapter, but the two big wipeouts come in chapters 19-21.

At the last Jesus returns and "smites the nations" (with a sharp sword which issues from his mouth?), and rules them for a thousand years. But the casualties of that "battle" are described as being not only the armies and their kings, but "all mankind" (19:18). (Who was left to be ruled?)

After this Satan is allowed to gather the nations (what nations?) together for an attack on the Jesus people--one more "last time." They make it right up to the camp of the saints, but no fighting takes place--not even Jesus with his sword this time. Fire falls from heaven and consumes them all. Then comes the "resurrection" (the second one, I should say).

You'd think Judgment Day would be the "end" of things here on earth, but in the final chapter the "nations of the world" (still doing business) are to be "renewed" by a "healing ministry" (21:5 and 22:2) administered by the people of a "heavenly" City--which has come to earth.

My effort here is not to explain all this, for there's not space--and it could be taken as "just one more preacher's opinion." I want my readers to gain an understanding for themselves of the apocalyptic literary writing form used in the Bible--and it can be easily done. The main problem is unlearning one's traditional view of Revelation's "end-of-the-world-ism."

This book is a good place to begin, for it is a formal Apocalypse, and it addresses something going on in history right at the time (and would get worse). Then one is able to move into the Gospels, where Jesus is portrayed mainly as the apocalyptic "Son of Man." Since it is this apocalyptic Messiah who is "resurrected, ascended, and to return," this has a different meaning than the one the Church "literally" laid on Jesus.

If this seems to be very far out, it is only because it has so long been totally neglected. Why?

The Bible Says...

By Floyd Hale

Question: If the Old Testament is not a religious law for Christians, why do we have it in our Bible?

Answer: I'm glad you asked this question, for it is troubling to a lot of people who have no way of finding the correct answer.

The Jews called the first five books of their Scriptures the "Law." This volume was written (ca. 500 B.C.) for the Israelites in Babylonian Captivity, to tell "the story of the people of the law of Moses," so that, by keeping the sacred traditions of their ancestors recorded therein, they would know and preserve their identity-- "in a foreign land." They were promised that if they did this their "holy land" would be returned to them (which--they were also told--was taken away from them because they had not kept these "laws of God").

Ezra brought these five scrolls, called "Torah" ("The Teachings"), back from Babylon (ca. 400 B.C.) and got the people of Jerusalem to adopt them as "God's law"-- mainly to have "Scripture" for running all the non-Jews out of town. (That today would be called "ethnic cleansing.")

This became the first Jewish Bible. Many of the Jews would never thereafter accept anything (the "Prophets" and the "Writings") as Holy Writ.

The Church, at first being Jewish, inherited all this as its Scriptures for all purposes of "faith and practice." But when the Christian writings soon came to be used more than their "Bible," there was a move on out in the Gentile Churches to canonize these into a "New Bible" to replace the "Old" one. You can imagine how this went over with the oldtimers but it should have been done--keeping the Old Testament as resource material only.

But the New Testament is not "religious law."

I could go on--and people in the Church ought to be taught all this--and a lot more about their Bible--but in the meantime the Fundamentalists, by declaring the whole Bible is "God's Word," perpetuate the confusion inherent in your question.

The Fundamentalists have done the same thing to our New Testament the Jews did to their Torah--made it into "Law."

170

The Bible Says...

By Floyd Hale

Question: Why does the book of Acts have so much about Paul in it and so little about the other apostles?

Answer: This is because by the time Acts was written the Church was strictly a "Pauline" institution far out in Europe. (The "tradition" that Peter went to Rome after Paul was martyred there, is an unlikely story, made up to support the later claim that Rome was the seat of Christ's first "vicar" of the Church.)

The other fanciful traditions about the Disciples going out as "apostles" to establish Christ's Church in far places are also apocryphal. The only report of any of them getting outside Jerusalem was to try to counter Paul's liberal ("heretical") teaching in Antioch and Galatia. Paul, who had never been with Jesus personally, was rejected by the Disciples and told, in so many words, to "go to the Gentiles." The author of Acts tries to put a good face on this rift.

It was Paul's extensive missionary work in the "West" which actually founded the "Christian Church." And that was not on the teachings of Jesus; it was on his own teaching that God had sent Jesus to earth from heaven to die for the sins of the world--and salvation was only by faith in him. Later on (when "resurrection" got questioned) he added that Christians must also believe that Jesus rose from the dead or they'd still be "in their sins."

It would be most interesting to know exactly what those other "apostles" believed. It couldn't be much other than what Jesus taught them in the first three Gospels (when these are rightly analyzed). The Fourth Gospel and the Epistles bearing some of their names were composed after their death, and all bear Pauline flavor.

I have said many times in various ways in this column, Christianity will become Christian when its primary emphasis is on the teachings of Jesus and not on the doctrines of Paul. But the Pauline "gospel" is so deeply embedded in the whole litany and hymnology of the Church that it can come about only in a world crisis which makes it "necessary."

171

The Bible Says...

By Floyd Hale

Question: According to Acts 16:30-31, what must one do to be saved?

Answer: You have answered your question in the asking: "Believe in the Lord Jesus, and you will be saved, you and your household." But like any other religious subject, "salvation" doesn't always mean the same thing throughout the Bible. Neither is lining up all the passages where it is mentioned, forming one "doctrine," true to what the Bible says. This can also miss the central truth.

To the great O.T. prophets--and to Jesus-- "God's salvation" was a condition of "community" (nation--or the whole world) in which God's children could exercise the rights and privileges He intended for them in the beginning. This would complete His "Creation"--and not until then.

The words "justice" and "righteousness" are the same word in the Hebrew language. But the less hope there was in Israel's becoming a just society, the more individual righteousness got promoted. Paul took this kind of righteousness out into the Gentile world--where Gnosticism had conditioned people to want to be "saved from this world" in order to go "up above" (from whence their "spirits" had originally come). He told them "righteousness" was the way--through faith in Christ.

Paul could not "find salvation" the Jewish way. He found it in what he believed was Jesus' atonement for sin. That experience of God's free gift of "grace" (nothing Paul could do to deserve or receive it) was so overwhelming he thought God had changed. But God had always been gracious; the Law made it hard to find.

Regardless of what Acts 16:31 says, Jesus did not teach that God's grace came through him or his death, but from God's unconditional acceptance of everyone (Mt. 5:45). Jesus wanted people not to get hung up on "getting saved," but "losing themselves" in helping God save the world.

Christianity has been pretty fast on "being righteous," but rather slow on working for "what's right." And the world hasn't been saved yet.

LETTERS TO THE EDITOR

To the Editor:

"The Bible Says" reads like a funnybook. Hale's answer to the question, "Where is Hell" comes across to me like he doesn't believe there is a place for the departed spirits of mankind to go after they leave this sphere of existence.

The Bible, a Greek word meaning a collection of scrolls, books, or scriptures reveals to me 29 verses describing a place for the unjust to go. This place was called hell, etc., etc.

There were twenty five verses that described a place for the just to go. This was called heaven, third heaven or paradise. That was enough to convince me the spirit that vacates its body goes somewhere, and it was not to some valley in Israel.

If Mr. Hale is correct in his column "How did the Bible begin?", he destroys the law of mercy and justice, not to mention all hope of salvation in heaven. He suggests the Bible is a hoax perpetrated by a prophetic party in the 8th century that went underground and drew up some lengthy document of laws in the name of Moses, then conveniently had them found in the temple.

He completely discredits the Bible by suggesting that Jewish priests, while in captivity, wrote Genesis, Exodus, Leviticus and Numbers and attached them to Deuteronomy.

If this is true, Christians can put their money in the bank, forget their belief in God, and drive down to Shawneetown and party.

A Reader

The Bible Says...

By Floyd Hale

Question: Could Jesus have been born in Nazareth?

Answer: He not only could have been, he was, I believe.

All the scripture references to Jesus' birth are in the two Nativity Stories--in Matthew and Luke. You don't treat "stories" as factual, for that fouls up their meaning. These two birth stories--written about fifty years after Jesus' death--teach something about the unique person he was. Treating them as true literally, not only misses what they teach, but it gives rise to false doctrine.

Jesus was looked upon by some as the Messiah, and the popular view of "Messiah" at the time was that he would restore Israel to its once great Davidic Kingdom status. Anyone accomplishing that feat-- even if he were not a Jew-- would be acclaimed as another ("son of") David.

This Messianic claim was incorporated into these two Birth Stories by having Jesus born "in the city of David"-- Bethlehem. Micah 5:2 is a poetic remembrance of King David, stated to inspire hope in the "restoration." And it ought to be obvious that Jesus was not the Son of David Messiah, for he did not "sit on the throne of his father David."

In one Gospel, Joseph and Mary live in Bethlehem (in a "house"), and take up residence in Nazareth only because it's not safe for the "child" to remain in Judea. In the other, Joseph and Mary go to Bethlehem so Jesus can be born there. Not only was Jesus about ten years old when this "enrollment" took place, the Romans never required the immigrants ("over the whole world") to return to their ancestral origins to be taxed.

Being Myths (which is a very legitimate literary form) the two accounts can not (and should not) be harmonized into one statistical report. One stresses the kingly Lordship of the bold Galilean, and the other the humanness of the humble Son of man. They celebrate *why* Jesus was born, not explain *where* or *how*.

I think it is sad that the beautiful Christmas extravaganzas every year about the "baby Jesus" start our children off on a false view of the Bible?

The Bible Says...

By Floyd Hale

Question: Was Martin Luther King, Jr. "foretold" in the Scriptures?

Answer: Dr. King gave a much remembered speech, "I have a dream (all racial discrimination will one day end)." On his tomb stone in Atlanta, Georgia is inscribed the words of Genesis 37:19-20, "Here comes this dreamer. Come now, let us kill him. . . and we shall see what becomes of his dreams."

If Martin Luther King had lived and died in Jesus' day, this could well have been quoted as "prophesying" him and his mission. But it is actually in a story about the boy Joseph dreaming that his eleven brothers would all bow down to him, and he would rule over them. This made them conspire to kill him, which they did (according to the story).

When you think of the Scriptures promoting justice and human rights--which they do, and Dr. King's inspiration coming from the Bible--which it did, you could in a real sense say his work was "prophesied." But to say this passage in Genesis "foretold that," would be midrashing the Scriptures. Midrashing was the "Rabbinical" way of (mis)interpreting a passage to make it prove something or other as "scriptural."

The early Christians did this to many Old Testament passages to make them "foretell" Jesus and his ministry--even his coming back to life. Jesus was the embodiment of everything good and redemptive in their Scriptures, and this is mainly what they were saying. But none of the passages cited were written with the man Jesus in mind (even the "young lady's child" in Isaiah 7:14 was to be named "Immanuel").

I think the writers of the New Testament can be excused for this--if we understand why they did it--without this suggesting they were fostering a hoax on the world. After the most critical analysis is made of the Gospels, I believe God's will is clearly seen in the life, teachings and death of Jesus of Nazareth--for those who can stand to know God's will.

Dr. King was one of those who knew God's will and certainly dared to do it. He was not "prophesied," but he certainly was a "prophet."

174

The Bible Says...

By Floyd Hale

Question: Why are the Israelites called Jews later on in the Bible?

Answer: In the 8th century B.C. the Northern Kingdom (which retained the title "Israel") fell to the Assyrians. Those "tribes" were never heard of again. Over a century later the Southern Kingdom (made up mainly of the tribe of Judah) was taken captive by the Babylonians (having taken the world away from the Assyrians). Being more tolerant of captives, the Babylonians let the Judeans remain a "colony" in Babylon. That being a prosperous place, many of the them never returned to Judea when allowed to. It was these exiles who put the first Jewish "Bible" together.

The title "Judean" was shortened by the Babylonians to its first syllable, "Ju," and laid on them as a put-down nickname. (Calling the Japanese "Japs" during World War II was sure not to praise them any.) Thus the name "Ju", spelled "Jew" in the English Bible, and it stuck. In most places today this name is yet used in not exactly a complementary fashion by non-Jews. Citizens of present Israel refer to themselves as "Israelis."

The modern Zionist movement, in its determination to retake their "homeland"(?), renamed it "Israel," claiming it to be rightfully theirs from the beginning (or before). "Israel," you know, was Jacob's name after God decided (?) to make of him a great nation. This name (and not "Judea") would be the umbrella under which all the Jews in Diaspora (dispersion)--even "the lost tribes"--might again gather (return).

Speaking of nicknames, did you know the title "Methodist"--and even "Christian"--were at first nicknames. The students at Oxford chided John Wesley's holy club there for being "methodical" in its pious activities, and it stuck. John detested the name for years, then for a while would refer to his following as "the people called Methodist." He finally just dropped "the people called" part.

At Antioch those who lived Jesus' "way" were derided as "Christ imitators" (Acts 11:26). The name stuck, but the imitating has dropped off.

175

The Bible Says...

By Floyd Hale

Question: Was the Apostle Paul mistaken about Adam being the first man?

Answer: Paul could have spoken of Adam figuratively as the "first man"--as the representative of humankind, for he didn't take scripture as literally as the literalists do today. But all indications are he really believed Adam was the father of all humanity.

That Paul mentions Adam as the "first man" does not help prove the Garden of Eden story is true. It only adds to the volume of similar problems in our Bible literature that need critical attention. By "critical" I mean the same kind of wise scrutiny all other valuable documents undergo--as to when, where, why, by whom, and especially in what literary form each piece was written. This should not be feared by people of faith--it should be demanded. For this is the way the great truths in the Bible are discovered and winnowed from the chaff.

Paul found in the Adam and Eve story the answers to two theological questions which plagued him (and a lot of other people): where did this damnable and mysterious stuff called sin come from?, and why must people die? His "Bible said"-- by editing Gen. 2:15-3:24 just a little--sin came into the world through this first man, and death resulted from his sin (Rom. 5:12, I Cor. 15:22). I have to say this is just not so.

Here a midrashed "scripture" in the Old Testament contributed to a further misunderstood "scripture" in the New Testament. The story of creation (Genesis 2:4b-3:24) is a "story"--properly called a *literary* Myth. Treating it as literally true Paul unwittingly created a *real* myth. This tells us (if we have ears to hear) we need to know a whole lot more about how to understand our "Scriptures."

This is not the effort of a smart-aleck preacher to destroy the Scriptures, nor the faith of believers. It is a bold attempt to get those who know I am right to do something about it in their respective groups. Error is a crack in the kingdom structure--and cracks get bigger in time.

176

The Bible Says...

By Floyd Hale

Question: Who was Melchizedek?

Answer: The author of the book of Hebrews uses about six chapters of his thesis ("Christ is better than any and all things Jewish") to explain Jesus was "better than" the Jewish priesthood (4:14-10:18). In it he repeats a number of times from Psalm 110:4b, "You (Jesus) are a priest for ever after the order of Melchizedek." This was to claim Jesus' priesthood was before--thus superior to--the first Israelite order of priests.

Abraham (returning from slaughtering a bunch of kings) was "blessed" by this king of (Jeru)Salem. He was a priest of "God the Most High" (a Canaanite ?). This pagan priest passed the plate and Abe put in a tenth of all his portable estate (Gen. 14:17-20). This legend (trying to push tithing back before Moses to the "father of their Faith") held a place in Israelite lore, and a Psalmists incorporated it into one of his Royal Hymns (110).

This is the most quoted Psalm in the New Testament, because of its messianic coloring. It was composed in the Post-Exilic period when the hopes were strong for a king, ("anointed of God") who would rise up and restore the kingdom of Israel. In this hymn "the Lord (God) promises that the Psalmist's Lord" (this dreamed of king), would trample his enemies underfoot and rule over them, in a very violent fashion.

At the time of this writing, the people were ruled over by priests, and this promised king would also fill that role--on the ancient order of the one who blessed Abraham.

By midrashing Psalm 110, misquoting Psalm 40, and going through a lot of other linguistic contortions, the author of Hebrews lays all these on Jesus--as "scriptural types."

Ignoring what is actually said of Melchizedek this "proves" Jesus was God's "perfect" blood sacrifice for sin--the blood of the priest himself being the offering.

This is a good illustration of how twisting scripture out of socket to make it support a preconceived conclusion can end up including something rather unorthodox. In putting the Jewish priesthood down a Canaanite priest is made the perfect type of Jesus.

The Bible Says...

By Floyd Hale

Question: What power did Jesus give up when He came to earth?

Answer: All kinds of "scriptures" can be quoted to show that Jesus was Divine and laid aside all prerogative (power?) as God's equal, to come to earth and die on a cross in the form of a man (Phil 2:7-8 etc). But all this-- and much more about the person of Jesus--is "faith language" which evolved in the New Testament Church as a result of Jesus' great life and martyrdom.

Taking all this literally led to major controversy in the 2nd and 3rd centuries in the Church, over whether Jesus was "man" or "God." When Constantine became emperor (A.D. 323) he saw the fast-growing Christian Faith as the unifier of his crumbling Roman Empire; so he called all the church leaders ("bishops") together at Nicaea (in 325, to what has been called the First General Church Council) and coerced them to "get their Faith together." After days of heated wrangling the majority finally compromised by agreeing (in essence) that Jesus was both God and man. The few who abstained were banished into exile and the Emperor received Christian baptism (the first one to do so). This resulted in the Nicene Creed and the Roman Catholic ("One") Church

Instead of solving the problem, it made this issue more confusing, for Jesus could not have been "fully human" and "fully divine"-- but that's about where we stand today. The "fully divine" folks run the show and the "fully human" folks have to keep their minds (and mouths) closed.

The only "power" Jesus ever had was the soul-power of his godly compassion and courage. This caused his followers to conclude he was "anointed of God." (The word "anoint" was pronounced "messiah" in their language, and this led to his title, "Christ.") One of the many evidences that he was "fully human" was his requirement that his disciples "follow" him--live his way. A human being can not imitate a god.

The "power" (the Greek word "dunamis" from which our word "dynamite" comes) in Jesus was the combination of his Gospel, "God is in charge," and his courageous living that way totally.

178

The Bible Says...

By Floyd Hale

Question: Are there priests mentioned in the New Testament Church?

Answer: According to my Strong's Concordance the word "priests" (where it applies to believers) appears three times in the New Testament--all three in Revelation 1:6, 5:10 and 20:6. But these have an apocalyptic interpretation (which I don't have space to get into here), and they really don't apply directly to the "New Testament church."

The above passages do affirm something very important in the Christian Faith--the "priesthood of all believers." This not only means that believers may (and should) minister to each other's spiritual needs. And it also means that a believer does not have to go through anyone to God-- he/she has direct and open access to his/her heavenly Father.

Since Jesus taught this, why do we claim there is access only to God through him? Here Jesus and the writings the Christians later canonized as Scripture (the New Testament) don't agree. I have to agree with Jesus.

There are several reasons why Jesus became "our high priest." Being "sinners"

people feel they can not approach the Deity directly-- they must have an "advocate" to plead their cause.

Since the first Christians were conditioned by their Jewish traditions to believe a person could come before God only with a "blood offering," they soon saw Jesus as that "Lamb slain"-- his death allowed God to "forgive sins." How come Jesus didn't teach this? He was most concerned that none of his followers exercise (priestly) authority over the others.

This is why there were no "priests" in the Christian beginnings. Anti-priest feelings were much more pronounced later in the Protestant Reformation.

But calling a pastor a "priest" does not make him/her one. I think too much emphasis can be placed on this, making it an empty issue of words, titles and names. Calling a horseweed a rose doesn't make it smell like one.

The Bible Says...

By Floyd Hale

Question: Why did Abraham lie about his wife being his sister?

Answer: In his foreign travels Abraham (according to the story) was afraid some man might kill him to get his wife Sarah. So he convinced her that posing as his "sister" would be the best thing for her--because it would keep her dear husband alive. Sure enough, on one of their trips to Egypt her beauty (at age 65?) won her into the heart--and household--of the Pharaoh (Gen. 12:10-20). This seemed not to bother either Abraham or Sarah, but it did God, for he sent plagues on the estate of Pharaoh. It is rather odd that God was not displeased with Abraham's conniving, but with Pharaoh's philandering. It is odd also how the plagues revealed to Pharaoh that Sarah was Abraham's wife. Even odder yet is the pagan Pharaoh's having a better conscience than God's man Abe.

Those who have researched the literature of the Old Testament believe this tale was first told on Isaac and Rebekah (Gen. 26), and then later (during oral transmission) moved back onto the Father of all Faith. There is even another version of this brother-sister act in Gen. 20, but there Sarah is only half-sister. (I guess that made Abraham a half liar.)

Why did the authors of Genesis mix fiction in with history? There are lengthy answers to this, but the main one was to continually support current claims by inventing past promises.

You will notice running throughout these accounts that God gave the land of Canaan to Abraham and his descendants--long before the Exodus.

Abraham's son Ishmael by Sarah's despised maid Hagar accounts for the Arab nation--"a wild ass bunch whose hand shall be against every man" (16:12). The two nations which gave the Israelites the most trouble, Moab and Ammon, were (according to the story) founded by Lot's two sons by incest (Gen.19:37-38). This was an Israelite way of writing (rewriting) history.

All of this was good propaganda for the Jews, but it certainly is not the Word of God for us.

The Bible Says...

By Floyd Hale

Question: Where will I go when I die, if I have accepted Jesus as Savior and been baptized?

Answer: You'll go nowhere. Your body will "return to dust," but your "life" --what you have lived--will go on in life. It is a person's "life" and not his/her "ego self" that's immortal. It is the kingdom of God that goes on--right here in life. We finite mortals have the good privilege of contributing our "lives" to that great and holy enterprise. If we do this we won't have to worry about--even believe in--an afterlife.

It is our self-centeredness which causes us not to realize what our "life" is. Our "self" is not us; it is the temporary instrument given us to guide our "living."

Bringing the "hereafter" into this does one of two things. As figures of speech heaven and hell can help prick the mind open to go on quest of the meaning of "this life;" or cause the week-minded to fear or fantasize "another life"--and miss this one.

Religion, which was meant to help people discover the will of the Creator and do it (and thereby "know life"), also tempts good people to get their eyes on a world "above." But I have noticed those who yield to this temptation usually keep one eye firmly fixed on this world "down here," causing them to become somewhat cockeyed. This world is not a prison from which to escape. It is where the Creator's kingdom is "coming."

Jesus lived his life the most meaningful way possible, by giving himself unreservedly to the doing of his heavenly Father's will--in life--for the good of others. Because this took his whole life--mind, body and soul--he became the most immortal person who ever lived. History, I believe, attests to this; and the book of Revelation, when understood, explains this very clearly.

Instead of asking people to believe in him as Savior and be "saved," Jesus called them to "lose themselves" in helping him save the world. But he warned that if people tried to do this, they'd get into trouble with, of all people, the religious folks (Mt. 10:17).

LETTERS TO THE EDITOR

To the Editor:

Your decision to give an open editorial space to a person is your business and no doubt made to further the sale of your newspaper. However, I take exception to the truthfulness of the heading of one of your guest editors.

WHAT THE BIBLE SAYS is not "What the Bible says." It seems to be more the opinions of a modern critical "scholar" who neither believes the Bible nor the God of the Bible. It is outside the realm of sound Bible interpretation to take literal language and ascribe figurative meaning to it, or take figurative language and ascribe literal meaning to it.

The former seems to be the case of Mr. Hale in answering the question about "hell" and the miracle of the water turned to wine, and then later the case in answering the question about "pearly gates."

I find Mr. Hale's stab at humor in his article as insulting and demeaning to serious believers of the Bible. My question for him would be: "Do you believe the book we call the Bible to be the inspired word of God, and the only inspired word of God?"

I suggest you title this editorial space, "WHAT A MODERN THEOLOGICAL CRITIC BELIEVES ABOUT THE BIBLE." It would be far less misleading.

A local Pastor

0

LETTERS TO THE EDITOR

Dear D. (Editor):

My annual letter to the editor is coming a little early this year and without the renewal check, because I wanted to give you and Floyd Hale the benefit of my support, however slight that might be.

I was raised in the dogma of the Methodist Episcopal Church but my father also said that I should use my head for something other than a hat rack, and I have tried to do that even in matters of religion.

When in Bible classes at the ME Church in Bone Gap, Bert Walton could always count on me to take an opposing view point just for the sake of livening up the discussion.

I never read "The Bible Says" or "The Bible Speaks" columns until those attacks on Mr. Hale showed up in letters to the editor. Now I wish I had saved that February 9th issue. I believe controversy (in moderation) is both healthy and beneficial. It keeps the gray matter active and it is possible that an open minded person might become enlightened. Your detractors who want you to discontinue "The Bible Says," should consider that if it were not for differences of opinion there would be no Christianity and among Christians there would not be any Protestant Churches, let alone the plethora (of freedom) that we now enjoy.

If there is a hereafter and if there is any connection to events that transpire here on the planet we call Earth, you can imagine how Martin Luther, John Wesley, John Smith and all the other religious rebels view what is going on in the guise of religion. Just look at Bosnia (Christians vs Moslems), Ireland (Roman Catholics vs the Church of England) and Israel (Jews vs Arab Palestinians).

Why not Floyd Hale and the Fundamentalist right here in Edwards County? I like it. Keep the column. If it can't be "The Bible Says" perhaps it shouldn't be "The Bible Speaks" (another column in this paper) either. You know we must be politically correct or face the wrath of the California delegation of the ACLU.

I enjoy the letters to the editor but am saddened that so many are from widows-- perhaps the result of too much controversy?

An (out of town) Reader

p

The Bible Says...

By Floyd Hale

Question: Do human beings have an eternal soul?

Answer: Soul, spirit, mind, etc. are each terms used to describe a certain function of one's personality. They (however these terms may be played with by quoting what "the Bible says") along with the physical body, make up the "whole person" for the purpose of "living" in this world. It is one's life--what one lives--which never dies (it can't anyway).

When any of these human characteristics are singled out and treated as the "real self," the real self is missed--and so is life. For a "soul" to be eternal it would have to have been in existence from the beginning of time, for "eternity" goes backward as well as forward.

The Gnostics brought this idea into the Church. At birth a "spirit" (or "soul") from above (the spirit world) was caught and imprisoned in "this (evil) physical world"--in a "body of death." If it were "made alive from above" (born again), at death it would "escape" back to its "home" above. This made death liberating, adding to further misunderstanding of life.

To treat the human ego (the self-centered self) as though it were here only to prepare for another "life" can be a very religious way of missing life. Jesus called people to "find" the real purpose of living by giving ("losing") themselves in God's kingdom; and do this not to save oneself, but "use oneself" in getting God's will done. This takes one's "life"--lived out in society (where else do we live?). If one were to do this in the radical way Jesus did, it might literally "take his/her life"--as it did his. Those who talk of getting a reward for this in an "after life" are not using the words of Jesus. To get one's life given back later is not really to have given it.

Life as a whole, with all its sophisticated systems, is the result of all the "lives" which have been "lived" so far. If people saw this world as God's kingdom (which it is), and lived in it as Jesus taught, they would come to full maturity as human beings. And. . . this would be heaven on earth.

The Bible Says...

By Floyd Hale

Question: Did the animal sacrifices under the Law of Moses absolve sins?

Answer: No, even though "the Bible says" they did (Lev. 4:26, 31, etc.). And don't fall for the explanation that these sacrifices were the "type" of Jesus' blood, and that it was really "Christ" who worked in and through those sacrifices back then. The Israelites borrowed the custom of animal sacrifice from their neighbors--it was common superstition at the time. Their priests said their God Yahweh required them. If Moses had anything to do with it, it probably came from his father-in-law priest Jethro (who was certainly not an Israelite), who advised him in religious matters and offered animal sacrifices (Ex. 18:12).

At the death of Jesus God did not change his way of forgiving sins (or doing anything else). The forgiveness of sin has always been one of the blessings of God's free g r a c e - - w h i c h unconditionally covers everyone (whether they know it or not). To "discover" this is the essence of the traditional experience called "being saved." True "repentance" is the "change" caused by God's grace, not a condition met to receive it (Rom. 2:4).

It was in and through whatever influence of hearing about Jesus' sacrificial death that Paul finally "felt his sins forgiven." This was such a revolutionary experience in his faith that he went out and preached that it was "only in Christ one can be forgiven of his/her sins-- the old sacrificial ordinances involving animals were nailed to his cross." When Paul's writings became "Scripture" this was taken as "commanded by God." Jesus would be the first to rebel at this. Jesus taught that God "received sinners."

Not letting people know about the unconditional (thus amazing) grace of God is somewhat like the Temple priests' keeping God's forgiveness depending on those sacrifices to be brought in. (The priests got their share of those burnt-- "barbecued"--offerings, Lev. 6:26, 7:6, etc.)

Treating everything in the Bible as "God's truth" can get pretty confusing.

The Bible Says...

By Floyd Hale

Question: What references could one go to in history that refer to Jesus?

Answer: The historian Tacitus wrote (ca. 110) about Nero persecuting "Christians" in Rome, an indirect reference to Christ. The favorite historical reference to Jesus is by Josephus who mentions (XX.ix.1) the stoning of James "the brother of Jesus, the so-called Christ." The longer passage in Josephus (XVIII.iii.3) where he mentions Jesus as "This man was the Messiah," was certainly edited by Christian hands. There is a Slavonic version of Josephus' Wars (much edited by later Christian hands) which mentions Jesus in several places--even describing his personal appearance.

In the Babylonian Talmud (Sanh. 43a) there is a reference to "Jesus of Nazareth who was hanged for leading Israel astray." There's another reference or two to Jesus outside the New Testament (which I can't recall at the moment) but the only value of all these is "secular witnesses to the fact that Jesus actually lived." None of these "historians" ever met Jesus, and writing long after he was dead. None of them say anything about his life-- except that Pilate had him crucified. What they knew was mainly from Christian influence which was growing.

I believe Josephus' Wars is the only one of the above writings yet in existence. The other quotes from them about Jesus have been handed down in Christian literature.

The most rigid critical analysis of the New Testament Gospels does not even suggest that the main character of those books was the creation of the authors' imagination. No scholar today would claim that Jesus of Nazareth was not an historical person, nor that he was too much different than the Synoptic (first three) Gospels portray him.

This has nothing to do with proving what we know as traditional Christianity was founded by Jesus, for it bears little of the mark of the one in whose name it was established.

History really took no note of Jesus, but he has effected history as no other man. That little gem, "One Solitary Life," says it so well.

The Bible Says...

By Floyd Hale

Question: Did Jesus cleanse the temple at the beginning of his ministry, or at the end?

Answer: "The Bible says" both. John's Gospel puts it at the beginning (2:14); the first three Gospels at the end (e.g. Mt. 21:12). There is no way to reconcile these contradictory reports. But they need be explained,

All evidence indicates it came at the end, for it led directly to Jesus' arrest and death. Why then did John put it at the beginning? He wanted to end his "story of Christ" with something to climax his theme, "New Life." He is not just writing "another Gospel"; he's writing an historical novel in Gospel form (to "up-date" Jesus for the Greeks), which gives him the literary freedom to do this--and much more.

In John the final showdown in Jerusalem "with the Jews" is not the temple cleansing but the "raising of Lazarus." This perfect "sign" of New Life was the final threat to the religious hierarchy, and for which they decided to finally "destroy him" (11:53).

To show that they "killed the Life-Bringer" John (using his literary freedom) makes up this "story" about "the raising of Lazarus" in which he has Jesus saying, "I am the resurrection and the life." (If Jesus had actually performed a miracle like this, it most assuredly would not have been overlooked by the other Gospel writers.)

I have pointed out so many times in this column that the Gospel of John must be understood in keeping with its unique literary form. Taking it as another Gospel it has become the "Christian Gospel"-- replacing the gospel of Jesus, and most quoted when referring to Jesus. Until John is understood for what it is, "believing in Christ and being saved" (3:16; 20:31) will be central in the Christian Faith, rather than "doing God's will" according to Jesus' gospel, "the kingdom (rule) of God," ("God is in charge!"). The rest of the New Testament follows John's Gospel--and so do we.

But how can the true gospel of Jesus be believed and its *power* work in and through believers *when it is not proclaimed?*

The Bible Says...

By Floyd Hale

Question: Did Moses write the first five books in the Bible?

Answer: Even Jewish scholars no longer believe this is true. Its a little hard to see the author of a book describing his own burial (Deut. 34:6).

Why and *how* the Pentateuch ("five books"), written in the name of Moses, was composed in Babylonian Captivity in the 5th century B.C. is a most amazing, interesting and inspiring story. It molded the survivors of the Jewish nation into a "church state in exile" and created the first "Bible." That "Book" (adopted as "God's Law" ca 400 B.C., Neh. 8 and 9) organized Judaism into a formal religion and replaced God with its own "Divine Authority." This gave birth to "Biblicism," which is very much alive today in Judaism's stepchild, Christianity.

The "Story of the People of the Law" filled four scrolls (later called Genesis, Exodus, Leviticus and Numbers). The practice of these "traditions of their ancestors" in that volume would save their "holy race" for the future-- when they hoped God would return their homeland to them (and them to it).

Since He had "taken it away from them" because they had "not kept His Law," they took real interest (for the first time) in that Law. It centered in a book called Deuteronomy, composed by the prophetic party as "Mosiac," and decreed by King Josiah as "God's law for the nation," just one generation before they were shipped off to Babylon (II Kings. 22 and 23).

To compile that four scroll "story," the priesthood used many ancient and current, written and oral sources. This they prefaced onto the fifth scroll (Deuteronomy, much edited) and called it "Torah" ("teachings"). These sources consisted mainly of four blocks of material: a 9th century B.C. History of Judah (symbolized by "J"), an 8th century B.C. History of Israel ("E"), the Prophetic traditions ("D"), and the late Priestly traditions ("P"). It was the later which dominated this tremendous literary project.

To know something of how this all came about is necessary to understanding the whole Bible.

The Bible Says...

By Floyd Hale

Question: What evidence can you show that Moses did not write the first five books in the Bible which bear his name?

Answer: When the Bible literature was first taken seriously by the scholars, in the 19th century, many inconsistencies were found in the Pentateuch ("five books" of Moses), which indicated that it could not all have come from the same hand. I can point out here only a few examples.

In Genesis 1, man and woman are created at the same time and after the animals; in the next chapter (a whole different story) Adam is created first, then the animals--and then Eve. Regardless of all the double talk about the second story just adding details left out of the first one, Moses would not have directly contradicted himself.

Neither could he have described (in the last chapter of Deuteronomy) his own burial. The author of this last paragraph refers to Moses and what took place immediately after his demise in such a way that Moses could not be writing that.

I could go on and on pointing out hundreds of indisputable literary evidences that neither Moses nor any other one person could have written the whole Pentateuch. But this does not discount it as being a hoax.

Scholars have found at least four major, ancient and current, written and oral sources (called by the symbols "J," "E," "P," and "D,") the priesthood used in composing this five scroll "Torah" ("teachings") late in Israel's history. Knowing how--and more especially why they did this in exile in Babylon about. 500 B.C., would make this great document more of a source for faith, rather than a lengthy volume God dictated to Moses.

When a lot of other "scriptures" are quoted to prove Moses wrote these Five Books, this only further illustrates how *we need to know what our whole Bible really is.* As long as people are not educated on this important subject, some of them are left with the unreal but emotional problem, of either having to believe Moses wrote the Pentateuch, or the whole Bible was written by a bunch of liars to deceive people.

The Bible Says...

By Floyd Hale

Question: Why study "about" the Bible, and not just what's "in" the Bible?

Answer: There is a tremendous amount of information built up by Bible scholars "about" the Bible which is treated by the Church as "classified" (not for laypersons to see). Believe it or not, it is based mainly on what's "in" the Bible. The difference is it is analyzed open-mindedly and in light of other historical data.

If we did not have scholars to point out--and explain convincingly--that the story of Jonah was a parable written by some unnamed teacher in ca. 350 B.C., to counteract the strong anti-foreigner feelings of his people, we might take it literally to have been the product of an 8th century B.C. prophet, who spent three days and nights in the belly of a whale, and was later "angry unto death" because he was the most successful missionary-evangelist who ever lived.

If we did not have higher critics to point out that Revelation is an Apocalypse, written to inspire the persecuted Christians at the end of the 1st century to remain faithful unto death, we'd think it was a time table of the future--right down to the return of Christ and the end of the world.

We don't have to take the scholars' conclusions on things like this, but if we studied their findings, we would discover fact after fact which would lead us to our own better enlightened conclusions. And what's good in all this, we would find out two things: What the Bible really "says," and how to discern the Truth in it.

Quoting several "prooftexts" from the Scriptures doesn't teach one thing "about" the Bible--or much else actually. Until we get an education in Bible, we will be subject to the Fundamentalists, who, treating the Bible unrealistically, not only mess up its whole message, but are forceful--and successful--in scaring interested people away from learning the truth. We talk about the biblically illiterate. It's the Bible literalists who keep the Bible a hidden Book--from those who love it most.

LETTERS TO THE EDITOR

Editor:

Your paper's Saturday edition page 2 feature, "The Bible Says," raises a lot of people's eyebrows, among them ours.

Floyd Hale apparently classifies himself as one of those "modern Bible scholars in the know!" (Nov. 2, 1996 column). We see him as one who enjoys looking for myths and discrepancies, fabrications (by the early Christians) and raising doubts over prophecy, angels, miracles and even the resurrection of Jesus Christ from the dead.

He desires to straighten us out on what he decrees as errors, misconceptions and wrong interpretations he finds in the scriptures.

Throughout nearly 20 centuries there have been so-called enlightened minds trying to explain away the Bible, but God still speaks His Word through it, despite all the detractors. We affirm our Faith in the Living Word as He comes to us through His inspired Word--the bible.

We believe in the sure word of prophecy as the Bible reveals God's plans for the future; we believe in miracles, for they have occurred among us, even to the dead being restored to life, and we anticipate, as has the church throughout nearly 2,000 years, the coming of our Lord Jesus Christ to His earth again--in the fulness of time.

If an atheist would content himself with casting doubt on the Bible, we might understand that, but a minister of the gospel?

(This letter came in just before this paper stopped my articles. Signed by 29 members and the pastor of a small rural church.)

9

The Bible Says...

By Floyd Hale

Question: What was the "rock" Jesus promised to build his church upon?

Answer: Your question assumes that Jesus made the statement in Matt. 16:17-19 to this effect, but I am convinced he did not.

Matthew (as did Luke) used Mark's gospel as his primary source. He quotes Mark 8 almost verbatim up through v.29 where Peter confesses Jesus to be the Christ. Then instead of going ahead with Jesus telling the disciples to "tell no one this," he inserts something not in Mark (his own three verses 17-19). Jesus says (according to Matthew) he will build his church on this "rock"-- either Peter himself (his name meant "rock") or his confession about Jesus being the Messiah--or both if you like.

What follows this should make this saying very suspect, to say the least. Jesus says God had revealed this to Peter. And Peter is given the authority to make binding in heaven what he (Peter) binds on earth, and to loose in heaven whatever he looses on earth. This coming from Jesus?

Then after this blessing and charge, Matthew picks up (v.20) where he left off from Mark--Jesus telling them to tell no one he is the Messiah, for he is going up to Jerusalem and suffer rejection and death. Peter rebels against the very idea, and out of concern for his Lord says "God forbid!" Jesus sees this as the satanic temptation--not to go all the way in his mission--and tells Peter, "Get thee behind me Satan!" Just after he blesses Peter and credits him with speaking via revelation? Jesus commends him and calls him the Devil?

As in other places where Matthew inserts later traditions into Mark's older account, he leaves telltale literary blunders like this. This addition was certainly not simply to "round out the full story" sketched by Mark.

I could explain further how this statement in Mt. 16:17-19 is foreign to the text, but only to say: At the time Matthew wrote there was beginning to be a claim in Rome that Peter was the first "vicar of Christ" on earth. This interpolation was to support that popish tradition.

And too, Jesus did not found the church; Paul did.

The Bible Says...

By Floyd Hale

Question: Does Palestine rightfully belong to the Jews?

Answer: Up till now everywhere there has been one rule of ownership for any territory; it belongs to those who take it and hold it. If this were not the rule we would have to give "our Land" back to the Indians (who were not really Indians). This applies to Palestine also, in spite of the fact that the Old Testament (which the Jews wrote) says "God gave it to them." They took it from the Canaanites, the ancestors of the present Palestinians, by warfare-- which is an odd way for God to give somebody something.

It has been the Christian evangelists, in their preaching that the Jews are going to return to *their* Holy Land ("the Bible says so"), which conditioned the world to condone the establishment of the new nation of Israel in modern times. The Israelis have Christianity to thank for spreading their nationalistic Scriptures all over the world for eighteen centuries as "God's Word."

The Zionist ("Return") movement began in Babylon in the 5th century B.C. by the rewriting of all their previous history with two dominant and related themes: 1) God gave Palestine to them to begin with, and 2) He promised they would get it back (after the Babylonian Captivity). All this "editing" of their traditions was done before the "Five Books of Moses" became Scripture--in fact that document was the product of the Zionist movement, and became the first Bible--the "Law"--in ca. 400 B.C.

The present swing back to conservatism in the government of Israel is allowing the Orthodox Jews to keep taking over East Jerusalem (Palestinian territory). Some of this is being done ("legally") by individual purchases, financed by a wealthy Jewish physician in the United States. Jewish soldiers picket the project to make it work. If the poor Palestinians keep on selling, the wealthy Jews of the world could before long buy the whole West Bank. The Biblicists--Jewish or Christian--might say, "Jehovah works in mysterious ways, His wonders to perform."

1

190

The Bible Says...

By Floyd Hale

Question: What is "the ark of His covenant" in Rev.11:19?

Answer: The original ark of the covenant was lost. It was probably captured during one of the many Israelite wars. Since it's main purpose was to insure divine protection, it was carried into battle by designated priests. At the time it was a common practice of most armies to carry such a palladium--right up front.

In II Maccabees a popular belief is expressed that Jeremiah had safely hidden the ark in a cave (and sealed the cave), and its discovery would come at the time of the "restoration of Israel" (2:4-8).

The ark of the covenant John "sees" in his vision is the archetype of that ancient ark. He mentions it here because of its "protecting power," which he is promising to the Christians under persecution by the Roman government. That protection will not keep them from death, but if their faithfulness--recognizing ("worshiping") Christ and not the Emperor Domitian as "Lord"--leads them to martyrdom, that will be "victory" (as promised at the end of the "Seven Letters").

This "victory" is symbolized by their coming back to life--in a "special resurrection" (not the general one at the "end")--and ruling with the "returned Christ." This is the apocalyptic way of saying their faithfulness (even in death) will influence the world for God, as did Christ's.

Jesus never promised protection for those who did God's will. Jesus believed the kingdom (rule) of God in the world was worth the suffering--and even death-- of those who dared to live accordingly. (We believe this about our nation's security.) This is one of the many differences between the Christian and the ancient Hebrew Faith. Carrying a box into battle which was supposed to contain "God's presence" is just one of the many religious superstitions reported in the Old Testament. The story of the "ark of the covenant" is not to be taken seriously. A good way to see this is in it's being described all the way from a plain wooden chest (at the beginning) to an elaborate golden shrine (by the later priestly editors).

191

The Bible Says...

By Floyd Hale

Question: What happened to the religion that Jesus lived and taught? Is it on the earth today? Where can it be located? All of the other ways are started by man.

Answer: I recognized this as being the very same question(s) sent in to me (evidently by the same person) about eighteen years ago, when I was then writing this column in this same Evening News. (If I've changed my answer since then, will the one who sent this in please let me know?)

Jesus didn't start a new religion; he asked the religious people of his day to fulfill the original prophetic purpose of their religion-- *get God's will done in the world.* There was no doubt in His mind that this would save the world. (And would it not?) Jesus believed any flak caused in doing this would only help the cause--if it were humbly accepted (as a "cross").

As the result of his having made such a courageous effort to get God's will done himself--and teach others to--Jesus was rudely rejected by the religious community. Since he would not go away, they finally had him put away--but permanently (they thought). This caused his followers to do two things. They made the very highest claims possible for him as a person, within their religious traditions. And they, at grave risk, continued for a while to live his "way"--doing "what's right," even where doing "what's wrong" was the rule.

Jesus' death, willingly accepted by him, was spoken of as "sacrificial"--which it certainly was. A young very religious Pharisee picked up on this and made it the theme of his gospel out in the Gentile world (where he grew up), explaining that "sacrifice" as something "God had made for the sins of the world." Paul, a "man," thus (unwittingly) started a new religion, "Christianity." But it was a religion "about Jesus," not quite "Jesus' religion."

Jesus' religion can be located anywhere in the world God's will is being done--whether those doing it know it is God's will or not.

192

The Bible Says...

By Floyd Hale

Question: What does the Bible say about witches?

Answer: Kill 'em!

Black magic was considered the work of the Devil--and worked. When Jesus was accused of casting out evil spirits (a form of sorcery) "by Beelzebul," Jesus is supposed to have said this was an "unpardonable sin"--showing just how evil witchery was considered.

There are a number of shady practices including sorcery mentioned in the Bible which fall under the category of "witchcraft." Ancient cultures in the Middle East were shot through with all forms of voodooism. Because it was of the "old religion" of the territory it was to be completely eradicated. Its practice was punishable by death (Ex. 22:18).

Although men practiced witchcraft in the Old Testament, the sentence of death on the guilty mentioned in Exodus applied only to a "sorceress." Witches carry a feminine connotation, while the angels in the Bible are all male. Women who believe God wrote the Bible sure swallow a big lump.

They didn't quit killing witches when Christianity came along. In less than an hour 400 of these unfortunate women were once publicly burned in France. A French judge boasted that in his sixteen years on the bench he had sentenced some 800 of these women to the stake. Some authorities say thousands of witches were put to death by both the Catholic and Protestant churches between the 15th and 18th centuries-- all done where the Bible dominated civil law.

It took the heat of American decency to stop the Puritans--our "spiritual forefathers"--in the New England colonies from burning girls, wives and mothers accused of witchery.

Christians ought to be at work on a lay method of Bible reading whereby God's Word in the Scriptures could be separated from the chaff therein, instead of having to believe it was all "inspired by God"--from cover to cover. I don't think the average Christian is aware of where Fundamentalism is leading. One good way is to see what it is doing in other parts of the world in other religions.

The Bible Says...

By Floyd Hale

Question: After Jesus' birth did his parents take him to Egypt, or back to Nazareth?

Answer: According to what "the Bible says" they did both--and at the same time. In Matthew's Birth Story, Joseph (warned in a dream by an angel) whisked Mary and Jesus away to Egypt to escape Herod's merciless effort to kill the infant. In Luke's Story (the only other account of Jesus' birth) they take him a few days later--openly--to the temple in Jerusalem for his mother's ceremonial cleansing, and then back home to Nazareth (where I am convinced Jesus was born). Those who say each writer filled in what the other left out, is to ignore what these stories actually say. Isn't it odd that the Literalists often refuse to see what the Bible literally says.

Let the contradiction stand, and know that myths about the same thing do not have to agree. The whole thing of getting Jesus born in Bethlehem was to add support to the claim (made years after Jesus was dead) that he was the "son of David." By midrashing Micah 5:2 Matthew makes it "prophesy" this, but that text was about David himself--a poetic harking back to his rise in power.

Matthew casts Jesus in the role of the "giver of the new Law"--another (but more superior) Moses. This is why he has Jesus being taken to Egypt--so he can come from there. Hosea 11:1 is midrashed to support this, but that poetic poem plainly speaks of Israel as "God's son" whom he called out of Egypt, about twelve centuries earlier.

I am in no way accusing Matthew and Luke of falsehood when I say these Stories are myths--Matthew and Luke both knew they were. Only when treated as myths can what they teach be seen--something very beautiful about Jesus.

When the myth about Jesus' birth is "quoted" in constructing creeds to be believed literally, damage is not only done to the facts, but superstition poisons faith.

Each of the four Gospels is a "Story of Jesus," told to portray the character the author has in mind. If these two "stories" at the entrances to them are not recognized as such, that character will be missed.

LETTERS TO THE EDITOR

Dear D. (Editor)

Enclosed is a check for another years's subscription to (your paper).

Surely the readers of your paper now understand what Mr. Hale has meant all along by his expression, "The Bible says."

In the last issue reaching Cincinnati he declared the Matthew and Luke accounts of Jesus' birth an "u n e x p l a i n a b l e contradiction."

I'm truly sorry for Mr. Hale, and I am sorry for you, dear friend D., as you give your silent approval to his words by continuing a column which he says is to help people to understand the Bible.

If any of the other readers of this newspaper wants an explanation of what Mr. Hale calls "u n e x p l a i n a b l e contradictions" of Matthew's and Luke's account of Jesus birth. please write to me and I'll explain how the two accounts do not contradict each other, but, being put together, actually give us within a few days the actual birth date of Jesus

A Pastor in Cincinnati

<u>Editors note</u>: I appreciate your letter, despite your promise to "write no more letters," several letters ago, I want you to have your say, but have taken out the parts of your letter where you state what Mr. Hale believes--let's let him speak for himself. Regarding the apparent conflict in the Matthew and Luke accounts of Jesus' birth, I'm disappointed you did not explain putting the two versions together in your letter of 300 words, the length of Hale's columns. You are a skilled writer and I know you can do it. Our readers would be interested, and so would I. Dialog is the best educational format. D.B.

r

LETTERS TO THE EDITOR

To the Editor:

In answer to Mr. Hale's "u n e x p l a i n a b l e Contradiction" between Matthew's and Luke's accounts of Jesus' birth.

Putting these two reports together gives a better understanding of the event.

1. Joseph and Mary make the trip to Bethlehem and Jesus is born there (told by Matthew and Luke).

2. The shepherds are told of the birth and went that very night to see him (told only in Luke).

3. The "wise men" from the East search for and find "The King of the Jews" (told by Matthew only).

4. The escape to Egypt (about 50 miles) to avoid Herod's plot to kill Jesus (told by Matthew alone)

5. The circumcision of the 8 day old Jesus, either on the road to or in Egypt (told by Luke).

6. The return from Egypt at Herod's death (in Matthew) and the ceremonial cleansing in Jerusalem forty days after Jesus' birth (in Luke). Luke did not say they went from Bethlehem to Jerusalem.

7. Joseph with Mary and Jesus, afraid to stay in Judea, go from there to Nazareth (as told in Matthew).

Thus the "unexplainable contradiction" is explained, and a more complete story, giving us more knowledge of the early days of our Blessed Savior, the Son of God."

A pastor
Cincinnati

Editor's note: I think it is obvious you simply rewote the two accounts into one story, instead of explaining the explicit contradictions between the two. Thanks for your try. D.B.

The Bible Says...

By Floyd Hale

Question: Did Jesus promise his disciples that they would know and teach his teachings inerrantly?

Answer: While Jesus was with them they seemed rather slow to catch on, primarily because his teachings were so different--and radical. To expect them to remember it all literally would seem a little much.

There is a reference in John's Gospel to Jesus telling his disciples "the Holy Spirit would bring to their remembrance all he had said to them" (14:26). This seems very much like the author--posing as the Disciple John--wants to claim that his Gospel is passing on the true teachings of Jesus, but when you understand the unique literary form of this Gospel you discover it does not contain Jesus' teachings (nor written by the disciple John).

Matthew, Mark and Luke all report that Jesus teachings centered on the theme of "the kingdom of God." Whereas in John Jesus teaches about himself as the Christ. This not just another Gospel--and there is no way to mix this Gospel up with the first three to "fill in what the others left out."

The only other place (I can think of right now) is where Jesus supposedly told his disciples "Teach people to observe all I have commanded you." This is much closer to what Jesus would have said (28:19-20).

To think that all the teachings of Jesus in our Gospels are strictly authentic is not quite true. That a few of them do not agree clearly tells us this. Then too, the authors of Matthew and John's Gospels were not among the original disciples of Jesus--not eyewitnesses to what he did and said. They take on these names to give them authority.

Anyway, Jesus' concern was not that his disciples be inerrant in doctrine, but that they "live his way"--and pass that on by example--that their influence might save--change--the world into a just and nonviolent society. To this cause he gave his life. Don't you think Jesus was right?

It becomes almost painful to come to this conclusion.

The Bible Says...

By Floyd Hale

Question: What is the purpose of Holy Communion?

Answer: Many take it because they believe it's the way to "receive Christ"--pure superstition. Some take it "in obedience to Jesus," thinking he instituted it as an ordinance in the Church--he didn't. Some take it for various sentimental reasons: it makes them "feel better," "closer to God," etc.--a substitute for real spiritual growth.

In the first place Jesus would not have prescribed a memorial ceremony honoring ("in remembrance of") himself. Neither would he have known it was actually his last meal with his disciples, etc. This is not just "liberal reasoning," for Literary (Form) Criticism reveals that Mark 14:22-24 was composed by the early Church and placed on the lips of Jesus--not to deceive but to provide a ritual used in "honoring Jesus."

Paul's account of this "supper" (I Corinthians 11:23-26) disagrees radically with Mark's in its wording. The early Christian traditions (Jesus' sayings, etc.) were often "reworded" before they were reduced to writing. This makes it rather easy for literary scholars to decipher back through a Gospel account to what was most likely said or done at the first.

I'd say the disciples, in their first "meeting together" after the crucifixion, "broke (crusty) bread and drank their (cheap) wine" (a complete meal away from home), not as a "remembrance" of Jesus' death (how could they forget that?), but as a *blood covenant* they entered to carry on his dangerous mission. It had nothing to do "symbolically" with their own "salvation," but with their discipleship.

In Palestine "salvation" had a community meaning and relevance. Out in the Greek world (where the Church first took shape) it applied strictly to the individual--there the "gospel" became "Jesus died for (individual) sinners." Then the "Supper" became the celebration of "Jesus as Savior." This subtle switch would not have been so bad if it had not replaced Jesus' real role as "Lord"--a leader to be followed.

The Bible Says...

By Floyd Hale

Question: What is basic in religion?

Answer: Jesus is good authority on this very important subject.

He did not teach Judaism, and he did not teach Christianity. In fact he did not teach "religion." He taught people they should love one another, and said all Scripture was a commentary on this (Mt. 7:12, where he restates this "basic rule" in different terms). Luke quotes Jesus as making this (loving others) the "law of life" (10:28).

You may say "loving God" is more basic. The people in Jesus' day believed this, but they religionized it into something which missed life. There is no shortage of religious folks who love God, but hate people. This is why Jesus (very shrewdly) made the "second commandment' explain the "first" one. He even said the way you love your self can be the guide.

If you think this rule of "loving others" lets you settle down into just being nice to those around you, you have missed the many ways self-love "works" itself out in all of life. One wants for others all the good things one wants for one's self. Every community condition you desire in which your freedom can be exercised is desired for the whole community. This is really the only way you--or your children (and their children)--can be free and secure. This is precisely what Jesus was saying in Luke 12:31. Loving (caring about others) is the building blocks of civilization--the kingdom of God.

If self-love is really love, it will give itself. God loves the world, and Jesus gave himself to save it. It is the world--the whole of society-- which is to be saved, not just a few individual souls rescued for "another world" (which is the product of fantasy anyway). We seem to think Jesus said "Do God's will so you can go to heaven," when he really said, "Get God's will done on earth as it is done in heaven."

The teachings of Jesus, and not man's teachings "about Jesus" (even though they are in the Bible) is what's basic in the Christian religion.

The Bible Says...

By Floyd Hale

Question: Will those who do not accept Christ go to Hell?

Answer: "Hell" is a figure of speech--and a very good one.

In the Old Testament the word mistranslated "hell" in the King James Version is "sheol," meaning simply that mythical place where all dead people go.

In the New Testament the Greek word "hades" (also mistranslated "hell" in the KJV) has a similar meaning. The other Greek word for "hell" in the New Testament, "gehenna," was invented by the Apocalyptists a short while B.C. as a "lake of fire" into which God would toss their oppressors. This became the traditional Christian meaning of "hell."

"Gehenna" is the only one of these words translated "hell" in the Revised Standard Version. Of the eleven times this term appears in all the whole Bible, six are in the First Gospel. Matthew liked to "quote" Jesus on hell every chance he got. Matthew (and only Matthew) also has Jesus describing this place as "outer darkness." Fire and darkness don't go together. Mark, in the only place where he attributes this word to Jesus, adds, "where the maggots never die and the fire is not quenched." Maggots could not work in fire. One scripture says the soul and the body can both be "destroyed" in hell (this eliminates the "for ever and ever"). Jesus said a convert to Judaism was made "much more a citizen of hell" (while he's still living). All this surely shows this to be a figure of speech--it's not just some "liberal" view.

I'd think any minister would be overjoyed to proclaim to his congregation the good news that there is no such place as hell, but this would take a big stick out of his hands. It would also take away the reason for many being religious.

A few years ago a little elderly lady--a saint I am sure--confronted me about my saying in one of my books (Christian Superstitions) there was no hell. She said, "You don't believe there's a hell?" I said, "Yes, I don't." And she responded--with a little flame in her eye, "You just wait!" I offered to buy the book back, but she said she wanted to show it to her preacher. I hope she did.

The Bible Says...

By Floyd Hale

Question: I'd like to know, does Jesus really love me?

Answer: It is more proper for me to say God loves you.

Jesus died almost twenty centuries ago as a martyr in God's cause--for the good of the poor, sick, depressed and repressed who were being denied the "good life" God intended for all His children.

Most of what was said about Jesus by the New Testament writers could be said about God--which if why they soon made a god out of him. This unwittingly elevated Jesus to the level where some think he is yet "living and ministering" to individuals just like he did "by the sea of Galilee." This accounts for the many hymns which fantasize all kinds of personal relationships and experiences with "Jesus." Little children are begun on the tune, "Jesus loves me, this I know. . ." Then later they are told God had Jesus killed so He could love them.

What's wrong with this? It is very hard to see this as "wrong," until it is seen as hiding the real image of the historical Jesus, a courageous leader who wanted followers. This "lovey-dovey" image of Jesus has even changed the original meaning of the name "Christian" into "being like Christ" in disposition, instead of "imitating Jesus" by doing what he did. Those who had this first laid on them as a nickname (Acts 11:26) were trying to "live the *way* Jesus had." They were known only as "people of the Way"--for that very reason (Acts 9:2, 19:9, 19:23, 22:4 etc., RSV).

I honestly believe a lot of this popular "Jesus loves me" religion is a substitute for answering the call to "follow Jesus" (see Mt. 7:21-24). It's not only easier but more enjoyable--and a lot safer. It ends up with the self-centered self "getting saved;" while the latter leads to heroic living for others-- that they might know "God's salvation."

You can be assured God loves you. But I'd suggest you take another look at the real Jesus. This will require a critical study of the Gospels. Because this has been neglected so long, it probably will take the help of a Bible scholar.

The Bible Says...

By Floyd Hale

Question: Are those not for Christ actually against him.

Answer: "The Bible says" so, in Matthew 12:30--"Those not with me are against me." But what about Mark 9:40, which says, in essence, just the opposite, those not against him are for him? A lot of rabbinical twisting of these two "sayings" can make them say the same thing in a different way-- supplement each other-- depending on the situation Jesus was facing at the time, etc. But such commentary is usually motivated by the defense that everything "the Bible says" is the Word of God, and not to find the Truth in the Bible.

I'm glad for the contradiction in these two texts, for it prods us into discovering the true attitude of Jesus--and thus the disposition his followers should have toward nonbelievers.

Matthew was published later than Mark, and in a very "churchy" situation, where a "Synagogue" was trying to become a "Church." You can imagine the conflict going on within that fellowship. Changing one's fundamental religious views is not easy or swift, and fence-straddlers always make up the silent majority in any group. Matthew sees these "neutrals" as aiding the opposition, which accounts for this "what Jesus would say about 'em" (often a Gospel writer's way of "quoting Jesus").

Mark's account being the older version is strong evidence that it is what Jesus actually said. And, what is convincing for me, the optimism in it reflects more the attitude of Jesus. He took the long view, and was patient with opposition--it would prove to be a force for good in the end. This is why he told his disciples they should put up with mistreatment--turn the other cheek, return good for bad. That takes optimism *plus.*

There is a sense in which the pessimistic view is true, but within the Christian witness that's another thing. It tends to treat as enemies those who are your friends. This is a form of paranoia-- worse than pessimism.

The moral in this is: if you don't learn to love your enemies, you'll have a hard time tolerating your friends.

200

The Bible Says...

By Floyd Hale

Question: What Bible proof do we have that there is really going to be a Rapture?

Answer: The one verse in I Thes. 4:17 mentions believers being "caught up . . . to meet the Lord in the air" (at his coming). This has been called "The Rapture."

To quote this verse (or any other) as "proof" that the Rapture will really take place is to misunderstand the Bible. It mistakenly takes for granted that the Bible is literally true, and that God wrote ("inspired") it. The proper interpretation of this verse requires that the student of the Bible first understand the apocalyptic form of expression (very popular in that day) which permeates this whole passage (4:14-17). This end-of-the-world lingo was also misused by most of the other New Testament writers.

There is one complete Christian Apocalypse in the New Testament, the book of Revelation. It's futuristic (and very militant) language is most certainly not to be taken literally--the author did not intend it to be. In it Jesus (not the real Jesus, but the "apocalyptic Word of God") returns and smites the nations with a sword and rules over them a "thousand years." The "144,000" martyrs ("raptured" to heaven as they were beheaded) return with him (in the "first resurrection") to help in this junta. After that comes the "second resurrection," when-- instead of those who make it through the "Judgment" going to heaven--God comes down to earth to lead them in "making all things new" in the world.

Paul used most of the apocalyptic jargon freely, but he adapted it (unwittingly) to the Gnostic doctrine of salvation--the "going to heaven" kind-- which was very popular in the Greek world where Paul preached. If you look closely at this passage in I Thessalonians you will see it's full of apocalyptic terms, but unrelated to the true apocalyptic aim, which was to see the nations of this world "become the Kingdom of God and His Christ."

Properly interpreted, the Bible itself proves there will be no Rapture. I fully realize some of the Bible can be quoted to "prove" otherwise.

There's that old saying, anything can be proven by the Bible.

201

The Bible Says...

By Floyd Hale

Question: Did King Solomon write any of the books in the Bible?

Answer: He gets credit for writing three.

The main reason for this is it would help the Jamnia Rabbinical Council (A.D. 90) get Ecclesiastes, Proverbs and Songs included in their "Scriptures." The Law and the Prophets were already canonized. Several other books--thirteen in all-- (especially Psalms) had become very popular and were among these, called the "Writings."

Ecclesiastes began as a foreign (probably Moabite) treatise questioning any divine purpose in life. It had become so popular with the Jews that it was given an acceptable ending and attributed to Solomon's authorship. The memory of him had embellished his "wisdom," making him the father of Jewish Wisdom Literature. (How could a man with so many wives be so smart?)

Proverbs is the compilation of the Jewish "wisdom" folklore which flourished under the Greek rule of the Middle East B.C. A few of them were old, but they had to have been written before 400 B.C. (when the Jews said "divine inspiration" with the Law becoming the first Jewish Bible, so Solomon qualified as the author--he had lived about six centuries before that.

Popularity was the major factor in any book becoming Scripture. This alone accounted for Daniel and Esther making it in, for the Rabbis didn't like either.

Am I saying the Bible was put together as a hoax? No-- certainly not. It was written and put together by people promoting and defending their religion (that's what makes its language so strong).

The same has continued down through the ages. In all this you have those who are on quest of God's truth. When the Scriptures are treated realistically and intelligently, that Truth may be discovered by people of faith and sincerity. Treated as "God said it all" and you have Him making some very stupid statements. For instance "God said" answer not a fool according to his folly (Proverbs 26:4), and then in the very next verse "He says" do just the opposite.

202

The Bible Says...

By Floyd Hale

Question: Please explain the 53rd chapter of Isaiah?

Answer: This chapter in the Old Testament was quoted by the early Christians as foretelling their crucified Master as the "Suffering Messiah"--and that is very understandable. But like so many of the other so-called "prophecies," when you examine it closely and in its historical context (when, why, how, and to whom it was written) you see that the author did not have Jesus of Nazareth in mind--or he would have said so.

To understand this chapter one should know something of the background of this second section of Isaiah (chapters 40-55) which was added to this great portfolio of preaching called "Isaiah." The adversity suffered by the Jews in Babylonian Captivity and Exile just following (to whom this was written) seemed so meaningless. It was addressed to "God's chosen people" who were being treated as anything else but.

The author is dealing with the "suffering of the righteous," and encouraging Israel to make their adversity redemptive rather than senseless fate. This would be the most humiliating of the "servant role"--to which this student of Isaiah was calling them.

It would be good if you reviewed those Servant Poems (42-52 etc.). In these God's servant Israel is referred to sometimes poetically as one person, which has made it easy to say this is foretelling Jesus. But "messiah" is mentioned in this literature only once, and then it was applied to King Cyrus (45:1) in its primary meaning, "an anointed one"--he was "doing God's will" in freeing the Jewish captives (according to II Isaiah).

A big problem is created by quoting this poem literally as theology--especially applied to Jesus. When that is done its Jewish subChristian phrasing is sanctified--such as "smitten of God," "his chastisement making us whole," the "iniquity of us all was laid on him," etc. In his compassion Jesus perfectly exemplified the spirit of vicarious suffering in this passage, but its theology has cheapened our Christology.

The Bible Says...

By Floyd Hale

Question: Who is "Immanuel" in Isaiah 7:14?

Answer: Read the whole of Isaiah 7. The prophet was trying to get Ahaz (King of Judah) not to worry about the two nations up north (Israel--the northern kingdom--and Syria) threatening him with war, to force him into a defense pact against Assyria. Isaiah believed if Ahaz took care of God's business in Judah, God would take of Judah's international affairs.

To assure the king of this Isaiah said a child would be born and given the name "Immanuel" (Hebrew for "God is with us"). Before that child would be old enough to know right from wrong (in 6 or 7 years) those two kings who were giving him trouble would be deserted (they soon fell to the invading Assyrians). Judah was saved temporarily because Ahaz had secretly made a pact with Assyria not to resist her control.

The "young woman" (RSV, the Hebrew word here does not mean "virgin"-- there was another Hebrew word for that) must have been Isaiah's young wife (who, according to the grammar, could have been "already expecting").

Otherwise the prophet would have had nothing to do with the "naming." He gave two other sons "prophetic names" like this also (7:3 and 8:3).

Just as Isaiah took his young son Shearjashub to the king's court with him (as a "sign"), he would keep little Immanuel visible to the king--reminding him as a "sign from God" to trust in Him alone (not in war).

Matthew plainly midrashed this verse in Isaiah to make it say what some of the Christians were claiming for Jesus--"God revealed in the flesh." Putting a spin on a scripture verse this way was a common rabbinical practice in Matthew's day--some preachers yet do it.

Reading into this verse a "second meaning" changes what "the Bible says." Jesus was called "Jesus" (Mt. 1:21)--not "Immanuel" anyway. And too, Mt. 1:23 is in a "story" (eulogizing Jesus long after his death) and therefore not to be taken literally as true.

All of the above does not take one thing away from the historical Jesus. It actually helps identify him.

204

The Bible Says...

By Floyd Hale

Question: Who was Mahershalalhashbaz? How did he get that name?

Answer: He was the third son of the prophet Isaiah, and his father laid this moniker on him as a "sermon title." That way, everywhere the little boy was seen, or his name called (especially in the presence of the king), his father's prophecy was "preached"-- *"The prey is hastening to make quick spoil."* That is literally what Ma-her-shal-al-hash-baz says in the Hebrew language.

At that time (8th century B.C.) Assyria (the present area of Iran-Iraq) was trying to become the first "world state." To accomplish this it would have to knock out the other "world power," Egypt. In between the two lay the small Palestinian buffer states, Syria (Damascus), Samaria, Judah etc. Isaiah (living in Judah) was warning his king that these other two nations (nearer to Assyria) would be overrun--the "spoiler" was already headed their way.

Isaiah's young wife (the "prophetess") was "with child," and Isaiah was going to give it this monstrous name. According to Isaiah, before Mahershalalhashbaz was "old enough to say papa or mama," Syria and Samaria (also called Israel) would be wiped out.

A few years before, he had told king Ahaz that he should not worry about those two nations "up north" pestering him. As God's "sign" to the king back then, Isaiah named his second son a "sermon title" also--"Imman-u-el," which in Hebrew means *"God is with us"* (on our side). He had said "before that child is old enough to know right from wrong those two kingdoms will no longer exist." Stay home and take care of God's business, and God will take care of you, was Isaiah's strong faith.

The prophet had also named his first boy a sermon title, She-ar-jash-ub,*"A remnant shall return."* We are not told the occasion of that christening, but it appears to have been a "sign" to the king also.

You can read all about this in the 7th and 8th chapters of Isaiah.

The prophets sometimes talked in a "futuristic style," but they were speaking to the issues of their day. That is what prophecy is all about.

The Bible Says...

By Floyd Hale

Question: What one book would you recommend (above all others) to read about the Bible; and where can I get it?

Answer: Some would say read only the "Good Book" itself, but it depends on whether you want an intelligent understanding of it or not.

In the line of commentaries I would suggest you use "The Interpreter's Bible." I think it is the best, but its twelve volume set is too expensive to purchase. Each book of the Bible in it has a scholarly introduction--this is most important. Most city libraries have this set. They may be in your church's reading room. Abingdon is the publisher.

Speaking of publishers, beware of anything put out by Eerdman. They publish only stuff written by traditional conservatives who pose as scholars (they have all the academic degrees but didn't learn much).

As for one book to own, I recommend John S. Spong's "Rescuing the Bible from Fundamentalism" (1991, Harper Collins Publishers, 10 East 53rd Street, New York, NY 10022), $12. paperback. You'll not find it in most religious bookstores--it's too truthful. The one chapter, "Christmas and Easter: Ultimate Truth and Literal Nonsense," is a masterpiece, and worth many times more than the price of the book.

Spong uses straightforward language, but he is not tearing down the Scriptures nor trying to destroy faith--just the opposite. He is not only a true scholar but holds a very responsible office in the Episcopal Church. He is the loved and respected Bishop of the Newark Diocese.

Instead of making any more remarks about this book or its author, I will list some of the fourteen chapter titles (as space allows): "Raising the Issues"; "The Pre-Scientific Assumptions of the Bible"; "The Formation of the Sacred Story"; "Prophets, Psalms, Proverbs, and Protest"; "Christ, Resurrection, Grace: The Gospel of Paul"; (Three chapters on the unique characteristics of each of the first three Gospels.); "Who is Christ for Us?" And a most interesting Preamble and Epilogue.

This book is for our times.

The Bible Says...

By Floyd Hale

Question: You say there is myth in the Bible. How can that be?

There are several Myths in the Bible. When I say this someone usually responds, "Do you mean the Bible is a myth?" Of course not. The confusion comes because it has been hounded into our heads (from birth) that "the Bible is literally true--and every word in it is God's Word."

The Creation Story is a good example of Myth in the Bible. It bears all the marks of ancient mythology: woman is created because man could not find a "helpmate" among the animals; a certain forbidden fruit which if eaten would give one the knowledge of good and evil; a snake talks to a woman; the man hides from God because he is naked; a curse is put on the snake, woman, man--and even the ground itself.

The Story of Jesus Birth is another example: angels (mythical characters) delivering messages to all involved; the Holy Spirit (God) impregnates a virgin; the infant Savior is supposed to be called Emmanuel but is named Jesus; Joseph doesn't "sleep with" Mary until after Jesus is born; a star leads the Wise Men to the the newborn king of the Jews; etc.

These two myths alone, right at the beginning of the Old and the New Testaments, if not understood as such and interpreted accordingly, will handicap one's understanding all the rest of the sacred Scriptures.

Answer: The word "myth" has a double meaning. It can be a false story, sometimes told to mislead. It can also denote a very legitimate literary form, in which a truth is taught, but the story itself is not literally true. Jesus told parables which were not literally true, but they taught powerful truths. But parables are not properly called myths.

This subject does not need a lot of double talk, quoting a whole string of other scriptures, and relying on centuries of tradition. It just needs to be faced up to and discussed intelligently. When the truth about the Bible (such as the above) is applied to the study of the Scriptures, then--and only then--can the central Truth in the Bible be revealed. Where this is not done the Bible continues to be used mainly to make people feel guilty.

The Bible Says...

By Floyd Hale

Question: Why did Jesus want his disciples to keep it quiet that he was the Christ (Mt. 16:20)?

Answer: Since Matthew relied on Mark (8:30) as his source for this passage, let's look at this in its original context, for Mark structured his whole Gospel around this "Messianic secret."

Why did the Jews reject Jesus--if he was their "promised Messiah"? Why was he executed as a criminal? The first Christians had some tough explaining to do, since Jesus' "success" came after his death. Mark assumes Jesus planned it this way--it was preordained that he be rejected and die--"giving his life a ransom for many." His death, the big question, became the bigger answer; it was "God's plan of salvation" (according to Mark).

At his baptism the voice from heaven tells Jesus, "You are my Son" (in Matthew the whole crowd is told). The next three times he is recognized as "the Son of God" it is by demons (1:24, 3:12 and 3:12). The first two are told "not to make him known" (the last one is just refused discipleship). Demons--supposedly members of the Spirit world--considered knowing what went on in that larger arena of life. So Mark uses their "sure authority" for identifying the real Savior.

Jesus is not mentioned as the "Christ" until the 8th chapter, where Peter blurts it out. And here Jesus responds by advising him to "tell no one" (8:30).

Finally, in answer to the high priest's direct question, "Are you the Christ," Jesus answers flatly, "I am" (the only Gospel in which this clear confession is made by Jesus). Jesus is to die--the primary purpose of his life (according to Mark). Now the secret can be told--and from the very mouth of the one who fulfilled it.

Throughout Mark Jesus is identified (and identifies himself) repeatedly as "the son of man." Mark's reason for this is most interesting. In the early Christian theology the unrecognized Son of God takes on the role of a heavenly figure, the Son of Man, which rescues his "failure" and makes him (because of the way he "failed") the Lord of the continuing Christian movement.

The Bible Says...

By Floyd Hale

Question: What is meant by "Repent for the kingdom of heaven is at hand" (Mt. 3:2)?

Answer: Matthew (being a good Jew) uses the word "heaven" in the place of "God." This phrase means "the reign (rule) of God."

When you look throughout the Gospels you see that "at hand" has two slightly different meanings, "near" and "present but unobserved." John Baptist, to whom this statement in Matthew is attributed, meant the former; but Jesus meant the latter. This was the major difference between Jesus and his mentor--to the disappointment of John.

John was an Apocalypticist, which meant the "rule of God" was soon going to be ushered in through some cataclysmic and sudden stroke of God's taking direct control of world affairs. It would be the "end of the (old) age." He is reported as believing Jesus (one of his converts) was going to do this as Messiah.

One of Jesus' major differences with his mentor was on this very issue. Jesus proclaimed the good news that "the kingdom is here"--God was already in charge, and those who followed him in the radical doing of His will would make it a reality in society. Jesus not only "preached" this gospel, he "practiced" it. This is exactly why Jesus was killed--his gospel was a threat to those in charge--the religious and political leaders.

To John "repent" meant get forgiveness of your sins (be baptized) so you'll not go to hell when Jesus comes. "Repent" to Jesus meant change (the real meaning this Greek word) and conform to God's rule.

You asked only about John's statement, but I wanted to place Jesus' use of this appeal along side it; otherwise you could mistake John's gospel as "Christian"--for it's in the New Testament. This is what the New Testament Church did, and unwittingly left Jesus' gospel unheeded. I really think the first Christians' (subconscious if not conscious) preference for John's gospel had a lot to do with this. They set the pattern for us.

The mixing up of all those Old Testament "prophecieis" (which didn't apply) with John and Jesus' relationship left this in a confused state in the Gospels.

The Bible Says...

By Floyd Hale

Question: Was Jesus of Nazareth the "only begotten" son of God?

Answer: The Bible says so, and for the Literalists that settles it. And they can quote a lot of scriptures to prove it. (Something in a document cited to prove something else in that same is true is flawed argument--but, "God wrote it all," etc.) Usually the proof text that Jesus was fathered by God (and not by a man) is Matthew 1:20, the "Virgin Birth." But this is in a "story." A story written to call attention to the magnanimous spirit that was in Jesus, not to report on how his mother actually conceived him.

It was not until the Church elevated Jesus to a status above human that this phrase was used in describing him. What do the Biblicists do with Jesus calling himself "a son of man"?

Some have said to me, "Oh you believe Jesus was just a man." To which I answer, "There is no such thing as 'just a man--or woman'." That "just" reduces human beings to something less than sacred. Jesus believed all people were sacred and to be treated that way-- children of their heavenly Father all. It was because of

Jesus' radically different teachings--and revolutionary way of life-- that he was "seen" as more than human. It is those sacred things about Jesus' life we need to "see"--and live with (if not by), instead of pass him off as a god to be worshipped.

On the question of Jesus being 'the only begotten son of God' the Christian leaders ("Bishops") fought with each other all during the second and third centuries. In doing so they displayed a spirit very unlike that of the Jesus they were fussing about.

It was when Emperor Constantine got all these "preachers" together (with travel pay) at Nicea in 325 and forced them to come to an agreement (for his own political purposes) that there was "one belief." The conservatives who said Jesus "was God" and not just "like God" won out, for they were the loudest. The liberals, Bishop Arius and his small group who did not agree had a curse laid on them and chased. And, I might add, it's been like that ever since on this issue.

210

The Bible Says...

By Floyd Hale

Question: How did ministers come to be called "Reverend"?

Answer: I don't know the history of this, but I assume it was intended by people as a title of respect for "preachers of the gospel."

There was a time when a minister made a sacrifice to serve as a clergy person, which probably accounted for some of that respect. A half century ago (plus one year) I entered the ministry. Having a wife and two children, and with college and seminary to get, I took it for granted I'd be poor all my life. I have been a "poor preacher" but never missed a meal nor wanted for anything I needed. Now retired I'm on a rather good pension--got it made (I'm praying Social Security holds out at least a few more years.).

I soon let people know it was all right to call me "Floyd." I think they appreciated that. (Some of my best friends call me "Dumb ol' Floyd.) I'd rather be called "Reverend" though, than some things I've been called, but that's another answer to a whole different question.

So much for me, but I had some space to waste, for there's not much to be said on this subject. I am aware that some think "Reverend" should not be ascribed to a human being, because only God is to be "revered," but calling a dandelion a rose does not make it smell like one.

The term "Reverend" is actually not a title but an adjective--one is not "a Reverend." The term is supposed to be preceded by "the"--"The Reverend So-in-so." I do think being addressed as "The Right Reverend" is a little much. (Now I'll probably get some mail with that on it.)

At the church where I attend, on the worship bulletin the minister's name appears after the title "Pastor:" Then below that is "Ministers: All Members." I kinda like that. I never thought of it before, but I guess that means we have a lot of female ministers in our church--more than male!

Sorry I don't have a better answer for your question. As with the title "Priest," I think too much can be made of the "name" issue.

The Bible Says...

By Floyd Hale

Question: What does it mean to be "justified by faith" in Romans 5:1?

Answer: This phrase has to be understood in the context of Paul's own religious experience. Paul wanted so much to be righteous, and thus saved from the wrath of God at the Judgment Day. He had been raised in the tradition that the way to be righteous was to "do all the Bible says." (Paul's Bible was the Law--the first five books of our Old Testament). But try as he may he could never feel "saved" in doing that.

He found that "trusting in the atonement Christ made in his death" God would attribute Christ's perfect righteousness to him. This freed Paul from the burden of guilt which had so plagued him. This made a "new man" out of Paul--as his life and work very plainly demonstrate. There has never been another like him. He (through his work and writings) founded what we know as the Church.

"Justified" is a legal term and comes out of the Old Testament idea that God--being a just God--could not be merciful to a sinner unless someone paid the price of (took the punishment for) his or her sin.

I do not want to down faith--for it is a life-changer--nor the great Apostle; but his religiosity reduced Jesus to an Old Testament "type"--the Pascal lamb. Paul was actually trying to revise his religion, Judaism, not creating a new one. This made Jesus the "perfect sin offering," allowing God to act graciously (instead of out of wrath) toward those of faith. Now this is the rub. It used up all of Jesus as this "sacrifice," leaving what Jesus actually did and said out of it.

It is not false humility to say that one cannot stand before God justified. Being "justified" is a false goal--it turns one inward on a never ending quest. It is even worse to believe one is "justified." Being just is the task, for that turns one outward to others and the whole social system in which we live together.

Paul's speaking of his being justified by Christ's righteousness did show his own quest was futile, but it put a wrong interpretation of Jesus into the scriptural record.

212

The Bible Says...

By Floyd Hale

Question: According to the Bible what was to happen to an illegitimate child?

Question: In Deuteronomy 23:2 it says, "No bastard shall enter the assembly of the Lord" (KJV). Not only is this illegitimate child ostracized, but his or her legitimate descendants are also excluded--"even to the tenth generation" (which really means forever). I don't care how you explain it, to say God inspired this law is to say God is unjust.

The "law" just above this one (v. 1) restricts a man from the assembly of God's people if he has had his testicles crushed or is sterile (a eunuch). Now that's even more absurd. Just a few verses above this it says a man who "is found lying with the wife of another man and the woman also, shall be put to death" (22:22). According to Jesus this would be sinners killing sinners for being sinners, Jn. 8:5.

Probably the most absurd of these laws is the one which says if a groom does not find the "tokens of virginity" on the wedding bed he can have his bride "stoned to death." Nothing is said about the groom's virginity?

To add more male chauvinism to injustice, how about the law on rape (vv. 22-29). If it is done in the city the victim shall be put to death (along with the man) because she did not cry out (taking for granted she would have been heard). If it happened in the open country, where no one could hear her cry, then she is to be spared the punishment. That's real mercy.

There are good laws in the Old Testament--many of them. But it is "what's right" in them which is supposed to motivate us. It is that "what's right" we learn from the scriptures which we are to promote in our society and not in the name of God or the Scriptures--but because they are right.

The tendency is for legalistic minded religious people to want to force their "holy laws" on society, thinking it is their religious duty.

This is what's wrong with the Christian Coalition. Fundamentalism is the same in any religion. What the Fundamentalist Islamic terrorists are doing in the name of God is a good example of where this leads to. (Abortion clinics get bombed and doctors shot.)

The Bible Says...

By Floyd Hale

Question: How should I study the Bible?

Answer: You hear so much about people being biblically illiterate-- knowing nothing or very little of what's in their Bible. This is because it has been promoted unrealistically.

You should first know something about why and how a chosen book in the Bible was written--and then much later included in the volume (library) of books declared to be "Scripture." This exercise is a matter of going to the right sources-- and it is most interesting.

To select (or have selected for you) a bunch of verses from throughout the Bible, and put them together in some kind of theme or "Bible doctrine," is to violate the literary form of each. Once the background of two or more different verses is understood, they may be compared, but to make them complement or supplement each other is usually to make the Bible "say" something it does not.

Let me illustrate. On the subject of the Holy Spirit, to make the Gospel of John and the book of Acts commentaries on each other is to homogenize and distort this "Bible teaching." John saw the work of the Holy Spirit as bringing "Jesus and God" into the religious experience of the believer (14:15-23). In Acts the work of the Holy Spirit was to empower Jesus' followers in their living out his revolutionary life style in the world. The literary forms of each book are very different.

I have said many times before in this column, you have to know the truth about the Bible to learn the Truth in the Bible. I have no doubt about the Truth in the Bible, and I am criticized regularly for not stressing that. But somebody has to put the breaks on the traditional (mis)use of the Bible long enough to reveal the Book for what it really is. If what I do shocks people that is all the more evident to me that a radical change must be made.

Good books on Bible background are not in "religious bookstores," because they would be "scholarly"--which is synonymous with "controversial"--which is synonymous with "bad." I'd be glad to help--just give me a call.

The Bible Says...

By Floyd Hale

Question: How did King David become such a saint?

Answer: By having a good press. The dynasty he established lasted for four centuries. And after it ended another one like him ("a son") was longed for who would "restore" that great kingdom. All this embellished his memory (from generation to generation) for the better. Only the prophets told of some of his sins.

Saul--who had no political legacy to praise him (no press)--was much the better man. David's "writers" went to great length to show that his (David's) ruthless rise to power over Saul was all "God's doing." To weaken Saul's position as king, David once (with his own private army of hoodlums) fought on the side of the enemy Philistines. He once sold the Philistines an Israelite border village, and then for fear word would get back home, had every inhabitant of the town slaughtered.

If God had Saul replaced with David as king, why did one of Saul's son's, Ishboseth, reign for two more years? During this time David got the Philistines (who controlled the whole area) to set him up as governor over Judah. From this political base his army fought the army of Saul's son in a lengthy struggle (II Sam. 3:1). With Ishboseth's army general, Abner, going over to David's side (at God's request of course), David won the war--and the crown. He then rewarded Abner by setting him up to be slain by Joab, his own general.

When II Samuel was written (four centuries later) David was becoming a pretty good fellow. By the time the Chronicler wrote, three centuries after that (and the Israelites were without a country), he had become a saint--the Patron Saint of Judaism no less. The "last straw" in this improving on the character of David was attributing all those beautiful and worshipful Psalms to his authorship..

Those who say David repented of his sins and was "much loved by God" would pull their hair if they found out their preacher--even though "forgiven" of it--had a man killed so he could marry his "widow" (whom he had already gotten pregnant).

215

LETTERS TO THE EDITOR

Dear Editor:

In his article, "The Bible Says," from Saturday, April 22, Floyd Hale states, "Those who strongly defend the 'inspiration of the Scripture' say that every statement in the Bible is to be taken literally--true, 'God said it!' But those who are informed in Bible background realize that this is not only erroneous but damaging to biblical truth in many instances."

I suppose I am one of those uninformed people in Bible background. I take the account of Jonah in the belly of the great fish literal, but not because I do not understand the parabolic nature of scripture, but because Jesus used the account of Jonah to teach the fact of His death, burial and resurrection (Mt. 12:39-40). I do not believe that the death, burial and resurrection of my Lord was some sort of symbolic parable from which I learn a higher spiritual lesson. I take it as the facts of the gospel that one must believe in order to be saved (1 Cor. 15:1-8).

However, Hale did answer my last question to him. He evidently does not believe in the inspiration of the scriptures. Incidentally, I do not take all the Bible literal and I know of few people who do. Truly, knowing the "background" of the Bible is to understood that there are parables and symbolic language used in the scripture. But once again, literal language must be taken literally and figurative language must be taken figuratively; and the difference between a parable and a fable is that a parable comes from something that is literal and may be true. Just because a miracle occurred which I cannot duplicate does not mean it is not literal.

A local Pastor (again)

t

The Bible Says...

By Floyd Hale

Question: Does Jesus pray that he not have to "drink the cup," or does he accept it without question?

Answer: This depends on whether you read John or Mark's gospel on this question. In Mark Jesus, "greatly distressed and troubled," prays three times that he may not have to die. But he goes ahead with it. In John there is no such prayer. Jesus goes out and surrenders to the arresting mob--even before Judas can kiss him. When his disciples encourage resistance, he coolly asks, "Shall I not drink the cup which the Father has given me?"

By misusing the other gospels this can be all "filled in" to eliminate the "contradiction," but if God had wanted "one full story," would He have had four different ones composed? Each of the four gospel writers had his own view of the meaning of the life and death of Jesus, which is revealed when they are compared in detail. Mark saw Jesus as "dying for the sins of the world," but he allowed for Jesus' willing participation in this as a human being.

With John the whole "plan of salvation" was cut and dried between him and the Father back in heaven. His "coming to earth," living and dying (and returning to the Father), was simply a matter of "going through the act." Jesus (according to John) knew all that was going to happen--even helped manipulate its procedure. For Jesus to ask God to change his mind about any of this would have been far out of character (according to John).

Editing Mark and John together is a literary violation of the two, which destroys the unique emphasis of each. John was not even interested in what Jesus actually said or did (except his death). He was interpreting Jesus to provide a "Gospel" to go with Paul's gospel--on which by then the church had been founded and was growing.

"Cup or no cup" is just one small way I have continually tried to get people to see what the Gospel of John really is--and then look for the real Jesus in the first three. It would be startling--if not shocking--if he were found.

216

The Bible Says...

By Floyd Hale

Question: Can a person be lost eternally, and what do preachers mean by that?

Answer: In the earliest Gospel, Mark, Jesus says: "For whoever would save his life will *lose* it; and whoever would *lose* his life for my sake and the gospel's will save it" (8:35). This is a play on words not to be played with, for it goes to the heart of Christian discipleship-- which is more than just believing a lot of stuff about Jesus and staying out of trouble.

What did Jesus mean about being "lost"-- eternally.

Jesus said this to those who would "follow" him. That narrowed it down to those who would actually "live the same way he lived." They had been warned that was risky business--could lead to death. But if they lived his way, for his cause and the gospel's--which was one and the same ("the kingdom (rule) of God"), their "lives" would be saved. A "life" is what one "lives" during his or her "lifetime."

What one lives is *"lived into life,"* whether that's good or bad. And it makes life as a whole better or worse for others (for generations).

According to Jesus if a person who does not "live" to help God be in charge of life ("His kingdom come on earth"), his or her "life" will be "lost," wasted. If one "lives" to see God's good will done, one will have to "lose" (give up) his or her own way of "living." Either way a person is a "loser." So why not live in such a way that one's "life" will last forever- -be "saved"?

This has nothing do with an "afterlife." There is no such thing anyway--life is everlasting. As God's Creation it goes on forever. We either go with God or we don't go anywhere. The human ego, which is often mistaken as one's "self," may try to find some other way of "saving itself"--even to becoming religious.

This is radical language but it should be understood if one wants to be a Christian. That "name" means "imitating Christ." That's not just being good, but being good for something--which will last, *eternally.*

Our traditional concept of "salvation" was injected into Christianity by the Gnostics in the New Testament days, and it remains popular because it appeals to the self-centered self.

217

The Bible Says...

By Floyd Hale

Question: What is meant in Romans 1:16, "the gospel is the power of God unto salvation"?

Answer: Paul meant: "His gospel (about Jesus dying as God's sacrifice for sin) was powerful enough to save a person from sin--if they believed in Christ and repented." Much of the rest of the New Testament can be quoted to support this. But Jesus used the terms, "power, gospel, and salvation" with a slightly different meaning.

"Salvation" to Jesus had the prophetic meaning of changing the way the community (world) operated to give people the freedom and rights God willed for them. Individuals would then benefit from "God's salvation." Individual salvation came in through the Christian Gnostics (to whom Paul unwittingly catered).

Jesus' "gospel" was "God is in charge." That's what "the kingdom (or rule) of God" meant to him. That was his one and only preachment. To those who were not in charge of anything--which was most of the people in that day-- that was "good news." That's why they came out in droves to hear him. But this was "bad news" to those in charge--the religious and political leaders. He was killed for being a threat to the "old time religion" and "national security"--his gospel was too "powerful" for them.

"Power," to Jesus, was in his followers' who "lived his gospel." When you read about this in the first five chapters of Acts you see they first got in trouble for doing a good deed--out in public-- in the name of Jesus. Peter protested--publicly--at least four times the "unlawful killing" of Jesus. When they told the magistrates they were taking their orders from God and not from them, they were practicing--in public--"legal disobedience." In continuing to "speak out boldly" they practiced--out in public--"freedom of speech." The disciples gave credit for their courageous "obedience" to the "gift of the Holy Spirit" (5:32). A new age was dawning.

But Paul (who boasted he did not receive his gospel from Jesus' disciples in Jerusalem) preached "another gospel"--which we like a lot better--and call it "The Gospel of Christ."

The Bible Says...

By Floyd Hale

Question: Why does the Christian Bible yet contain the Jewish Scriptures?

Answer: This is a good question and deserves a much fuller answer than can be given here. I'll try to sketch it briefly.

Christianity began on Jewish soil as a Jewish sect (looking upon itself as the "True Israel"), by those who had accepted Jesus as the "promised Messiah." The believers were Jewish and used their Scriptures (what is now the Old Testament) to "prove they were right."

Paul, the self styled "Apostle to the Gentiles," took his own version of the "Christian Faith" out into and to the Greek world. It was not long until the widespread Church was almost entirely Gentile, using Paul's writings and the four gospels for their spiritual guidance--to the neglect of their (Jewish) "Bible."

A strong movement arose to create a "new Bible" out of Paul's writings and one of the gospels (an edited version of Luke) to replace the "old (Jewish) one." A few (but loud) old timers headed this off--as you might guess--but the newly proposed documents (with a few more added) were soon "included" into their Bible--as a "New Testament" (along side the "O.T.").

By its very title and contents it replaced the "old covenant." Once years--centuries--passed, tradition ("that democracy in which the dead vote") solidified this into one "Book," causing Fundamentalism to hold that "God wrote it all."

The first five books of the O.T. (the first Hebrew Bible) was originally called "Torah"--the "teachings" (of Moses). Under Ezra it was made "the Law" for all Jews (ca, 400 B.C.), and was soon being obeyed literally. (Sometimes the whole O.T. is referred to in the N.T. as "the law.")

Those now who defend the whole Bible as "Holy Writ" will say it's all "God's Word." But when its many ceremonial (e.g. animal sacrifices) and outdated (if not unjust) laws are cited, they will say they don't apply to Christians--"we are not under the Law." Then why is it in our Bible? You can't have it both ways.

It all depends on what authority you believe the Bible has.

LETTERS TO THE EDITOR

To the Editor:

I have hesitated to write to you for a long time about the Hale articles on the Bible in the paper. I am not a letter writer; but I notice very few of the letters you print said anything good about Mr. Hale. In fact they were more accusative of him than what he writes.

A lot of my friends appreciate those articles. We discuss them a lot. The Sunday School Class I attend discusses them more than we do our lessons. All those who speak up say they are getting a better view of their Bible. I ask them why they don't write you and say so, and they ask me right back, Why don't you? It was sorta agreed I would speak for the group.

Whether Mr. Hale is right on all points or not, I commend him for his courage to continue to write. He must have thick skin. I found out he doesn't get paid anything for this.

It alarms me that those who condemn him do it in the name of God and quote their Bible. I believe what he says about fundamentalism being a bad thing. It seems to me religion is getting back to that more and more.

The thing that bothers me is that preachers who went to school, and all of them are supposed to, didn't seem to learn what Mr. Hale did. If they did they keep it to themselves. I can understand why though, some people in church would run them off.

I've said too much, so I had better shut up. I feel better after writing you, and I plan on telling preacher Hale that I think an awful lot of him.

A reader

u

The Bible Says...

By Floyd Hale

Question: Does the Bible say all the stars will fall to earth someday?

Answer: Yes. The author of Revelation says in his First Vision (6:12) this will happen in the end-time. Can you imagine all the stars landing on earth? Each of the thousands of stars, you know, is a sun--most of them much larger than ours. If only one of them came toward the earth, its heat would incinerate this little planet into a cinder even before it got here. If God was in the habit of revealing scientific data to the writers of Scripture, He forgot to tell John about this.

People of all times have been familiar with "shooting (or falling) stars," but we know now these are rather small meteoroids burning up as they enter our atmosphere. When I was a child my father believed the stars were little lights God had hung in the sky--like Christmas ornaments-- which were not too many miles (even feet) above the earth.

Then too, if the stars all fell to earth in John's first Vision, how could a third of them fall again in his second Vision (8:12)? We accuse people of being biblically illiterate, but how many who think they know so much about the Bible really know what it says? Revelation does not foretell the end of the world, the return of Jesus, and Judgment Day. It is an "Apocalypse" (the Greek word translated "Revelation") written to Christians who were being put to death for their faith.

John used this way-out literary form (as had the author of Daniel) to literally "scare the faithful into remaining so"--when under persecution and threatened by death.

About A.D. 70 Mark inserted a "Little Apocalypse in between his "ministry of Jesus" and the last "passion week" in Jerusalem (Ch. 13). In it he has Jesus saying (he didn't actually say it), "Just before the Son of man returns you will see (among other things) the stars falling from heaven" (v.25).

The apocalyptic language permeates the whole of the New Testament, and it has nothing to do with what Jesus taught--and asked people to believe.

The Bible Says...

By Floyd Hale

Question: Why are there so many contradictions between the Resurrection stories at the end of the four Gospels?

Answer: Let's first look at a few of these. The list of women who came to the tomb differs in each account. In one report they came "while it was yet dark"; in another "when the sun had risen." In one "a young man" sitting in the empty tomb told them to go tell the disciples Jesus would meet them up in Galilee; while in another Jesus appears to the women there at the empty tomb. In one account Jesus appears to the only woman who came to the tomb and told her "not to hold him, for he had not yet ascended." In another the women "took hold of his feet" without his objecting.

It was "one man" at the tomb, "two men" in another gospel, while in the remaining two "one angel" and "two angels." In some accounts Jesus demonstrates his physical presence, while appearing and disappearing at will as a ghost in others. In one Jesus' first meeting with his disciples after his death is in Galilee, and his last word to them is, "I will remain with you always." Another Gospel ends with them staying in Jerusalem and going with him out to Bethany on the afternoon of his resurrection (not forty days later) where he ascends. I could go on, but this is enough to show that these are not four different ways of describing the same event. Neither do they supplement each other--to give "the whole story."

These stories (properly called "myths") grew out of the apocalyptic affirmation of the disciples that "God raised the Son of man to his place of power in the heavens as Lord." The "resurrection" of Jesus had nothing to do with his body (physical or spirit), but about his continuing Lordship--which his death had threatened.

We discover Jesus' role of authority in the Gospels and "believe it" or "not." Believing it and acting on its claim of discipleship is what makes a Christian--the only thing that does.

Learning what our four Gospels are all about is far overdue--that is, if we really want to know who Jesus was and what he did,

The Bible Says...

By Floyd Hale

Question: Was Jonah actually swallowed by a big fish?

Answer: It has been mistakenly taken for granted that anything in the Bible is true--otherwise it would not be in the Bible. Truth depends very much on the *expression form* in which it is phrased. The "truth" in Jesus' parables is not to be found in the literal stories. Jesus was not teaching about a treasure found in a field, nor about a landowner going on a journey. But such stories could have been true, which would help make their "hidden truth" more easily "seen." For instance Natahn's "story" to King David about the "one ewe lamb" was so true to life that the king seized upon its literalness, thereby condemning himself of its hidden truth-- taking Uriah's "only wife" (Bethsheba), while he had "a whole flock of 'em" in his palace.

"Jonah" was a similarly devised story, about a foreigner-hating prophet (thus a "good guy") who wanted to see the Ninevite "foreigners" burn--even after they all became religious. The author has God seemingly agreeing with Jonah at first against the Ninevites, but then He "repents" (changes his mind). Then Jonah wanted to "die" rather than change his mind. In this perfect parable the reader is subtly forced to change his/her mind--along with God, or remain a racially prejudiced religious bigot like Jonah. The punch line "truth" is "seen" (for those with eyes to see) in the last two verses.

This pamphlet must have had some effect on its day, for it was treasured and later included in the Scriptures. I have no problem believing this story was inspired of God. It stabs to the heart of racial prejudice and bigotry.

The "reader" to which this little masterpiece was addressed lived at a time when Jerusalem was being " ethnically cleansed" (of foreign wives) during the Ezra Reform--"because their Bible (the Law) said to."

Those who insist on Jonah's being swallowed by a fish, God repenting, all the Ninevites accepting Jewish religion, etc., because "the Bible says so," foul up the Truth in this small gem of a story.

222

The Bible Says...

By Floyd Hale

Question: Have the two witness of Revelation 11:3 come yet?

Answer. No, and they won't, for this is not a future event of history foretold. They are characters in this extravaganza drama told in visions.

The only thing John "foretold" was that "faithfulness unto death would win the victory." And it did. The killing of the Christians finally made the Romans sick at their conscience. When the Roman Emperor Constantine came to the throne he lifted the persecution edict in 313 (or 323), and received Christian baptism himself. This wasn't the "end of the world," but the "beast" had been tamed, and a "new age" began--in which the Western World took off on a whole different course.

John draws on several "end-of-the-world" stories (Apocalypses) at his disposal--and there were many of them circulating in the first century. One Bible scholar has detected parts of twenty-three different sources used by John. That's one reason Revelation is so lengthy.

The "measuring of the temple" comes from Ezekiel. This scene is suggested by Zachariah with the seven-branched candlestick changed to two lamp stands. These two prophets in 11:3 are not named but easily recognized as Elijah and Moses (the authorities on "no rain" and "plagues." It was believed then by some that these two would return to earth "in the last days." (They appear in the Transfiguration story also.) John builds around their martyrdom a very gory ordeal. The "forty-two months" (3 1/2 years) comes from Daniel. Even with its symbols explained it ought to be obvious that such an event is fantasized. This--and all the other wild "visions"-- are set before John's audience as illustrations that victory comes to the faithful through suffering and martyrdom, and those who "really die" are those who partake in evil--"worship the Beast."

I hope you read this column last two weeks for in it I gave some background information for the understanding of Revelation, which is an Apocalypse, not the future foretold in symbols.

The Bible Says...

By Floyd Hale

Question: Why does John in his gospel replace the Lord's Supper with Feet Washing?

Answer: This is one more of the many differences between the Fourth Gospel and the first three.

By the time John wrote the Christians and the Jews had become bitter enemies. "The Jews" appears over sixty times in John, and usually has a derogatory slant to it--Jesus (who was certainly a Jew) even refers to his enemies as "the Jews" in this gospel. John sought to expunge all Jewishness from the Christian "gospel."

To keep the Lord's Supper from being mistaken as a Christian Passover Feast, John moves Jesus' "last supper" one evening earlier and institutes "Feet Washing" (not a bad badge of discipleship). The same "do this" said to the disciples in John 13:15 appears in his instituting the Lord's Supper in Luke 22:19 (KJV).

The "eating my body and drinking my blood" in John 6:52-63 is not referring to a communion meal of bread and wine, but to the "spirit" of Christ himself. This appears in John's metaphor of Jesus as "The Bread of Life," and to point out that this is not a sacrament, John adds (in the words of Jesus),
"The words I have spoken to you are spirit and life." This was also to correct the accusation being made at the time, that the Christians were practicing cannibalism--feasting on their God.

Many times I have pointed out the uniqueness of John's Gospel. Its contents are not to be mixed in with quotes from the first three, to "tell the whole story of Jesus." John has a story all his own to tell, and it ought to be understood in detail, for it is a Gospel written to and for the Greeks, after the Church had become mainly Gentile, and founded on Paul's "gospel."

Neither is Jesus to be quoted from John, unless one knows that "his words" are John's placed on his lips, for a whole different purpose than the first three evangelists wrote.

If you have a question on any of this, send it in.

The Bible Says...

By Floyd Hale

Question: What do you think is the most misunderstood book in the Bible?

Answer: For a long time I thought Revelation was, but I now am convinced the Gospel of John is. Each is written in very unique but different literary forms; but it is the harder to detect in John.

The reason the literary form of John's Gospel is so easily missed, it is treated as "just another Gospel"--which it is not. When John wrote there was no need for another Gospel--they had three good ones. John was writing for a Greek audience, to which the three "biographies of Jesus" did not appeal. They were written in the Jewish idiom-- about a Judaic Messiah, nationalistic Son of David, apocalyptic Son of Man, etc. John wanted to interpret Jesus as the "Logos God" come to earth to give "Life." Also, out in the Greek world the Christian Faith had not become unified.

To interpret "resurrection" as "eternal life--now," John scripts a conversation between Martha and Jesus in which Martha expresses the old Jewish idea; Jesus corrects her with the new, *"I am* the resurrection and the *life."*

John then composes an "action parable," the Raising of Lazarus, to "illustrate" this. (To make it a complete "Gospel" John does add the Resurrection Stories-- though much changed.

It is my guess that John really wanted his Gospel to "replace" the first three-- which for all practical purposes it did in the Church. I think this is why he, though familiar with Matthew, Mark, and Luke, he never "recognizes" them directly by quoting them.

John had the literary freedom to put his own "interpretation of Christ" in as the "sayings of Jesus," and his readers (who might compare his with Matthew, Mark, and Luke) would easily see they were reading a kind of "devotional" in the form of a historical novel.

When the Gospels were later canonized as a part of the "New Testament," this "Gospel" was included because it was so popular in the Western church. It remains so because we like it; it explains Jesus "totally" as our God-sent Savior. Discipleshipis is then reduced to "believing in him as the Christ."

225

LETTERS TO THE EDITOR

To the Editor:

There is a story about an old woman that goes something like this. Seems one Sunday morning after church as the pastor was shaking hands with the people he noticed the old woman's Bible, or what was supposed to be her Bible, for all she was carrying was the cover.

"Why, Mrs Brown, what on earth has happened to your Bible?" he asked. "Well Rev." she answered, I have been coming to church for a good while now. It seems like, that, in each sermon you preach you say a certain part of the Bible is not inspired or does not really mean what it says. So, after each sermon I have torn that part out. Well, as you see, after you preached this morning, this is all I have left." We have a man in Benton that writes a column entitled the Bible says. Perhaps it should be entitled The Bible Says (?). It seems to me, this man must have attended the same church as the old woman mentioned above. I think maybe he needs a new Bible also.

Proverbs 3:5

Trust in the Lord with all thine heart and lean not unto thine own understanding.

Proverbs 14:12, 16:25

There is a way that seemeth right unto man, but the end thereof are the ways of death.

A Reader

To the Editor:

And to the Christian people of (this town). In the past month or so a column has appeared in our newspaper every Saturday called "The Bible Says."

In our opinion, his explanations of the Bible are completely different to our understanding of the Word.

We, as a result of this man's column, are canceling our newspaper, and would like to see other Christians who agree something should be done, do the same.

If enough people cancel their paper I'm sure some action will be taken to have his articles removed.

Mr. and Mrs. (Reader)

V

The Bible Says...

By Floyd Hale

Question: Exactly what is the Bible?

Answer: I was reminded the other day that I sometimes say the Bible needs to be understood for what it really is, and then I don't go ahead and explain what it is. I guess I figure each one of my articles adds to the lengthy answer to that question.

The Bible is a very priceless item, because it is the ONLY resource literature we have for gaining an understanding of the origin and development of the Christian Faith.

It was written as separate books--some in ancient times--over a very lengthy period. Each of these was addressed to a certain group, at a certain time, to meet a certain need. Five of these books made up the first Jewish Bible. Three other groups of Jewish documents were considered sacred and added later. The "Prophets," then the "Writings," and finally the twenty-seven books we call New Testament.

Each of these books meant something to the faith of the people who treasured them. This had the most to do with them being preserved and centuries later declared "Holy Scripture" (by an "official committee on canon"). Learning about when, why, by whom, and especially *in what literary form* these were composed, you may learn what they meant to their original readers. This is the proper way to gain from them insights and strength for your own faith today.

The works of the great and dedicated scholars in this field should not be overlooked as resources in your study. Reading the Bible believing it was written for us today, and taking it all literally, has led to a lot of erroneous "Bible beliefs."

You may say I have not yet explained "what the Bible is" (and I haven't), But it really "IS" what it becomes to the individual who understands it.

I have been accused of writing this column to say "What the Bible is not," but my aim is really to help interested people learn how to understand it. The "good" in the Bible is like the "goodie" in a nut; you have to crack the nut to get it. I am a nut cracker.

Those who say swallow the nut whole (even with water) thinking they are doing you a favor, are not.

The Bible Says...

By Floyd Hale

Question: Who are the "144,000" in Revelation 7:4?

Answer: I want to stress that understanding anything in the book of Revelation requires an understanding of the unique literary form in which this most peculiar book was written. It is an Apocalypse, and is not "the future spelled out in symbols." It used "end of the world" language to dramatize the need and effect of faithfulness "right now."

It was written to the Christians at the beginning of the Roman Persecution and must be understood in that setting. Its basic message is "keep the faith even if they kill you." And If they kill you that will help all the more to gain the :victory."

Writing in apocalyptic, John had the freedom of portraying Jesus as a most violent Lord, who not only comes back and slays all the peoples (nations) with a sword, but threatens to come any time and punish those who advocate recognizing the emperor as Lord-- "worshiping the Beast."

John prepares his brothers and sisters for the long haul--144,000 (a lot) will die before the "Beast" is defeated. In the first vision martyrs begin to arrive in heaven and cry out for God to avenge their blood on the earth people (vengeance is a 'good' apocalyptic term). They are told to rest and wait until the "number is complete" who will also be martyred for their faith and witness (6:9-11). In the next scene of this same vision these 144,000 are "sealed"-- they will be faithful unto death; celebrated here as if they were already martyred and in heaven (7:4-14).

These 144,000 are not only all men, they "had never defiled themselves with women ("chaste," 14:4). "Fornication" is the old prophetic symbol of being contaminated with anything foreign. The 1200 from every tribe says faithfulness will come from all across the Church (the "new Israel").

Note that these martyrs don't get to stay in heaven; they come back (are "resurrected") to help Jesus "conquer and rule the nations." This is the apocalyptic way of saying their faithfulness and martyrdom is helping bring victory for the Church.

It worked.

227

The Bible Says...

By Floyd Hale

Question: Where is the Garden of Eden?

Answer: According to the Bible (in the Adam and Eve story) it was a place on earth. Since it is near the Euphrates River (Gen. 2:14), that puts it somewhere in the present Iraq. Eden is mentioned again (4:16) as just west of Nod, but since Nod is mythical ("a place of wandering") that's no help-- except it does help us see that Eden is of mythical origin also.

There was a "tree of life" there which bore fruit ending up being guarded by an angel armed with a flaming sword--lest man eat thereof and live forever in his sinful condition. That it is guarded makes it sound as though it is yet here on earth somewhere. Understood as an actual place--then, if not now-- treats this whole story as literally true, which mistakes human fiction for divine Truth.

To begin with, one should understand what this story actually says (Gen. 2:4bf.). God made a man and then the beasts. The man could not find among the animals a "help meet," so God made him a female man. He put them both unclothed in a garden ("paradise") and

they didn't know they were naked. He told them not to eat the fruit of a certain tree in that garden, for if they did they would "know good from evil" like Himself. A snake tempted the women and the woman tempted the man and they ate of the "forbidden fruit"--and then discovered they were naked. They didn't die (as God told them they "surely would on the day they ate thereof"), so He drove them out into a world full of sticker weeds--where she would suffer labor pains in birthing and he would suffer hard labor in making a living. For its part in bringing "sin" into the world the snake had its legs amputated and made to eat dust.

By analyzing this myth one can easily see the answers to many puzzling questions which plagued the ancients (and some moderns yet), but the myth is not "where it's at." Eden is the world "as it ought to be." Jesus asked his followers to help him restore it. More has been done on this project than most people realize, but there's a long way yet to go. A sign on the gate to that garden reads: "Help wanted!"

The Bible Says...

By Floyd Hale

Question: My son sent me an article, "From Mark to John," out of one of them liberal religious magazines. I found it very confusing. What was it trying to say?

Answer: I'd have to see the article, but I can imagine it pointed out how the early Christian Faith changed from the time of Jesus to the completion of the New Testament. During that first century there was no central control over the developing Church and what Christians believed, partly because its basic doctrines grew up out in the Greek world.

Mark was the first Gospel written (about A.D. 70). John was the last (near the end of the first Century). Mark presented Jesus in his Jewish setting. John "doctrinized" Jesus into a mystical Christ which went along with Paul's gospel to the Gentiles. Jesus (in John) is no longer a teacher using short parables and "preaching the kingdom (rule) of God"; he claims he is the Christ and tells lengthy metaphors about himself (the "I Am's").

I hope the "liberal" author of that article pointed out that all the red-letter words in John are actually John's, placed on the lips of Jesus. Jesus was no longer a "son of man" who was martyred because he did God's will--and asked his followers to do the same; he came from heaven to "be lifted up" on a cross as the Lamb of God slain for the sins of the world. In Mark Jesus asks people to follow him (do what he did); John asks people to believe in Jesus as the Christ. There are many other examples of this change in Christianity before it became "catholic" (unified).

The main thing which keeps people from seeing this is the long tradition of mixing chosen texts from all four of the Gospels together into "one complete story." These documents were never written to be put together that way and treated as "Holy Writ." They are the only written resources we have which, if examined critically, will tell us what the Christian Faith was in its beginning.

Would you send me a copy of that article (if it is not too much trouble). I'd like to see how much I missed what it is all about.

The Bible Says...

By Floyd Hale

Question: Why does Matthew contradict some of the things Mark said in his gospel?

Answer: The authors of these two gospels didn't have the slightest idea their books would appear someday side by side in a "Bible"--and be considered "God's words."

The Christian movement was evolving rapidly between Mark's writing and Matthew's (a period of about 20 years). In Mark Jesus tells his disciples (as he sent them out) to take only a staff and sandals. Later Matthew's version of this has Jesus telling them to take nothing--not even these two items.

If Matthew misquoted Mark in this place, then what does that say about his (Matthew's) writing being "inspired"? If he deliberately corrected Mark's report, what does that say about Mark's writing being "inspired"?

A contradiction can not be explained as two versions complementing each other. If each were "telling it as he saw it," this makes both documents to be human products. (I don't find anything wrong with that.) Making too high a claim for the Bible ("it's infallible and inerrant") fouls up the method by which the Truth in it is discerned.

The scholars who could help us get our Bible straight are ignored by being branded as "critics." A literary critic does more than point out "what's wrong" with a book; he/she makes a full analysis of the work, so the facts about that document may help one understand it.

For instance a good Bible critic might point out that the stories about Adam and Eve, Job, Jonah, Daniel, Esther (and some others) in the Bible are not historical accounts--literally true. Knowing the unique literary form of each (and when and why each was written) one may discover what the authors were actually "saying." Otherwise serious misinterpretation results-- and much of it has. One sad result of this is missing the true image of God, right in the Bible.

If one applies literary criticism to the gospels of Matthew and Mark, he/she will see that Matthew makes Jesus a more strict disciplinarian (e.g. Mt. 10:10 and Mk. 6:8).

The Bible Says...

By Floyd Hale

Question: Will the gospel of Jesus Christ as we know it today be preached during the thousand years of peace following the period of tribulation?

Answer: Your question relates to the last of the "seven Visions" in Revelation (19:10-21:8). Looking at it literally, at his return Jesus (the Word) slays all the kings and armies of the world with a sword. This vents "the fury of the wrath of God the Almighty," and the dead carcasses make a "great supper of God" for the birds.

Jesus then rules the nations a thousand years "with a rod of iron." At the end of this period (you call "peace"), the Devil is let out again and gathers all the armies of the world to fight the saints (one more last time). Fire falls from heaven and incinerates them, and the dead are resurrected for the "opening of the books." Note that those whose names were found therein don't go to heaven. Even those in the "first resurrection," who had gone to heaven when martyred (6:9-11) didn't get to stay; they came back (were "resurrected") earlier to help Jesus fight and rule.

I hope this raises some doubt in your mind about taking this literally. This book--like every other book in the Bible--was meant to be understood for what it says, "when" it said it, the "way" it said it.

When you understand the apocalyptic literary form in which Revelation is written, you see that the thousand years ("forever") begins now. They knew only too well that the "tribulation" was NOW. And the "Word" is the gospel of Jesus being preached--NOW. Jesus' "coming" is NOW (as expressed in various places throughout this apocalypse as "soon"). The sword by which he slays comes out of his "mouth" (not in his hand). The people who were getting this message were being shocked (scared) into remaining faithful NOW.

John's whole message is a *militant* version of Jesus' "gospel" of the kingdom (rule) of God--"GOD IS IN CHARGE!" It is too bad that today many take the vengeful and violent language of this literally.

The Bible Says...

By Floyd Hale

Question: How does one receive faith in God or Jesus Christ?

Answer: Paul said "It (faith) is already on your lips and in your heart--for the believing. . ." (Rom. 10:8). This is the simple matter of trusting God. But Paul went on to confuse the issue by adding on some things one must believe-- "about Jesus." Interpreting Jesus' death from his Jewish "Bible" (our Old Testament), he saw it as a "blood offering" God made for our "atonement" (at-onement with God).

All one needs to do to "be saved" is to believe one is. God has already taken care of that by accepting all (us sinners) and rejecting none--He always has. Jesus didn't have to die to get God to do that. Since Paul's God had changed his mind several times ("according to his scriptures"), this was just one more change He was making in His "plan of salvation."

By His free and unconditional gift of grace God has pulled the rug out from under the "seeker," and left him or her with only one thing to do--listen to the call of Jesus, "Follow me." Getting one's "self" saved is a self-centered exercise anyway.

Jesus made it very plain that following him was a very unselfish enterprise and makes him lord (boss) of one's life. The "self" is to be "lost" (quit trying to save itself) if it is to get involved in the real business of saving the world--by loving it the way God does.

Jesus called people to follow him, not have faith in him. I realize you can quote a lot of scriptures which disagree with this. "Believing in Jesus" is being convinced "he was right." The only object of faith can be and is God. "Faith in Christ" builds up a sophisticated doctrine "about Jesus," a part of which makes him "God." Jesus would say this is idolatry.

It is easy for those who read me very much to conclude that I harp on this string over and over. I do this to try to free the Bible from the traditionalists, that its truth may be discovered. It is not the Bible I try to destroy, but people's "faith in the Bible." God--and God alone--is the object of faith.

232

The Bible Says...

By Floyd Hale

Question: What is the "gift of the Holy Spirit" promised in Acts 2:38?

Answer: The teachings on the Holy Spirit differ from writer to writer in the Bible literature. In the last Gospel written (after Paul had pretty well established the Church out over the empire) the promised Holy Spirit "comes" to administer God's grace to individual believers (Jn. 14). But the way to properly understand what the "gift of the Holy Spirit" is, is to see what the followers of Jesus did with it (or what It did with them) in the book of Acts.

This is far too brief a summary of the first five chapters of Acts, but this is some of what happened. They went PUBLIC in "obeying God." This is the condition on which He "gives His Spirit" (5:32).

Not just once but at least four times they publicly PROTESTED the killing of their leader (2:23, 3:14-15, 4:10, 5:30). It is obvious they EXERCISED THE FREEDOM OF RELIGION when it conflicted with the traditional Faith. They not only PRACTICED THE RIGHT OF FREE SPEECH, but when beaten and jailed for it they prayed for "boldness" to keep it up. And this didn't have one thing to do with their own salvation; it had everything to do with God's program of saving the world--Jesus' way.

Although the Pentecost Story in Acts is about "the" gift of the Holy Spirit, nowhere therein does it say this was a permanent endowment. The Disciples were "filled" with It repeatedly as the need arose for the radical doing of God's will--out in the world.

Receiving this "gift" is a whole lot like the quarterback who raised his head out in the huddle and yelled to the coach, "Willie say he don't want to carry the ball." I think this is why we have made John's Water Baptism "Christian," while ignoring the Baptism Jesus came to administer. (If you want scripture for this: Mt. 3:11, Mk. 1:8, Lu. 3:16, Jn. 1:26-33, Acts 1:5.)

The only person I know of in our day who came near to receiving this "gift" (repeatedly) as the Disciples did, was Dr. Martin Luther King, Jr.

233

The Bible Says...

By Floyd Hale

Question: Does the movie "Armageddon" have anything to do with that battle in the book of Revelation?

Answer: I forgot exactly what he said, but the narrator at the beginning of the movie referred to this biblical account as an "end of the world" introduction to the story. From then on nothing even resembled Revelation.

In some loose fashion Bruce Willis may have played a "Christ figure"-- saving the world by giving his own life blowing up the giant asteroid headed for our planet. (Now I've done spoiled the movie for those yet going to see it. Take my advice and don't go.)

The first readers of John's Revelation were just entering the "tribulation" of being persecuted by the Roman government. Because they refused to take the pledge of allegiance to the emperor--"worship of the beast"--they were executed for being "enemies of the state." Those were very severe times, the kind of crisis which called for the distribution of an "apocalyptic pamphlet" (which Revelation was). John saw the Church in danger of being lost in its infancy to compromise.

The location of Megiddo is near a mountain pass in the Carmel Range which an army had to secure if it controlled northern Palestine. Thus many "decisive battles" were fought there--in the Plain of Esdraelon nearby. The mound (Tel) of rebuilt fortifications there is yet a maim tourist attraction.

In John's Apocalypse Armageddon (Mt Meggido) symbolizes the "showdown battle between good and evil." The Christians had begun digging foxholes. Many gave their lives and "Jesus (the Word) comes in riding on a white horse, slaying the enemy wholesale, with a sword issuing out of his mouth (his Gospel)." This will not be a future battle between nations; it was going on right then.

The Church in some nations today are fighting this very same battle. This makes it all the more urgent that Jesus' gospel, "God is in charge," be preached to every nation in a whole new and vigorous campaign.

The Bible Says...

By Floyd Hale

Question: Why does the date of Jesus' crucifixion in Mark's Gospel differ from that in John's?

Answer: A student of the Gospels soon learns that each Evangelist gave a theological interpretation of Jesus as he composed his "biography"-- that's why they wrote. If they had not, most of the "facts" would be without meaning for faith-- especially the death of Jesus. This is worked into the narrative in such a way that the uninformed reader is unaware of it.

In Mark Jesus keeps the (last?) Passover with his disciples, changing it into a (first?) Lord's Supper--as if he knew he'd be executed the next day. It is very likely Mark scheduled it thus to "take over" the Jewish Passover Feast--Jesus is "our Passover." (This is done in Acts with Pentecost.)

In John's Gospel Jesus' last meal with his disciples is just that, a "Last Supper." Jesus does not institute the "Lord's Supper" (if anything is instituted it is "feet-washing"). John explicitly points out that Jesus was crucified on the Day of Preparation, when the Paschal lambs were slaughtered, making Jesus the "Lamb of God"-- sacrificed but not necessarily eaten.

Most likely John dated his death of Jesus this way since he was against about everything Jewish. Some also think it was convenient for him not to mention a "Lord's Supper" for the Christians were being criticized for "cannibalism" at the time because of it.

In his sixth chapter the strong "eat my flesh and drink my blood" comment is not about a Eucharist. John points out that these "words" are *spirit and life.* This goes beyond "remembering" and any "hocus pocus" in a sacrificial meal, to Jesus as the very "bread of life"-- which is what that lengthy "I Am" lecture is all about.

Being aware of this contradiction in dates should incite the student of the Bible to learn not only the above--but much more about the many differences between Mark and John. The gospel truth depends on it.

235

The Bible Says...

By Floyd Hale

Question: How do you explain the contradictions in the three accounts of Paul's 'conversion' on the Damascus Road?

Answer: The contradictions to which you probably refer are in Acts 9:3-9, 22:6-11, and 26:12-18. In the first account the whole traveling party "heard the voice" from the heavens, while in the second one the men with Paul "did not hear the voice." In the third it says "they all fell to the ground," but in the first one they (other than Paul) "stood" speechless. In ch. 22 Paul is advised to go to Damascus where he "will be told all he is to do." In ch. 26 Jesus explains his "commission" to him right there on the spot.

Writing several years after the fact, Luke shows great literary freedom in reconstructing all the events in Acts. As was the custom of the day, he gave "history" a story form, adding dialogue to make it live. It was legitimate for him so to write, but the reader should know this--and understand it. The Literalists have spoiled the story, saying it is all literally true. It doesn't have to be.

Religious experience is without rational description. It requires a symbolic language fitting the individual--and adaptable to the occasion of the telling. If this is close to Paul's experience--and I think it is--it shows he was a desperate man at the time, facing the dilemma of either changing his mind or loosing it. A psychologist would see this in the bright light, his falling to the ground, and the temporary blindness. He had just left the stoning of Stephen, over which he probably officiated. The way Stephen took it (the way Jesus did) confronted Paul with the "Cross"--and he saw himself as a "crucifier." This is the way the Cross works, and it not only changed Paul, but thereafter dominated his teaching and preaching .

Never having met Jesus personally, Paul "knew Christ" only as "Savior." This differed with the way the disciples saw Jesus. The Christian Faith has gone with Paul's "religious experience," without realizing it leaves Jesus far behind.

The Bible Says...

By Floyd Hale

Question: What does the Bible say about capital punishment?

Answer: Anyone (or animal) coming near Mount Sinai while Moses was up there with God was to be put to death. So was anyone coming near the tabernacle while Moses and the priests were in there doing holy business for the camp. Anyone except a priest or levite caught doing tabernacle service was to die. Coming near while the tabernacle was being dismantled for travel was a capital crime.

In the "Law" (the five books of Hebrew Scripture) the crimes punishable by death are: 1. Murder. 2. Kidnaping. (I should say "man-naping," for it doesn't say anything about stealing a women.) 3. Giving one's child to Molech (child-sacrificing). 4. Blasphemy or cursing God. 5. Necromancy and witchcraft. 6. Working on the Sabbath. 7. Worshiping a foreign god. (This applied also to those who recommend such.) 8. Ox-goring. If a man's ox which was not kept up killed a person, he (and the ox) were to be stoned. 9. Also striking or cursing father or mother. (Even a "disobedient son" could be stoned.)

10. Adultery (both parties). 11. Rape of a virgin--in the open country. (The victim was also guilty if it took place in town.) 12. Homosexuality (women not mentioned). 13. "Lying with a beast," man or women (the beast was to be killed also). To save space I have not given scripture references, but with a good concordance you can look these up (if that interested).

These are not mentioned as punishment or paying one's debt to society. All this was in the name of keeping the community from "suffering God's wrath." Nothing is said about those casting the stones being "without sin."

Being in our Bible, do these "commandments" apply to Christians? If not why is it in the Christian Bible--and called God's Word? It seems to me things in the Old Testament are cited as "Scripture" when they fit into one's doctrinal designs, and rejected as an "older covenant" when they do not. We have yet to get our Bible straight. But as long as nobody pushes us we won't do it.

237

The Bible Says...

By Floyd Hale

Question: Was Jesus' mother still a virgin when he was born?

Answer: According to Matthew she was--that was necessary to the virgin "birth." The Church soon established the dogma that she remained such all the rest of her life.

This says something about how a character in a "myth" can end up becoming the "Mother of God"--which she did.

"Myth" should not be considered a bad word, when Matthew and Luke both chose it as the literary form for their stories of Jesus birth. It was--and remains-- a very legitimate form of expression. Taking it literally make what it says true, and misses the truth in it. This results in false doctrine.

In Matthew's search for all the "scripture" he could find to support the high claims being made for his Lord, he cited Isaiah 7:14, which says (in the RSV), "Behold, a young woman shall conceive (or 'is with child') and shall bear a son, and shall call his name Immanuel."

The reason the RSV replaces "virgin" (in the earlier KJV) with "young woman" is because that is what the original Hebrew text said. In the later translation of the Jewish Scriptures into Greek--for the Jews out in the Greek world the word meaning "virgin" (and not just a "young woman") was used. Since it was this later translation (called the Septuagint) which Matthew (and all the other Christians at the time) used as their "Bible," this seemed OK.

For Isaiah to be on the naming of the child it must have been his own (his wife was a young woman at the time), and he was in the habit of giving his sons "sermon titles" for names anyway (i.e. 7:3 and 8:3). "Immanuel" did not men "God has come in the flesh," but "God (is) with us." The sign of this to the king was "God is on our side"--against our foes who are threatening us. (Read the whole of this 7th chapter and you get what this was all about.)

This was a handy "scripture" for Matthew to midrash into an affirmation that said the Spirit was in Jesus, and God is with us. This had nothing to do with his mother's sex life.

LETTERS TO THE EDITOR

To the Editor:

On September 13 a question was asked of "The Bible Says. . ." which was this. Was there really a Virgin birth? The answer, given after a quite a few words, was, no, there was not a Virgin birth.

But let me say, God says in His word that Jesus was born of a Virgin. And we know His word is true.

He also says his word is forever settled in heaven.

But what is the Bible? It is the King James version of 1611. These modern versions that so many preachers and others are using today are not only a changed translation of the King James version.

God says in Rev. 22:19, "If any man shall take away from the words of the book of this prophecy, God shall take away his part out of the book of Life and out of the Holy City."

Preachers who are using these changed versions of God's word have their eyes blinded by Satan and cannot see afar off. Why don't you preachers get back to preaching the Bible, shake off the blinders and stand up and tell people there is such place as Hell for the wicked and Heaven for the righteous and that sin is in the world and must be repented of.

This nation of ours is the most sinful in the world. Our Supreme Court says abortion is legal, is O.K., but they are not Supreme. Only God is Supreme and He says it is murder. Yet I have never heard one preacher of today say one word against it to his church.

A Reader

W

The Bible Says...

By Floyd Hale

Question: Is Jesus coming back soon?

Answer: In the closing lines of the book of Revelation Jesus says--not once but twice--"I am coming soon" (Rev. 22:7 and 20). That was about nineteen hundred years ago. Since he did not--and soon meant soon--it is obvious that this is not to be taken literally. But then how is it to be taken?

First of all Jesus didn't say this--nor anything else in Revelation. John's book is an "Apocalypse." Since its message is supposed to have been "revealed" by God through Jesus (and a few angels), the English translators called it "Revelation." An Apocalypse is more than a message revealed in symbols; it is a most unique literary form in which fiction, fantasy, prophecy (foretelling the future) and any other literary form the author chooses, is combined to inspire fear and hope in his readers. That's legitimate in an Apocalypse, but the reader must know how to interpret it.

Since Jesus' gospel was "God is in charge," the kingdom (rule) of God, the author of Revelation emphasizes this by putting it in the most military and violent terms, unmercifully killing the enemy and whipping ("with a rod of iron") everyone else in line, The spirit of hate and vengeance breathes through almost every line. That's the apocalyptic way of saying it.

Knowing what each symbol symbolizes is not enough. The apocalyptic expression form must be understood and deapocalypticized--stripped of all its sub Christian ideology and venom. It is not foretelling the end of the world. It is not foretelling anything--except that victory comes through martyrdom--the way Jesus did it. The first readers of this book were being put to death as "enemies of the state" (Rome), and John was trying to inspire them to remain faithful.

Jesus is not coming back. If he did we would crucify him again. He didn't really go away (Mt. 28:20). He's still in the world, and occasionally where their is unjust suffering. a compassionate and courageous person (like Gandhi or Martin Luther King, Jr. picks up a cross, and follows him.)

239

The Bible Says...

By Floyd Hale

Question: Will the Jews rule the whole world someday?

Answer: The Bible says so (in Daniel 9:27). To say that "the saints of the Most High" in this passage refers to the followers of Christ (and his final victory over the world) is to force an interpretation on Daniel which is not true to that book. To show how Christians have traditionally done this to the Jewish Scriptures (which are in their Christian Bible), the King James revisors (in the 17th century) translated the Hebrew word "ma-shi-ach" in Daniel 9:25 and 26 as "Messiah." In all other places in the Old Testament they translated that same word "an anointed one"-- which when Daniel was written (2nd century B.C.) referred to the priests.

Here is where those who claim to take the Bible literally would have to say all Gentiles (non-Jews) will end up being the "servants" of the Jews. But the literalists don't go by what "the Bible says"; they quote a lot of the other Scriptures to make a particular passage say what they want it to say--and what has been traditionally believed.

Daniel was written as an Apocalypse to inspire the Jews to remain faithful to their holy customs, who at the time were having the Greek ("satanic Western") culture crammed down their throats at gunpoint by their Syrian overlords. Other nations (e.g. Babylon) had persecuted them before the Syrians, and God would see them through this tribulation (according to the author of Daniel). He would not only cause them to survive, He would--"in the end"--make all the nations "under the whole heaven" serve them. In an Apocalypse things like this can be said--while you are fantasizing you might as well go all the way. But that does not mean God said it.

If Christians really understood their Bible, they would remove the Jewish Scriptures (the O.T.) from it (and keep them as an Apocrypha, for "required reading only"). The religious leaders--who know this--won't suggest such a thing, for fear their members would leave and go to the fundamentalist churches--who teach that God wrote the whole Bible--He just changed his whole program in the middle of it.

The Bible Says...

By Floyd Hale

Question: What is the doctrine of "baptisms" mentioned in Hebrews 6:2?

Answer: I don't know, but the answer doesn't come from putting together all the other passages in the Scriptures where "baptism" is mentioned, building a "Doctrine of Baptism." The authors of the New Testament books didn't have all the others before them as they wrote. These had not yet evolved into one set of "Scriptures."

I doubt if the author was referring to the difference between water baptism (of/for repentance) and the baptism of the Holy Spirit (of/for witnessing). The extreme experience of persecution and death through which Jesus went is also called a "baptism."

I think it helpful that the RSV translated "baptisms" (in the plural) "ablutions" in this place. Writing to Jewish Christians the author is probably drawing a distinction between the "one" Christian baptism and the many Jewish rituals of purification. The "baptism of repentance" was a one-time thing, whereas the rituals of purification were to be repeated. This goes along with the strong warning which followed.

The main reason this book was written was to try to keep the Jewish Christians from "sliding back" into their old Faith. The Jews at the time were making it very hard on those of their number who became Christians. (You can understand that.) The author was using the old "Hebrew" tactic of "putting the fear of God into 'em," by telling them if they "back slid" they couldn't come back--be baptized again (v. 4). They'd be "crucifying Christ anew--holding him up to contempt." That's strong language.

Since this is obviously an unorthodox "teaching," I don't think if I were you I'd be too concerned about the meaning of the "doctrine of baptisms" in the book of Hebrews. I wish the Christians had left baptism at the Jordan River with John the Baptizer--where Jesus left it. He never baptized--except with the Holy Spirit. I think all the fuss over water baptism is a very subconscious "religious" way of ignoring Jesus' Baptism.

The Bible Says...

Question: What is the "time and times and half a time" in Revelation 12:14?

Answer: This comes from the apocalyptic traditions which originated with Daniel (7:25 and 12:7). When you look at that book you will see the author was predicting the time from his writing to the "end" of the Antiochan Persecution would come in "three and a half years" (forty-two months, 1260 days in other places). It is interesting that two "additions" were made to these "times" by a later hand to explain the inaccurate "guessing" (12:11-13).

The success of the Maccabean Revolt (against the Syrian overlords) in 164 B.C., the most celebrated military victory in all Jewish history, immediately made the book of Daniel (an Apocalypse) a most "inspired" document. It created the outburst of the apocalyptic way of thinking about the kingdom of God at the time of Christ, as our New Testament testifies. When the Romans set out to exterminate the Christians, John relied heavily on the book of Daniel in writing his Apocalypse (Revelation) to the Christians, to inspire them to keep the faith--even unto death.

When you read this verse (Rev. 12:14) in its context, you see that the dragon (the symbol of Satan) stalked the pregnant "woman" (Mary), waiting to devour her "male child" (Jesus). She is flown on "the wings of an eagle" (God's providence) into the wilderness for "a time, times, and a half time." Since the dragon can't get to the woman, it, in anger, goes off after the rest of her "offspring" (the Christians).

Evidently John was using Daniel's "time, times, and a half time" to tell his brothers and sisters that the "end" of their tribulation would surely come. It did (not in three and a half years, but) about two centuries later, after thousands of Christians were martyred. Instead of in a wilderness, these "souls" were kept safe in "heaven" (another good apocalyptic symbol).

Sometime the Bible student has to take a full course in Apocalypticism. There are good scholarly written books on it. Its literalism has to go.

The Bible Says...

By Floyd Hale

Question: Do you believe there is life after death?

Answer: According to a friend of mine he asked my wife if I believed in life after death. Her answer was (according to him), "Floyd doesn't even believe in life after supper."

"Everlasting life" means exactly what it says, *life goes on*. Death does not (and can not) stop it. The Bible writers had various ways of speaking about this in their ancient forms of expression. These tend to have gotten literalized into a "fire insurance" policy for the person who wants to "play it safe." Evangelists have often capitalized on this weakness.

Jesus said one must "lose" one's life in order to save it. In this the "self" (which has been granted temporary custody of one's "life") is "lost"--replaced by "Christ." He takes over and lives one's life his way. This is very heavy religious language, but it has a very practical meaning.

The "self" can not be saved. To speak of a "self" (usually called a "soul" or a "spirit") living on after death is to forget that the "self" is "lost"--one way or another. It is one's "life"-- what one "lives into life" (where else does one live?)-- which lives on in "everlasting life." One Gospel writer said Jesus came that we might get in on this (Jn. 10:10).

"One's life" merges into "the whole of life"--in this life (where others live)-- improving it or tearing it down. "Life" is bigger than one's little individual ego. God is in charge of it. That's why He is called the "Creator," and life is called "the kingdom of God." He rules in and over it, to the extent His will is done in and with it. That's why Jesus asked people to follow him in the doing of his Father's will.

Jesus put it to the religious folks of his day in very down to earth "secular" terms. I'd suggest you look closely at two of his stories which illustrate what I have been trying (all too clumsily) to say. These are: "The Good Samaritan" (Luke 10: 25-41) and "The Last Judgment" (Matthew 25: 31-46). In both of these God's will was done without anything said about religion.

I think Jesus is yet to be taken seriously.

243

The Bible Says...

By Floyd Hale

Question: I believe there is a law in the Islamic Bible that the hand of a thief is to be cut off. Is there such a law in our Bible?

Answer: The cutting off of the hand is mentioned twice as a penalty, in Deut. 19:21 and 25:12. In the former it is to be administered to the person who causes another to loose a hand. In the later it applies to a woman who "seizes the private parts "of a man who is beating up on her husband.

To show the awfulness of her crime, "she was not to be shown pity." I think the author of this "law" was the one to be pitied. I can't imagine a man standing by (in holy reverence) allowing his wife to be so humiliated and mutilated-- especially since she did that for his good. Surely she would know she was "breaking the law." Which would make her deed all the more commendable, I would think.

This "law" no doubt grew out of another "law," which said a man with bruised testicles could no longer be a member of the congregation (which was also stupid).

If Christianity had not come along, Israel would have remained one of those crazy Middle Eastern nations over there practicing stuff like this--and putting out "contracts" on anyone accused of blasphemy (Lev. 24:16), which some would say I just committed. In fact, if Christianity had not come along, there would be no nation of Israel over there now. For it has been the Christian Church spreading the Jewish Scriptures "as the Word of God" (in which it says "the Jews shall return") that has conditioned the Western world to condone the Jews taking that land away from the Palestinians (whose ancestors, the Canaanites, had it taken away from them by the ancestors of the Jews to begin with). How do you think the Christian Palestinians today feel about this?

The cutting off of the hand is commended once in the New Testament. In his typical hyperbole Jesus said, "If your hand offend you (cause you to sin), cut it off." But the Church was not to perform the surgery.

The Bible Says...

By Floyd Hale

Question: Does the Bible say God actually kills people?

Answer: God "commanded(?)" the Israelites to go out and slaughter hordes of people, but I can think of at least once where He "smote(?)" a man Himself. In II Samuel 6:6-7 it is reported God "smote" one Uzzah dead, for performing, of all things, what he thought was doing God a favor. Uzzah was helping move the ark to Jerusalem when the ox cart carrying it jostled, and he put his hand to the shrine to steady it. There is just no logical explanation why God would get "angry" with this man and kill him--yet this account is defended by Biblicists as "the Word of God."

My understanding of Bible literature, and especially its books of "history," convinces me that this incident never happened in the first place. The author (writing centuries after the fact, to make a strong theological statement) was promoting the "sacredness" of the ark--Israel's God was supposed to be present in it.

To emphasize fear as the motive for serving God the Israelite leaders liked to tell all the awful (and spurious) things their God did to literally scare the devil out of the people. The word "to hold in awe" does not fit into most of the passages where the "fear" of God is mentioned. It is regrettable that Christians incorporate into their image of God this kind of stuff from their Bible.

Our Old Testament was the "Bible" of the New Testament writers, which accounts for the author of Acts inferring God struck down two of the first Christians--for withholding some of their money from the Church and lying about it (Acts 5:1-10). My knowledge of why and how Luke wrote this "history of the new Church" assures me this incident also did not happen.

The God of the New Testament did not lay a mean threat of fear on the first Christians, but a heavy burden of love. It is high time we gain a knowledge of our Bible. I think the survival of the Christian Faith--at least its true content--depends on it.

LETTERS TO THE EDITOR

Dear D. (Editor):

After reading Mr. Hale's answers to questions sent to him about Jesus in your Feb. 9th issue of (this paper), all I can feel for this man is pity.

Also, I would like to ask that you take this man's writing out of your newspaper. We have put up with lies and the lack of morals from the White House, National newspapers, and television. I do not think we need this liberal atheistic view in our local papers put out by a "so-called man of God."

A Reader

Editor's Note: An atheist doesn't believe in God. I doubt if Rev. Hale would plead guilty, but if the jury is still out, it sounds like you might hang it. D.B.

Dear Friend D. (Editor):

Apparently your hardheaded, liberalistic thinking has overdone itself by allowing Floyd Hale articles to disgrace the religious page of your paper. No doubt the devil and his angels are all smiling.

You contend you print the articles to cause the reader to think. Why not just print hard-core pornography? I'm certain that would allow people to think. At least I bet that's what the rapists and sex offenders in prison would tell you!

I think it might be a good idea to let your wife screen your articles. To me she seems to display a lot of good common sense.

A Reader

Editor's note: You know me well enough to know I would encourage open discussion of opinions different than my own, but would not publish pornography. You admit in feelings for others we are both liberals. D.B.

Dear D. (Editor):

I would like to respectfully suggest that it is time you to gracefully retire the Floyd Hale column from your paper. It is an affront to the beliefs of the vast majority of the people of Edwards County. It causes one to question the motives of the editor as well as the writer of the column.

A Reader

Editor's note: Space has been given for Rev. Hale's opinions and for those who disagree. D.B.

The Bible Says...

By Floyd Hale

Question: Why do the gospels of Matthew and John disagree on how Jesus called Peter?

Answer: In the Gospel of Matthew Jesus invites Andrew and Peter at the same time (Mt. 4:18). In John's Gospel (1:35-42) he calls Andrew, and then Andrew goes and brings his brother Simon (Peter) to Jesus.

There are other differences in these two texts also. According to Matthew Jesus first met Andrew and Peter both up by the Sea of Galilee--where they were fishermen. In John Jesus met Andrew down near Jerusalem (at the Jordan) who was then one of John the Baptist's followers. Andrew then goes after Peter (who must have been nearby). The "next day" Jesus goes up into Galilee and calls other disciples. If Matthew and John were both disciples of Jesus how could they have gotten basic facts like this so mixed up? (Neither of the authors of these two Gospels were disciples of Jesus.)

The Fourth Gospel (John's) was written near the close of the first century, after it was concluded that Jesus was "the Son of God"-- in fact "the same as God." Thus he knows everything that's going on and how it will turn out (in John). He knew all about Andrew before he met him, telling him he was "an Israelite in whom there was no guile." This convinced Andrew that Jesus was "the Messiah." Things like this run throughout John's Gospel. He knew the Samaritan woman at the well had had five husbands (and lived with her present boyfriend). He told her he was the Christ (Messiah). I could go on about John's Gospel--which is actually not a Gospel at all. It constructs a "life of Jesus" (almost a century after he died) to support the faith of the Church that Paul founded--which became the traditional Christian Church. This is why the traditionalists like to "quote Jesus" from this Gospel. In it he "says" the very things they like to hear--although he didn't actually say any of it.

I have said many times before, the Gospel of John is the most misunderstood book in the Bible. And it will continue so, for it is the best liked book in the Bible. Just get borned again and you've got it made.

246

The Bible Says...

By Floyd Hale

Question: How could John the Baptist be the greatest among men but least in the kingdom of heaven?

Answer: Let me first say that Matthew, writing to Jews, usually substitutes the word "heaven" for "God" (as in this place), because they tried to keep from using God's name--afraid of breaking the third commandment. Other Gospels use the title "God" in this place (Lu. 7:28).

I don't profess to know what this text in Matthew 11:11 means. I (along with many Bible scholars) question its being one of the authentic sayings of Jesus. Although it could be a later "version" of something similar he said. This is not to deny the meaning of this passage; it just doesn't seem to fit into Jesus view of the kingdom.

The earliest reference to John was as "the Baptizer" (Mk.1:4). This (Mt. 11:11) is the only place where Jesus refers to him as "the Baptist," indicating this tradition originated after Jesus' time. Jesus would not have cited Malichi 3:1 as foretelling John, for it does not. (Neither does Isaiah 40:3, misquoted in Mt. 3:3.)

The Gospel writers made Jesus fit into their claims that he was the "promised Messiah." It would be most interesting if we had writings left by John's disciples to compare with what the Christians said about him. The "Baptists" continued as a thriving sect throughout the New Testament period. The last Gospel written makes a very concerted (yet subtle) effort to try to get them to "join the Christian band."

One popular interpretation of this passage sees John as the last (but "greatest") of the Old Testament prophets--the "old kingdom"--with Jesus' converts being the first ones in the "new kingdom." This too just doesn't quite square with Jesus' kingdom teachings.

Another problem with this text is the "kingdom suffering violence and being taken by force" (v. 12)--whatever that means-- also doesn't sound like Jesus.

This is not a straight answer to your question. But be consoled this doesn't have anything to do with your faith.

247

The Bible Says...

By Floyd Hale

Question: What is the unpardonable sin?

Answer: The Gospels differ on this subject, making it a bit confusing. Luke reports Jesus warning about blasphemy against the Holy Spirit as the unpardonable sin, but does not relate it to Jesus casting out demons (12:10). Where he says Jesus was accused of casting out demons by (the power of) the Devil (11:14-23), he says nothing about that being blasphemy against the Holy Spirit--nor unpardonable.

Matthew (12:22-32) follows Mark (3:22-30) on this warning coming as a result of Jesus being accused of casting out demons by (the power of) the Devil. Then Mark adds: "This eternal sin was committed by those who had said He (Jesus) has an unclean spirit" (v. 30). This seems to be a charge against Jesus--which had just been declared forgivable (v. 28). Since Jesus said he did it by (the power of) the Holy Spirit, I guess this makes it in a round about way against the Holy Spirit. If this really happened as related, that "unpardonable sin" could be committed only by someone during Jesus' lifetime. Right?

I remember as a youth, the last night of just about every revival meeting in our little church the evangelist preaching on this text would say, "You can resist the Spirit only so long, and He will cease striving with you." As a pastor I once counseled with a man who sincerely wanted to become a Christian, but thought he could not, for he was convinced he had committed the unpardonable sin in this manner years earlier. I could not convince him otherwise. I never felt so sorry for anyone in all my life.

The Apostle Paul was quite an expert on the subject of sins, but in none of the warnings he gave his many congregations does he ever mention this one. If he had known about it I am sure he would have.

Blasphemy was punishable by death in the Jewish Law, and that was in the "Bible" of the authors of the Gospels. That's how I think it slipped into this Gospel story. My understanding of how the Gospels were written gives me reason to believe Jesus did not make this statement.

The Bible Says...

By Floyd Hale

Question: Is Saddam Hussein the "anti-Christ"? (2-4-99)

Answer: Many rascals in history have been tagged with this infamous label. I remember when many were sure it was Hitler. For some Franklin D. Roosevelt filled the bill; the big blue spread-eagle on his NRA symbol was "the mark of the beast." (NRA stood for the National Recovery Act, not the National Rifle Association.)

There are various views in the New Testament on this subject. It was thought by some there would be a false messiah (pseudo-Christ) rise up "in the last days" and fool just about all the faithful into following him. Paul told the Thessalonians--whom he had got all excited about Jesus returning soon--that this would not happen till "that man of sin" ("that lawless one," RSV) was first revealed. This "son of perdition" would sit enthroned in the temple and rule as God. Jesus would then come down and slay him.

The author of I John told his readers they were living "in the last hour, for many antichrists have come." He says these were some (evangelists?) who had gone out from them, but they "deny Jesus is the Christ." (It would be interesting to know the exact details of that controversy.) John says his readers had been told that the antichrist was coming, "and (he) is in the world now." In his second letter John says "anyone who denies Jesus Christ came in the flesh is the antichrist."

It is surely obvious these scriptures can not be put together in one "Bible teaching"--especially pointing to such a figure in the future.

"Antichrist" was a part of the "end of the world" (apocalyptic) scare language which was popular in the early Church.

The fundamentalist view that everything in the Bible is true--God's Word--lets silly things like this (and many other so-called prophecies) be of prime interest, replacing the important matters of faith. I sure would help if people were told the truth about their Bible.

Saddam is mean, but I'm afraid he's not "the man."

The Bible Says...

By Floyd Hale

Question: Did God forgive sins before Jesus died on the cross? If so, why was Jesus' death necessary?

Answer: The Bible shows that God did a lot of forgiving before Jesus was killed. The mixup about this is a good illustration of how people can make a serious mistake by taking all that's in their Bible as "God's Word."

The Hebrew Scriptures (our Old Testament) was the "Bible" of the first Christians--they were Jews. This made them think they had to be "Biblical" in everything they proclaimed about Jesus. The Gospels are full of this--even put on the lips of Jesus after his death. Luke 24:25-27,46 is a good example of this. They even claimed things to be "scriptural" which were not. This was not to outright deceive; it was just their way of promoting religion. And, I'm sorry to say, it's still done today in some parts.

Their "Bible said" forgiveness came by "the shedding of blood." Although God had no part in the animal sacrifices (they learned this from their pagan neighbors), they believed those sacrifices-- especially the annual Pascal lamb--made atonement for the sins of the people. And these were not "types" looking toward the offering of Jesus. Since Jesus lived a sacrificial life, it was easy for his death to be interpreted as the perfect Levitical sacrifice--God's doing. This replaced a Jewish superstition with a Christian one. Paul (a Jew) developed his gospel out of this and founded the Church on it-- without the Jerusalem Church's blessing.

What is bad about this is, it promotes a mystical experience of "faith" based on a myth, by misrepresenting the life and death of Jesus--thus missing the real Jesus who asked people to follow him (even unto death) in getting God's will (what's right) done in this world.

Biblicists still pick from the Scriptures--long lists of quotes--what they want to believe, overlooking the most important part. When will people ever be told the truth about the Bible? Jesus was killed because his Gospel, "God is in charge," threatened the powers that be.

The Bible Says...

By Floyd Hale

Question: Does the Bible really mean to say that God created the first woman because there could not be found among the animals one good enough to be man's "helper"?

Answer: One thing is obvious about this Creation Story (Gen. 2:4b-3:24); a man wrote it, back when male chauvinism was a divine attribute.

The Story of Adam and Eve, not to be confused or harmonized with the first Creation Story (1:1-2:4a), is a "story"--properly called a myth. The author thought knowing right from wrong was for the gods only. (The business of "knowing" is yet considered evil in some religious circles.)

This story reveals many serious questions about life when it was composed. Why was the beautiful experience of birth marred by labor pains for the mother? Why did the husband have to labor hard from dawn to dark (back then) just to eke out a living? Why do sticker weeds grow wild and profusely, when vegetables have to be planted and cultivated? Why do snakes have to slide along on their "bellies"--can't walk? Since they believed God caused everything both good and bad, these must be divine curses.

This story makes for some interesting allegorizing, but it remains a "story." Its one main point is, ignoring what's right (disobeying God) is why the world is in the mess it's in--true enough. But woman is certainly not an afterthought of the Creator because no animal could quite fill her role. I would suggest the opposite is what happened; I think the woman came first. Since she was going to be tied down birthing and raising kids, she needed the "helpmate." Many women have had to live an animal's life, because men have enjoyed a false sense of superiority and freedom.

The Apostle Paul treated the Adam and Eve story as literally true. Recently the largest Church denomination in America quoted him in passing the resolution: "Women should obey their husbands." What does this say to you about where we are today in understanding the Bible?

251

The Bible Says...

By Floyd Hale

Question: Who was Zechariah's father, Berechiah or Iddo?

Answer: It really doesn't make any difference (except it probably did to Zechariah), but this illustrates something very important about the Bible.

Zechariah (1:1) says it was Berechiah (and he ought to know). Ezra (5:1) skipped over Berechiah and reported Zach's grandfather Iddo as his father. Small mistake but nonetheless a mistake. To explain this as any of his ancestors could be called his "father" is itself a mistake.

If you look closely at I and II Chronicles, Ezra, and Nehemiah (all one "History" authored by the same person, whom we know only as "the Chronicler"), you will find many such "mistakes." Most of them were the intentional changes of the older account, Samuel-Kings. Chronicles covers the same period of the history of Israel which Samuel-Kings does. But the Chronicler "rewrote" his history much later to make it support new religious thinking.

A good example of this is the older statement (II Sam. 24:1) that God told David to number Israel. The later History says the Devil told

him to (I Chr. 21:1). (Neither told him to "according to Hale.") Both of these "Histories" were written for religious purposes--long after the facts and not just to report the facts. A close comparison of Samuel-Kings with Chronicles reveals some different religious points of view. This is not what the "critics" say; this is what the Bible says--when it is let express itself.

Since the average lay person is not aware of such things about their Bible, someone like me has to point this out--not to tear down the Scriptures, but to convince people that they need to learn a new and realistic approach to their Bible.

The Bible--the one most outstanding book of world literature--is more and more being taught in the colleges and universities as literature. I hope this can one day be done on the level of secondary public education; because the Bible was the major force in establishing this great democracy we call America.

The Bible Says...

By Floyd Hale

Question: Did Jesus say he would rise again from the dead?

Answer: To get my answer you'll have to follow very closely.

How could Jesus continue to be "Lord" (Divine Boss) of the disciples after his death? By laying the apocalyptic title, "Son of man" (from the book of Daniel, a very popular Apocalypse at the time) on him this was done. This became a solid tradition by the time the first Gospel, Mark, was written forty years later. In it Jesus is continually called "the Son of man."

Mark even has Jesus "foretelling" his own resurrection as the Son of man (8:31, 9:9, 10:33). Since this mythical "Son of man" came from heaven ("on the clouds") he returned ("was raised") to heaven--after his martyrdom in the body of Jesus. The "ascension" myth in Acts is saying the same thing--not promising a Second Coming. Since Jesus had said he was "a son of man" (the way the prophets humbly referred to themselves), this must have helped them change that "a" to "The."

Resurrection being a popular belief (Paul believed in it before he became a Christian), helped give shape to the resurrection myths at the end of the Gospels. To treat these as literally true is to miss what they are saying about Jesus.

If you think I am playing fast and loose with the Scriptures, look closely at what that apocalyptic affirmation really means, "God raised Jesus to his right hand of Power--and gave him a name above every name (Lord)." "Lord" (as I said above) means Boss. The disciples "obeyed" Jesus because they believed he was right--about God and His kingdom. They believed it so strongly that they would continue to "follow him"-- after his death. This is the way he "appeared to them" after his death. Their experience of the "risen-ascended" Jesus--laid the heavy burden of a continuing discipleship on them. The same applies to a would be disciple today.

It sure would be a lot happier alternative, to believe "Jesus' rising from the dead" means I will too someday--just for the believing in him.

The Bible Says...

By Floyd Hale

Question: Was the Heaven's Gate group who recently committed suicide in California a Christian sect?

Answer: They were not a Christian sect, but their odd beliefs came mainly from Christianity. Their aim was to go to heaven, and so is that of the traditional Christian. They were not only willing but anxious to give their lives to go there--now. Christians want to live as long as they can here, and use their heaven insurance as a "death benefit."

If you added "on a UFO" to what Paul says about his followers being "caught up to meet Christ in the air" (in I Thes. 4:16), you'd be getting close to Heaven's Gate. The HG people were in the process of being "changed" to live on a "higher level." Paul said the "living (believers) would be changed" to make that flight.

Heaven sounds awful good for our dead loved ones, but Jesus asked his followers to apply their thinking strictly to this world. This is where he wanted God's kingdom (rule) to come-- through people doing His will. That sounds like pretty straight thinking to me, but Jesus said that would require "losing one's self." The HG folks were sure willing to loose themselves. They would have made very good Gnostics in the early church, for "this evil world" was not their home--it would soon "pass away."

All that fit right in with Paul's desire to live forever (don't we all?), so he bought into it (haven't we all?). Using the language he borrowed from the Apocalyptists (end-of-the-world folks at the time) he ended up making heaven fundamental to the traditional Christian Faith. It has stuck simply because we like it. "It'll preach"--as they say. This helps us ignore what Jesus taught, that "heaven" was for this world. Those who believe him--and work toward that end--can (and should) forget about a "next world." If there is another one, they-- and only they--will be ready for it anyway.

I think it interesting that the Heaven's Gate people financed their life style by selling computer skills to those who were going to stay behind in this world.

254

The Bible Says...

By Floyd Hale

Question: Why did Matthew say Jesus rode two donkeys into Jerusalem?

Answer: Mark (11:4-7) and Luke (19:32-35) both report it was only one animal Jesus rode, a "colt on which no one had ever sat." Its mother is not mentioned.

This is to "fulfill a prophecy," and Matthew (21:1-7) mistook Jechariah 9:9 for two animals, "Lo, your king comes to you; triumphant and victorious is he, humble and riding on an ass, on a colt the foal of an ass." This was a very popular way the Hebrew poets had of describing the same thing in two different ways--a "parallelism." One with which you are familiar is in Psalm 8:4, "What is man that though art mindful of him, and the son of man that though visitist him?" (KJV).

Matthew says when "they brought the ass and the colt to Jesus, the disciples put their garments on them, and he sat on them." Both the KJV and RSV try to soften this error a little by saying that Jesus "sat thereon," but the original Greek text is very explicit, "he sat on them." I once pointed this out to a minister who defended this, saying Jesus rode one a while and then the other--thus riding them both.

There is a famous painting of Jesus' entrance into Jerusalem. The artist used Matthew (probably thinking the other Gospels said the same thing), and shows Jesus actually straddling both the beasts. It is done from an angle so Jesus doesn't look too awkward.

I would point out two things we might learn from Matthew's error. First, don't be so hip on "fulfilled prophecies." It is obvious that the rest of those in Matthew did not apply either. It was actually this "prophecy" which helped create this Triumphal Entry story--not a fulfillment.

Second, this shows where "literalism" can lead a person. Matthew was so literal in quoting his "scripture" that he failed to see what it actually said.

Don't misunderstand me; I like Matthew. If for no other reason he illustrates very clearly--right in the Bible-- how one should not quote the Scriptures.

Literalism just doesn't stand up when it is applied to the whole Bible anyway.

The Bible Says...

By Floyd Hale

Question: What do preachers mean when they say sinners will be lost?

One of the early space shots by NASA almost failed to get a guidance operation to work as the craft neared the moon. During that problem a scientist interviewed by Walter Cronkite said if we didn't get it fixed, the gravity of the moon would sling the astronauts back toward the earth but miss it, sailing on past--forever. (It got fixed.) What's the difference between "missing the earth"--going on forever into outer darkness, and "missing life" while living here?

"Lost eternally" is an apocalyptic expression which challenges a person to "find" his/her purpose in this world. In a parable Jesus told about those who had compassion on their neighbors in need (Mt. 25:31f.), when he said they made it through "the Judgment" he was not telling folks how to get to heaven. He was saying that caring about (and for) others was the way to live here and now. If very many people did that, we'd have heaven on earth.

An everlasting string of scriptures can be quoted on this subject, but since the hereafter is a figure of speech, I have to relate its meaning to the right now.

Jesus has convinced me that life is "where it's at." God made no mistake in creating this world which he plans to correct in a "next one."

Treat this place like it is not God's kingdom, and you've "lost" it. Treat this world as a place to prepare for going to another one, and you've really "lost" it. If one seeks to do God's will in-- and with--this life, God can be trusted to take care of whatever might come later. A religion which tempts a person to "escape" from this life encourages a sick brand of thinking.

Jesus said one could find oneself by "losing" his or herself. Note that this works only when it is done Jesus' way.

I think a lot of good peoples' lives are "lost" in just wasted time, when they could be doing a lot of good with them.

The Bible Says...

By Floyd Hale

Question: What does the Bible mean by "fornication"?

Answer: Webster defines fornication as "voluntary sexual intercourse between an unmarried woman and a man, especially an unmarried man." The Bible carries about the same meaning, except in some cases it includes adultery. It was far more than a "personal sin." In Bible times (before "the pill") this had to do with protecting proper procreation of the race--maintaining the family role. Children born out of wedlock faced real insecurity. Can you imagine a civilized society in which the females parented children the way animals do? Even some animals mate for life.

The Israelites were so concerned about this they even made it a law (in the name of God) that illegitimate children ("bastards," KJV) were to be excluded from the "congregation"--which was non-citizenship status. This shows you how unjust people can become in promoting justice.

The prophets called going after other gods "fornication" (sometimes "harlotry"), being unfaithful in relationship to Yahweh (the Israelite God). This would create a race of infidels, who in Israel also held no rights of citizenship--the church was the state. In fact infidelity (and even those who suggested it) were punishable by death. (This is what makes Islam--a sister religion to Judaism--an enemy of democracy.)

There was no such thing as freedom of religion in Israel. The fundamentalist leaders in Judaism are making this a big political issue in the present state of Israel.

I might add right here that Christian fundamentalists, if they had their way, would pass and enforce secular laws aimed at making the U.S. "a Christian nation again" (which it never was). This begins as pushing for morality in civil affairs-- which is good--but when it makes morality a civil law on religious grounds it violates a higher law. Our founding fathers rightfully saw that true freedom of religion includes the right of freedom from religion.

257

The Bible Says...

By Floyd Hale

Question: What does "idolatry" in the Bible mean?

Answer: It meant (to the Hebrews) "worship of another god or an object (idol) representing another god" (Webster).

The Hebrews are credited with introducing Monotheism--the belief that there is only one God. There is evidence in the Old Testament that this evolved from the conviction that the Israelite God (Yahweh) was superior to all other gods. Living among and mixing with people who "worshipped other gods" did not help the Hebrews become "holy" ("a separate people").

This was not a matter of a particular "idol" being so attractive, but the benefits bestowed by the god it represented. The god Baal of the Canaanites, in whose land the Israelites were squatters, was the deity in charge of fertility in that territory. Worshiping Baal caused good and plentiful crops to grow, cattle to bear healthy and plentiful offspring, even wives to birth babies--especially boy babies. You can see why Baal had some appeal to the Hebrew farmers (which almost all of them were).

Before we pass this off as a silly ancient superstition, we should realize that the modern version of this cult is the worship of the Almighty Dollar.

Another form of modern idolatry is 'Bibliolatry.' Just as prosperity tempted the ancient Hebrews to worship Baal, religion tempts the Christian to worship the Bible. "Worship" may sound like a strong word, but this unwittingly makes God out of the Bible. Taking the Bible literally as "God's Word" sets a person up to be sucked into this cult--believing "God said" everything the Bible says."

If the literalists really saw what the Bible says, they'd see that it portrays and even praises a sometimes wrathful--even cruel--God. Jesus tried to get his brethren to stop worshiping their Bible (the "Law." After he was executed as a blasphemer (Mk 14:64) a few did change and follow him, but the writings they produced were soon canonized as "Bible" and then treated as "law." The average lay person doesn't know how to get out of this Bibliolatry

The Bible Says...

By Floyd Hale

Question: I believe that through Jesus Christ we have forgiveness of sins, but do we have to pay other consequences in life for our sins?

Answer: Sin is too much treated as being strictly against God. Most (if not all) of what we call "sins" harm people--one's self, others, and/or society as a whole. The consequences of sin (wrong doing) are many and of lasting effect. They do more than corrupt character. They hurt others. And they pollute the stream of life--"even to the tenth generation." All this should be the focus of any discussion on sin, not the punishment of the sinner by God.

Consequences are natural, and they fall most on the innocent. When the strict terms of justice are applied to sinning, the issue is confused. Sin can not be "paid for." That was the legalistic way of thinking applied to righteousness by the Jews which distorted the image of Jesus--he "paid" for the sins of the sinner by dying on the cross. In the Law (the first Christians' Scriptures) a blood offering was required for absolution. Since a sacrifice had to be a perfect animal (without blemish), it was claimed Jesus was "without sin" in order to "atone for sin." All of this leads the believer away from the real work of Jesus. He was killed because he dared to do the will of God (what was right), right where wrong was being done to the people--and asked others to do the same ("follow me"). That--and that alone--will remedy the sins of the world. Consequences work both ways.

To "pay other consequences in life for our sins" is unrealistic. First, because of the legalistic meaning of "pay" mentioned above. Second, the word "other" suggests (to me) there are "costs" (penalties) above and beyond the natural consequences-- which there are not. Third, this suggests a law of retribution (paying in this life), which is an old but false idea.

Let me repeat. Any discussion of "sin" should focus on its consequences in and on life--especially on the lives of others, not on the offender's punishment.

The Bible Says...

By Floyd Hale

Question: Should I forgive someone of a sin against me, if that person does not ask me for forgiveness?

Answer: For the Christian the answer hinges on understanding God's grace, which is unconditional--or it is not grace. God accepts everyone, saint and sinner alike (Mt. 5:45). It is interesting that the "saints" don't like this. This is perfectly illustrated in the story of the Prodigal Son. In this parable Jesus purposefully did not put forgiveness on the lips of the father when the boy returned. Jesus also purposefully had the father ignore (almost rudely) the boy's memorized prayer of confession.

It is knowing the grace of God which causes the proper kind of repentance (a change of heart). If repentance were required first, then forgiveness would result from something we did--"works." This is what Paul was saying in Rom. 2:4.

I said all of the above because Jesus said we were to forgive others the way God forgives us. This goes deeper than the formal and legalistic way of asking and granting of pardon. It has to do with curing offenders of their offensive ways--the purpose of "forgiveness" to begin with.

Jesus was speaking on this subject once when Peter said, "How often should I forgive my brother who sins against me--seven times?" Peter thought that would be going to the limit. Jesus responded (in his unique way), "Peter, Multiply your seven by seventy" (490 times?). You have to examine this closely or you miss what Jesus was saying. By about the tenth time the person offending you would surely see a forgiving spirit already in you--AS you were being offended--which might cause him to change his ways, stop being an offensive person. This is not "letting people walk on you." It is God's way of curing offenders.

I know this sounds extreme--impossible--but it can be applied in a small way in a lot of everyday relationships. People who hold a grudge are not likely to have their friends say they are sorry--and they shouldn't "have to"--which just might get them to.

260

The Bible Says...

By Floyd Hale

Question: Why did the prophet Jonah want God to take his life?

Answer: Because he had just been the most successful missionary of all time. He had preached God's message to the Ninevites, "Forty days and I am going to overthrow your city." But Jonah didn't want to see 'em "saved."

If you read this little story anywhere else but in the Bible, you'd see right off it was a "story," not a report on what actually happened. If all the people in the large city of Nineveth, from the king (of the Assyrian Empire) on down to the last inhabitant would have become dedicated Jews (as this book states), the history of the Middle East would have taken a much different course in that 8th century B.C. But this little pamphlet was written four centuries later to condemn the Jews for their hatred of foreigners--an ethnic cleansing was actually going on in Jerusalem--carried out by Ezra, against gentile women (Palestinians?).

It was a very bold effort on the part of the author, who was going completely counter to almost all the other Old Testament writers, so he hid his message in a parable. In this "story" God begins by being against the foreigners also, but He "repents"--changes His mind of the evil He was going to do to the Ninevites. But Jonah had rather die than change his mind. He has the audacity to hold God to his word. Then God says (in the author's subtle suggestion), "Foreigners are My people also. Would you expect Me to kill even the little children--and the animals" (4::9-11)? The author hopes the reader will blink and then change his mind about foreigners and go with God, instead of with the bigoted Jonah.

There was a prophet named Jonah mentioned as living in earlier times (II Kings 14:25). Being a contemporary with the Assyrians' ("Nineveth") giving the Israelites much pain, his name is used as the hero(?) in this story. Since all kinds of miracles and wonders had been attributed to God by earlier Bible writers, the readers of this story had no trouble taking this story literally--that's the mental trap set up by a parable.

261

The Bible Says...

By Floyd Hale

Question: Does the Bible put a blessing on hatred?

Answer: The Psalms are fairly well accepted as the authority on spiritual matters. In the 139th, which is a lengthy praising God and praying to Him, the author invokes God to "slay the wicked." He says "I hate them that hate Thee." He hates them "with a perfect hatred," and counts them "his enemies." It is rather obvious that the Psalmist here builds up a straw man out of the wicked (mainly because they are giving him a hard time) and says those "maliciously defy God" and "lift themselves up against" Him.

This is in the same Bible in which Jesus teaches, "Love your enemies and pray for those who give you a hard time" (Mt. 5:44). If the 139th Psalm is not Christian, why is it in the Christian Bible? That it was in the Hebrew scriptures is one thing, but to include it in the Christian canon is another. To say that God started a whole new program ("covenant") with the Jesus people is to excuse the "old" one as legitimate--for "back then." God never changed; his blessing was never on a lot of things the Israelites said and did--saying He said it or told them to do it. The O.T. literature rises to high moments of justice and mercy on occasion, but to claim the Word of God for it all is to confuse the Christian Faith.

Jesus even says, "You have heard that it was said," when referring to what they called Holy Scripture. "Men of old (including Moses) said, but I say." That is the same as saying "The Bible says but I say." This was not because Jesus had some divine authority; it was because he understood God's truth--and had the courage to speak it. The human mind has the ability to recognize truth--if it hasn't been conditioned by a lot of religious dogmas.

Those who say we need the O.T. because it prophecies Jesus ought to learn that Jesus is not foretold in the O.T. The several New Testament passages which make this claim change the original meaning of those O.T. texts. The great prophetic tradition within the Jewish culture was bound to produce a person like Jesus sooner or later. This can be discerned from reading the Old Testament.

The Bible Says...

By Floyd Hale

Question: Who killed Jesus?

Answer: Since the anniversary of that killing-- Good Friday--is coming up this week, let's take another look at this age old "murder mystery."

You have heard preachers say "God did it," but that's hard for me to believe. The most casual reading of the Gospels shows that a group of very religious folk had a lot to do with Jesus' demise. The governor, who was coerced into being the judge at the trial, found it politically expedient to let those making the charges be the jury. Could the good citizens of that community, who rose up en masse demanding quick justice for that out-o'-town breaker of sacred law have been wrong?

Where were all those people who had benefited so freely from the healing hands and loving heart of the accused? Where were his friends? Would not their failure to stand up as character witnesses be a "sin"? Could the soldiers who did the close-up bloody work on Jesus have been "sinning"? After all, they were just carrying out the orders of their government--which was there in that little foreign country to "keep the peace."

Who else was around that day? Who was missing?-- everybody else in that whole city! What kind of people is it that make up a community in which anyone can suffer unjustly without them getting involved? Was that a "sin"? But you say, "They didn't know about it." That's just it, they had been a long time in the habit of "not knowing" what was going on. Was that a "sin"? That was just another average day in the lives of those people. They had learned the best way to stay out of trouble was to stay away from where it was going on.

Maybe we have found out "who done it"--*sin did it!* But sin has no meaning apart from sinners. And it just might be we have found out, not only what is meant by "all of us are sinners," but what our "sin" really is.

Could it be that's why we like better the preacher's answer to this question, "God did it"?

263

The Bible Says...

By Floyd Hale

Question: Was it an even 2,000 years from Adam to Abraham, and an even 2,000 years from Abraham to the birth of Christ?

Answer: If you go by the figures in the Genesis 5 and 10 genealogy, Abraham was born exactly 1,998 years after Adam was ~~born~~ created, in 4004 B.C. You didn't miss it far. The only thing wrong with this is, Adam is a fictional character, not the first homo sapien on this planet. And, anything prior to the twelfth chapter of Genesis is not history.

Quoting Jesus and Paul to prove Adam, Enoch and Noah actually lived, only proves that we need a better understanding of our Bible.

When biblical chronology is followed, Abraham's birth would have been in exactly 2006 B.C. 2,000 years from Abraham to the Bethlehem manger event would bring us to 6 B.C. This is closer to the 2,000 years figure than you might think, for the best educated guess is Jesus was born sometime just prior to 4 B.C.

Your question suggests to me that you are aware of the once popular theory of some of the Millennialists. They figure the 2,000 years following the birth of Jesus is the "Christian Period," at the end of which Christ is to return to "rule 1,000 years"--completing the "seven millennium cycle." This would date the Rapture about two years ago. (At least you and I missed it.

As the year 2,000 draws near, I expect to hear more about the ushering in of the upcoming Seventh (Sabbath) Millennium. According to this the lights go out at midnight on the morning of January 1, 3001 A.D. (You and I won't have to worry about that either.)

I like Jesus' answer to questions like this, "God only knows!"

Time wasted playing the numbers game with the Bible would be a lot better spent trying to figure out what is relative in it.

264

The Bible Says...

By Floyd Hale

Question: Rev. Hale, why don't you ever say anything good about the Bible?

Answer: I guess the good I say about the Bible is in the small print--or the footnotes. There's no shortage of preachers saying good things about the Bible. The problem is most of them say it's all good--or infer it.

I know an awful lot of good about the Bible. That's why I say all those "bad things" about it. If you get the bad out of the way--simply understood it for what it is--the good gets gooder.

A lady once wrote a letter to the editor of this paper (about twenty years ago) about this column, telling a story about a woman who tore a page out of her Bible every time her preacher said something bad about it on Sunday morning, and finally she had no Bible. The false traditional view of the Scriptures sets a person up for this kind of fear.

It must be said, ninety-nine percent of what was on those pages was good--several pages had nothing bad on them. I don't want one page torn from the Bible. I want it all to remain just like it is. I just want it to be understood for what it is.

Most of what I say taken as "negative," is not about the bad in the Bible at all; it's about errors, contradictions, other inconsistencies and the *different literary forms* that have been so misinterpreted; otherwise the fallacy that its's all literally true--"God said it."

I find myself writing as though I were trying to change the minds of stubborn Fundamentalists. I know better than try to do that. I try to be so blunt and logical that the rest of the readers don't miss the point. It is mainly to them that I write. They need a spokesman.

The Bible can hold its own--even do much better if it is treated honestly. I find a lot of the letters which used to come in to the editor of the paper about me, were written as though to their Doctor, cussing him out for telling 'em they've got cancer--"You're not goin' to cut on me!" they respond.

I've said before, the Bible is not a piece of candy, it's a nut. And I'm a nutcracker--or just a nut--or just a "cracker." (I once lived in Georgia.). Anyway, I believe God wants me to keep on crackin'.

265

LETTERS TO THE EDITOR

Dear Editor:

Let me hasten to say Rev. Hale has done an excellent job with these columns, 'The Bible Says.' His writings are scholarly, honest and highly responsible. They indeed constitute perhaps the best general Christian education available at this time in Southern Illinois. I like so much the way he concludes one of the articles: "Until we learn to use our Bible intelligently we probably will go on blaming 'atheist professors' for the breakdown in the faith of our children." That's right on target! All this erudition may be too strong for many people in your area. . . but God bless 'em! You are rendering an outstanding service as an editor. You are to be commended for treating your readership to such enlightenment.

Another Minister

To the Editor:

You have been receiving so many letters against continuing the column "The Bible Says." I hope you do not yield to such pressure and discontinue it.

I enjoy it very much. When I read the column on the book of Jonah, I read the story in the Bible, and by disregarding it taken literally, I was more aware of the great moral lesson it teaches.

A Reader

y

INDEX

Questions are numbered by page.
Letters to the Editor are identified by abc's.

i

v

www.ingramcontent.com/pod-product-compliance
Lightning Source LLC
Chambersburg PA
CBHW060328100426
42812CB00003B/915